DEMOCRATIC GOVERNANCE IN INDIA

DEMOCRATIC GOVERNANCE IN INDIA
Reflections and Refractions

Editors
DIPANKAR SINHA
KABERI CHAKRABARTI

General Editor
Sobhanlal Datta Gupta

PUBLICATIONS
KALPAZ PUBLICATIONS
DELHI-110052

Democratic Governance in India: Reflections and Refractions

Rs. 690

ISBN: 81-7835-592-2

Published in 2007 in India by
Kalpaz Publications
C-30, Satyawati Nagar,
Delhi-110052
E-mail: kalpaz@hotmail.com

Lasser Type Setting by: Rudra Computer Graphics, Delhi
Printed at : Salasar Imaging System, Delhi

Contents

PART - II

PART - III

Acknowledgements

We wish to acknowledge the University Grants Commission (UGC) because most of the papers in this volume were presented in the UGC-funded National Seminar on *Democratic Governance in India States*, which was organised under the DRS Programme (Phase I) of the Department of Political Science, Calcutta University on 18 March, 2005. We also wish to take this opportunity to acknowledge our debt to the contributors of the volume, who, despite their extremely busy schedule, gave priority to our endeavour.

We were ably assisted by Gargi Bannerjee, Research Associate of our department, who was prompt enough to type some of the contributions which were handwritten. Madhushree Ghosh, the librarian of the Institute of Development Studies Kolkata, provided valuable information in preparing the Select Bibliography. We also received assistance from Pallabi Bannerjee, Indrani Baksi, Paramita Bannerjee and Shayani Chaudhury, enthusiastic students of ours, who were quite active in preparing the Select Bibliography.

Last but not the least, the Kalpaz Publications, and its Director of Publication, Mr. Amit Garg, in particular, have been extremely cooperative and supportive in making this publication possible.

General Editor's Note

The present publication is the first volume emerging out of the DRS Programme (Phase I) on Democratic Governance in the Indian States under the Department of Political Science, University of Calcutta, funded by the University Grants Commission, New Delhi. The volume contains.contributions of two categories, namely, the papers presented at the National Seminar on *Democratic Governance in Indian States,* organized under the DRS Programme, which was held on 18 March, 2005, and the papers which were invited from scholars at a later stage.

The title and the content of the volume indicate that efforts have been made to combine conceptual-theoretical perspectives on democratic governance with specificites of select Indian states. This approach has been adopted, keeping in mind the fact that the current volume is the very first in line. Democratic governance, both in its conceptual dimensions and in practical manifestations, is quite complex and, by virtue of being so, sufficiently controversial. The volume, by its focus on certain key areas, is expected to play its role in the ongoing debate and discussions on what is arguably one of the most provocative themes of the day.

Sobhanlal Datta Gupta
Coordinator, DRS Programme (Phase I)
Department of Political Science,
Calcutta University

List of Contributors and Editors

Javeed Alam: Former Professor at the Centre for European Studies, Central Institute of English and Foreign Languages (CIEFL), Hyderabad. He has written extensively on various dimensions of democracy and governance in India, including class, caste, minorities, mass mobilisation, social consciousness and autonomy movements. One of his more recent publications is *Who Wants Democracy?*

Amartya Mukhopadhyay: Professor of Political Science, University of Calcutta. His areas of research are public policy analysis, international relations, Indian politics, and cultural politics. His publications include *Politics of Implementation: Mass Transportation Policy for Calcutta* (2002). His forthcoming book is on *Alternative Tagore: Unconventional Politics of a Poet*. His articles cover a wide range of themes including postcolonialism, civil social institutions in India, human rights, electoral strategies and Indian federalism.

Asish K. Bhattacharya: Professor of Finance and Control, Indian Institute of Management Calcutta (IIMC). He is also the Faculty-in-Charge of The IIMC Centre for Corporate Governance. He obtained D.Phil from Allahabad University. Earlier he was the Technical Director at the Institute of Chartered Accountants of India. He is a Fellow of both the Institute of Chartered Accountants of India and the Institute of Cost and Works Accountants of India.

Asok Kumar Mukhopadhyay: Former Netaji Subhas Chandra Bose Professor, Department of Political Science, Calcutta

University. He received Ph.D. degrees from Calcutta University and London School of Economics. He has been Academic Visitor to the Department of Government, London School of Economics, and Senior Research Fellow, Frederich Ebert Stiftung, Germany. He has authored eleven books, and more than hundred articles in Indian and foreign journals.

Prabhat Datta: Centenary Professor of Public Administration, Department of Political Science, Calcutta University. A former member of the University Grants Commission Panel on Political Science and Public Administration, he is currently Hony. Advisor to State Institute of Panchayats and Rural Development and Institute of Local Government and Urban Studies, and Chairman, Jawaharlal Nehru Urban Renewal Mission, West Bengal. He has authored more than twenty books on governance and has written articles on the same theme in national and international journals.

Manabi Majumdar: Fellow, Centre for Studies in Social Sciences, Kolkata. She was formerly associated with Madras Institute of Development Studies. Her recent work examines issues of decentralisation reforms in education and the politics of local resource mobilisation. She has published widely in national and international journals and edited volumes.

Indrasish Bannerjee: Senior Lecturer in Political Science, Ramakrishna Mission Vidyamandira, Belur Math, Howrah. He specialises in Development Studies and Political Ethnography. He has contributed several articles in journals.

Ivaturi Ramabrahmam: Professor, Department of Political Science, University of Hyderabad. He is also the Hony. Director, Academic Staff College, University of Hyderabad. He specialises in and writes on public policy, administrative processes, higher education and training, and transparency in governance. He has co-edited a volume on *Globalisation: Contextualising Social Science Research in India.*

S. Sudhakar Babu: Assistant Professor, Academic Staff College, University of Hyderabad. He is currently engaged in exploring and evaluating, through empirical studies, the linkage of governance and technology at the grassroots-level in Andhra Pradesh.

Samir Kumar Das: Professor in Political Science, Calcutta University. A Postdoctoral Fellow (2005) of Social Science Research Council (New York), he is also the Deputy Coordinator of UGC DRS Programme on 'Democratic Governance in Indian States' in Political Science, Calcutta University. Earlier he taught in Presidency College, Kolkata. He has authored *Ethnicity, Nation and Security: Essays on Northeastern India* (2003) and edited *Peace Accords and Peace Processes* (2005). He specialises in issues of ethnicity, security and migration particularly with reference to India's Northeast.

Sobhanlal Datta Gupta: Surendra Nath Banerjee Professor of Political Science, University of Calcutta, and Coordinator, UGC-sponsored DRS Programme in Political Science, Calcutta University. His prime area of research is Political Theory. He has authored and edited a number of books which include *Justice and the Political Order in India: An Inquiry into the Institutions and Ideologies, 1950*-1972 (1978), *India: Politics and Society Today and Tomorrow* (1998) and *Com intern and the Destiny of Communism in India* 1919-1943: *Dialectics of Real and a Possible History* (2006).

Dipankar Sinha: Reader in Political Science, Calcutta University and Honorary Adjunct Fellow at the Institute of Development Studies Kolkata. His prime area of research is the communicative dimensions of development-governance interface. He has authored *Communicating Development in the New World Order* (1999): and (in Bengali) *Media Sanskriti* (2003). He has also co-edited *The Information, Communication and Technology: From Early to Post-Colonial India* (2005). His essays have been published in edited volumes and journals from India and abroad.

Kaberi Chakrabarti: Lecturer, Department of Political Science, Calcutta University. Her areas of research and teaching include Communication Studies and Development Administration. Her most recent publication is a co-authored (with Mohit Bhattacharya) volume (in Bengali) *Samajik Tatto Unnayan Prosasan* (tr. *Social Theory and Development Administration)*.

Editorial Introduction

Dipankar Sinha

Kaberi Chakrabarti

Democratic Governance in India: Beyond the Square-box of Views

Can an exploration of the core idea of *governance* be far behind if the main focus of the volume is on *democratic governance*? The apparently perplexing query assumes special relevance in at least two specific contexts: first, in the context of both the terms being framed and couched in the neo-liberal logic and discourse; and second, in the context of the still considerably blurred interpretations of the term governance. Since the last decade of the twentieth century *governance* has slowly but forcefully made an entry in the dominant discourse of development with so much vigour that it has now acquired the status of a buzzword, and no less, that of a political slogan. As teachers, our experience of the responses of the students in postgraduate classes and of various seminars and symposia also make us aware that in a number of cases the term governance— which is strategically located at the crossroads of political, administrative and intellectual developments, and sets the normative basis of government— is used even when the use of the term 'government' would have been sufficient and more appropriate.

The problem, however, is that like many other buzzwords in social science the concept of governance is used quite loosely, and even imprecisely, both by its ardent publicists and passionate critics. Governance, generally speaking, relates to "the webs of permissible behaviour of institutions and components of a society possessing a body politic".[1] Howsoever fluid, imprecise, diverse and amorphous its connotations could be, there is, paradoxically enough, some kind of *taken-for-grantedness* about the concept. One of the most evident manifestations of such *taken-for-grantedness* in the Indian context is the Tenth Plan document[2] itself which, in a highly celebratory mood, steers clear of any concrete terms of reference of good governance and uncritically declares it as "perhaps the single most important factor" in ensuring the achievement of the Plan. The Plan also points out that lack of it "could be the cause of immense disappointment and missed development opportunities". The complexity is all the more compounded if one confronts the main theme of our volume, that is, *democratic governance*, with the following question: if governance, as the current discourse goes, is all about transparency, accountability, responsiveness, rule of law and multi-level information networks, all of which individually and collectively 'internalise' democratic norms, why then use 'democratic' as an affix to governance?

What is more important than the temptation to answer the question is its inference. The question incorporates within itself, though not necessarily in a clear-cut manner, the problematic nature of the concept of governance in general and democratic governance in particular. Governance as an innocuous 'word' might have been existing in the dictionary for long but its reincarnation, followed by its ever-growing presence in recent times as a key concept, and its wide circulation in the policymaking circle are, to a great extent, associated with the growing pessimism about the State's capacity to influence the social structures and processes and, more specifically, its policymaking power. As Stoker categorically states,[3] the governance networks are not just about influencing government policies but are about taking over the business of government. Stoker's argument is echoed by Rhodes[4] and Box,[5] eminent theorists of governance. Thus, as part of its strategy the World Bank, for instance, takes utmost care in justifying the Market economy as the only viable path of development and as part of the process it has put the idea of governance at the centrestage, and that too as the key to the Market-based restructuring of institutions, rules and political processes. The immediate point of departure for the World Bank discourse on governance has, however, been the need to address and remove the allegedly endemic corruption and inefficient public services in the non-Western developing and transition states (the latter often described as post-crisis societies).

Be it governance or democratic governance, the focus has been, as pointed out by Jan Kooiman, on *interactions with a 'co-' public-private character, offset against a 'do it alone' government perspective.* As Kooiman further elaborates:

"Governing can be considered as the totality of interactions, in which public as well as private actors participate, aimed at solving societal problems or creating societal opportunities; attending to the institutions as contexts for these governing interactions; and establishing a normative foundation for all those activities.

Governance can be seen as the totality of theoretical conception on governing.'[6]

In course of time, governance has come to be the lynchpin of a radically different design-cum-configuration of the state-(civil) society complex, based upon a form of governing that involves numerous inter-personal networks, negotiated inter-organizational coordination, and decentred context-mediated inter-systemic steering. In the dramatic backdrop of the oft-cited reference-point, namely, of the "fall of the Berlin Wall and the global democratic re-awakening", such a perspective challenges the notion and status of the state as a 'primary actor' and visualizes a vast array of role-performance— primarily from individuals to community-building associations to transnational/global actors— for ushering in 'deep democracy', 'inclusive democracy' and so forth. The complexity is compounded by the fact that in the conceptualisation of democratic governance various issues and conditions— as varied as human rights and basic freedoms, rule of law, independent judiciary, transparency, accountability, social equity, effective representation of underrepresented groups, bribery and corruption busting, right to information, merit-based public service, independent and responsible media and so forth— are at the centrestage. No less provocatively, such coneptualisation goes beyond viewing democracy as a formal system— as a process characterized by widening scope for exercising political 'voice'. As the *Human Development Report 2002* notes:

"Democratic governance in this fast-changing environment is about more than people having the right to vote. It must be about strengthening democratic institutions so that they keep pace with the changing distribution of economic and political power. And it must be about promoting democratic politics that make participation and public accountability possible even when the relevant power and process lie outside the formal institutions of the state."[7]

But how far are they practicable as propositions if democratic governance privileges the 'efficiency' criterion, based on the single-minded promotion of Market economy, at the cost of 'effectiveness'? The question assumes particular significance insofar as it has a higher status than many of its sister-concepts in going beyond the objective of establishing efficient public institutions, economic growth-friendly predictable economic and political environment and effective functioning of public services to provide centrality to political freedom, human rights and removal of discrimination.[8] However, there is also a catch. It lies in the very exploration of relevant power and process lying outside the State. This point by itself is potent enough to make democratic governance a highly provocative concept. To refer back to Stoker, the seed-propositions of governance are problematic themselves.

Let us elaborate how Stoker develops his thesis.[9] Regarding the first proposition — governance as a set of institutions and actors that are drawn from but also beyond government—there is a divorce between the complex reality of decision-making associated with governance and the normative codes used to explain and justify government. Concerning the second proposition— governance identifying the blurring of boundaries and responsibilities for tackling social and economic issues— the blurring of responsibilities can lead to blame avoidance or scapegoating. In the case of the third proposition—governance identifying the power dependence involved in the relationships between institutions in collective action— Stoker argues that the power dependence exacerbates the problem of unintended consequences for government. About the fourth proposition—governance being autonomous self-governing networks of actors—the emergence of these very networks raises difficulties over accountability. Lastly, when it comes to the fifth proposition—governance recognizing the capacity to get things done which does not rest on the power of government to command or use its authority— even where the governments operate in a flexible way to steer collective action, governance failure may occur.

As hinted earlier, the cooption, 'sponsorship' and the consequent circulation of the concept of governance by the World Bank, specifically the subtle attempt to infuse the concept with 'social justice' along the Market-friendly way, have made it one of the most controversial concepts of the contemporary times. There are many amongst us who, citing the 'parentage' of the concept, argue that *governance* in general and allied concepts like d*emocratic governance* (or that of *good governance,* for that matter) in particular should be avoided and expunged from the ongoing development discourse. The main thrust of the argument is that concepts like these primarily seek to facilitate and promote the entry and circulation of the global capital and seek to distort and diminish the 'autonomy' of the State. One respects the spirit that lies beneath such radical argument as one also appreciates its apparent attraction. But the fact remains that the act of delinking ourselves from such concepts has at least three undesirable outcomes: first, it would prevent us from problematising the concepts and failing to test them to 'our reality'— which by any means is not a very good proposition for the social scientists for whom the problematisation of issues is linked to survival and credibility. Second, such delinking would mean that such key concepts are the 'property' of the institutions like the World Bank, the International Monetary Fund or the World Trade Organization and that there is no other vantage-point from which they can be approached, 'rescued' and provided with different connotations. Third, the first and the second would, in turn, reinforce the *taken-*

for-grantedness of the concept, mentioned in the preceding discussion, and would also lead us away from relating it, in our own ways, to the twin processes of democratization of public decision-making and utilization of pubic services for the common good. No less dangerous, such delinking would also come in the way of intense debates and discussions on the concerned themes which create an ambience of questioning and catholicity and induce us to go *beyond the square-box of views.*

This introductory write-up is not meant to delve into various manifestations of democratic governance in India, many of which have been discussed by the contributors of this volume. But at the same time, it being a sort of 'prelude' to what is to come in terms of the contributions in the volume we need to assert here that democratic governance is basically a *learning process*. To explain, we use the phrase *learning process* in an expanded context than what Tom Bentley has done in his extremely provocative essay on *Governance as Learning: The Challenge of Democracy.*[10] The essay, which has parliamentary democracy as its focus, rests on two primary referents as it discusses the consequences of governance as a *learning process*: first, the collapse of the age-old and sacrosanct distinction between politics as a policymaking activity and administration as a policy implementing activity; second, the extension, if not the replacement, of the existing mode of legitimation of policies through separation of powers and structures by a new mode of more direct and intensive relationship between the state and the citizens, realized through strategies and sophisticated networking. In our case however, the *learning process* is marked by continuing grassroots-level interactions and negotiations with the 'new reality' in India in which the rulers and the ruled are living amidst the retreating State and an aggressive Market. In our version of democratic governance as a *learning process* the changing parameters, identified by Bentley, constitute a necessary but not a sufficient condition. Living in the world's largest democracy and surviving probably one of the most complicated cases of governance the *learning process* has to take into account and assess the impact of the 'new reality' on the ordinary people of India. The contributors, from varying vantage-points, have a commonality— all of them share a serious and sincere concern about India and its ordinary people.

India, widely known as the "largest democracy in the world", is a fascinating and challenging space for testing the elasticity of (democratic) governance. The Indian State at the same time has been indicted, time and time again, by the scholars belonging to both the Left, Centre and the Right, for effecting a disjunction with the society. As the following observation goes:

"Questions have been raised about the relevance of democratic governance to the daily travails of ordinary Indians.... Democracy is...not seen as a mere 'spectator sport' where a handful of elected representatives 'perform' while millions of citizens 'clap from a distance.'".[11]

Since the advent of the Market reforms in the 1990s the Indian State, as the aforementioned excerpts from the Tenth Plan document show, has been trying to show a 'keenness' in bringing governance back in. Then again, this gesture by itself has not been enough to free itself from critiques. While it is true that these days we seldom come across critiques of the Indian State's 'class character' (as class has in course of time seems to have become an unfashionable category in social science!) the Indian State nevertheless is subject to newer routes of interrogation which seek to pin it down on the basis of democratic deficit. Such routes have a wide range and to mention some, general critiques based on its attitude towards the Civil Society and civic activism to more specific critique scrutinizing the carrot and stick policies vis-à-vis the non-governmental organizations and the media, critique based on its indifference and even hostility to the rights of the displaced, critique highlighting the utter underestimation of institutions of local governance and democratic decentralisation, critique resting on its efforts to find a short-cut to 'good governance' through mechanical and often mindless deployment of the information and communication technology and so forth. If that is not all, the State in India has also been accused of putting its people in *detention incommunicado* by denying them the Right to Information. But why concentrate only on the State in the days of Market ascendance? The Market is a major foundation-block of the edifice of governance, and corporate governance has come to acquire the status of a key determinant of the efficiency and effectiveness of governance. Back in 1991 India has formally adopted Market-led reforms, and the days of the Market in India remaining under the protection of the State is over. In fact, the Market in India has not only gained adulthood in directly determining the nature of governance and development there are cases in which it is acting behind the State to determine the parameters of what apparently seems to be the State-guided policies. It is high time that we shed the argument that the Market in India is too young to be brought under the scanner, and embark on interrogating it with greater vigour and critical outlook. In short, despite the emerging literature on the theme there is lot of scope to take a hard look at the Indian scenario in terms of the problems and prospects of democratic governance.

Technically put, the book is based upon contributions of mainly two different categories. On the one hand, it contains contributions which are the revised and expanded form of papers presented in the University Grants Commission-supported National Seminar on *Democratic Governance in India States*, organised under the DRS Programme (Phase I) of the Department of Political Science, Calcutta University, and held on 18 March, 2005. On the other hand, it also contains contributions which were invited from the scholars having (democratic) governance as their major or emerging area of interest. Drawing upon the insights of the contributors who are methodologically and conceptually negotiating their respective ways through the spectacular and often perplexing maze of governance in India the volume seeks to present itself as a modest but sincere attempt to explore and comprehend various forms, modes and contexts of governance. The essays, as the title of the book itself indicates, are a mixed bag of reflections on and refractions of democratic governance. They contain reflections in the sense of carving out careful thought about the theme. They also contain refractions in the sense of revealing the 'bends' at particular points of the trajectory of the theme. In this context we can treat India, in terms of its State-society-Market complex, as a medium-cum-metaphor—thus, in the case of reflections India is a 'mirror'; in the case of refractions India is a 'glass'. As the contributions would reveal to the readers, such reflections and refractions are, in many cases, not necessarily pleasant experiences for those who put much premium on democracy and governance. Then again, as critical social scientists we are destined to face them, simply because we ourselves are fated to reveal them and explore the ways and means of minimizing, if not eradicating, them. Let us briefly introduce the essays of the volume.

Quite against the set norms of mainstream scholarly papers, Javeed Alam's *Democracy and "Governance" in the Wake of Mass Upsurge* has a concluding conjecture which runs and develops itself throughout the essay. The conjecture is that the "democratic process, or the processes around democracy" has disengaged itself from the "institutional infirmities" and in the process has acquired "autonomy" of its own. Alam puts governance in double quotes both to differentiate it from the mainstream and hegemonic interpretations of the term and to register his own interpretation of the same. What acquire the centrestage in his radical analysis are the various instances of ordinary people-led protests and resistances, many of which are directly produced from the tension between the forces representing the nation-state and those representing the regions and the states. But Alam does not romanticize the "politics of the oppressed". He carefully notes how the inner dynamics of such politics also acquires oppressive character, thus for instance, in the case of marginalisation of women.

In his essay *Governance, Social capital and Governance: Views from the Wasteland* Amartya Mukhopadhyay takes off with the assertion, reflected also in the Introduction of the current volume, that it is not the best strategy of the social scientists to decry and discard a concept on the basis of its genealogy. Mukhopadhyay makes a *de tour*— through a critical assessment of some leading Western scholars of governance, including James Coleman, Robert Putnam and Francis Fukuyama to identify the methodological and substantive limitations of their analytical frameworks— and arrive at the 'wasteland', namely, India, to make a brief scan of its research on governance. While acknowledging the value of ongoing research on the theme he also locates some constraints, mainly emerging from the complex nature of the state-society relationship in post-colonial India, to advocate a process of rigorous rethinking to develop more meaningful analyses of governance.

Ashish K. Bhattacharya's paper on *State, Liberalization and Investment Question: Issues in Corporate Governance* provides a sort of theoretical background to corporate governance which has acquired the centrestage of contemporary practice of governance in terms of improving competitiveness and enhancing efficiency. However, corporate governance has not been provided much attention by social scientists many of whom relegate it to the background as a 'purely management issue'. Such a detached attitude denies the reality of the days of the Market-led liberalization in which we cannot explain the dynamics of capital and investment without referring to corporate governance. Bhattacharya's paper, at the micro-level, reveals the significance the firm, as nexus of contracts, and its growing role in the liberalized economy. At the macro-level, beyond the confines of the corporate world, it makes us aware of the role of the State vis-à-vis corporate governance as the provider of regulatory environment and institutions, and as one of the major hosts of foreign direct investment (FDI). Bhattacharya's paper sets the stage for further investigation in more concrete terms of the structure, culture, policies and strategies of corporate governance in liberalizing India.

Even if set in Part I of the volume Asok Mukhopadhyay's essay on *Hesitant Devolution: India's Tryst with Democratic Governance* is a sort of prelude to Part II of the volume, which has focus on some specific states in India. Mukhopadhyay has an overwhelming focus on democratic decentralization, regarded by many as the major 'scaffolding' of governance. But he, at the same time, provides a pan-India coverage, including the much-cited cases of West Bengal and Kerala, to show how, with the local bodies not constituting a tier of the Indian federal state, democratic decentralization suffers from certain inherent limitations. This, he further argues, takes its toll in accountability, technical efficiency and financial viability, thereby severely constraining the goal of participatory governance. In his overall assessment of the Indian polity, even keeping in mind the significance of the 73rd and 74th Amendments, Mukhopadhyay identifies a "Hamletian dilemma" on the part of the Indian rulers: to devolve or not to devolve powers, responsibilities and finances from the top downwards.

In *The Law and the Field: Citizen Participation and Urban Governance in West Bengal* Prabhat Datta's point of departure is the extremely significant 74th Amendment of the Constitution which, among various other landmark-provisions, has created the Ward Committees with the broader objective of institutionalising and democratising citizens' participation in the governing process. After a description of the powers and functions of the Ward Committees Datta has a dual focus on Rajpur Sonarpur Municipality and Behrampore Municipality— the first from the urban fringe of Kolkata and the latter from the district of Murshidabad— to reveal how lack of awareness about the War Committee on the part of both councilors and the ordinary people leads to a yawning gaps between the legal structure and the ground-level process. Datta's analysis, containing a number of issues and observations which are perhaps true in other parts of India too, thus, makes us aware that despite much recent hype all is not well with the urban local governance.

With West Bengal in direct focus Manabi Majumdar and Indrasis Banerjee in their contribution *Evolution of the Panchayati Raj System in West Bengal* probe the issues of fiscal discipline and accountability with a vital question in the background— whether the tax revenue-dependent state is more responsive to the needs and concerns of its tax-paying citizens in comparison to the counterparts which mostly rely on unearned income. More specifically, the focus is on the course of resource mobilization and micro-planning potentials and practices of the Panchayati Raj institutions (PRI) and the redistributive effects of the same. The narrative, however, does not confine itself to the dry analysis of the legislative acts and debates. Going beyond the surface-level reading of various relevant documents and proceedings it deftly weaves the 'political' at various layers and levels to highlight the nature of the party-PRI relations and the relations between the 'local power' and state-level politics.

Ivaturi Ramabrahmam and S. Sudhakar Babu also deal with the linkage of fiscal discipline and accountability in Andhra Pradesh in their essay on *Democratic Governance: Reforming the Accountability Domain*, with a somewhat different emphasis. The essay has a much-needed focus on public finance without which any meaningful discussion on governance cannot take place. With key focus on accountability, the essay scrutinises the reports of the Comptroller and Auditor General (CAG) vis-à-vis the Andhra Pradesh scenario of SMART (simple, moral, accountable, responsive and transparent) governance to expose how the accountability domain is either neglected or diluted through 'new measures', leading, in turn, to the sapping of the foundation of governance. The scrutiny ultimately narrows down to two key sectors—education and health. Leave apart the widely-shared view that no (human) development can occur without these two sectors made vibrant, the shocking instance is that the sanctioned money for buying teaching aids for schoolchildren remain unspent, that too amidst the recurring claims of efficiency in governance.

Righting Governance or Governing Rights? Tripura (2000) by Samir Das has a rare but necessary focus on a state in the North-East India, which often escapes the attention of even the most regular and supposedly rigorous analysts of governance in India. The essay, keeping Tripura in front, advocates a sort of counterpoint to the existing the philosophy and discourse of governance by making a plea for viewing rights through the prism of governance and not the other way round. Tripura in this essay emerges— beyond the complexities of its 'real' events and dimensions, such as, the relations of the Bengali settlers and the indigenous people— as a metaphor of the problematique arising out of the general failure of the analysts to take the rights into the framework of governance. Das contests and opens wide what we may describe as the *hidden agenda* of governance— governance coming in the way of rights by depriving the rights of the agency and subjectivity of the citizens. This, as Das contends, along with the hype that generally goes with governance, has grave implications because it develops a built-in process of imposing limitations to the institutional politics.

Part III of the volume contains a Select Bibliography based on the literature on the main theme and the text of the Right to Information Act. The latter has been incorporated because in our view this specific right is the fountainhead of democratic governance.

Back to our own exposition, we deem it appropriate to refer to John S. Mill who, writing in the latter half of the nineteenth century- Britain and taking upon himself the difficult task of defending democracy against the rising preference for enlightened dictatorship, had perhaps provided us with the best possible summary of the great complexities of governance though this classic remark in *Considerations on Representative Government*: *"A government which attempts to do everything is aptly compared...to a schoolmaster who does all the pupils' tasks for them; he may be very popular with the pupils, but he will teach them very little. A government, on the other hand, which neither does anything itself that can possibly be done by any one else, nor shows any one else how to do anything, is like a school in which there is no schoolmaster, but only pupil teachers who have never themselves be taught."*

Living at the crossroads marked by the Indian State's transition from the first depiction provided by Mill to the second the editors are quite clear in their mind that it is impossible to capture, within the two covers of a volume, every bit of the variety and complexity that governance offers in terms of its conceptual formation and practical manifestation. As social scientists knowing the absurdity of such over-ambitious venture we make no tall claim about the volume. But at the same time, we can venture to mention that an attempt has been made here to intellectually confront a highly elusive, provocative and controversial concept and to contextualise it, so that certain contours and parameters can be identified and certain clues and cues can be left for further consideration. The brief overview of the essays, provided in the preceding part, substantiates our claim. We would also like to add here that the value of the book would be further enhanced by the fact that its contributors have a varied background in terms of their disciplines, methodologies and perspectives— an essential precondition to giving shape to a concept that is still, so to say, 'under construction'.

References

1. Amiya Kumar Bagchi, "Governance— National, Corporate and International: The Indian Context", *South Asia: Journal of South Asian Studies*, XXVIII (2), August, 2005, pp. 265-281.
2. Tenth Five Year Plan, "Governance and Implementation", Government of India, New Delhi, 2002, p.177 and p.188.
3. Gerry Stoker, "Governance Theory: Five Propositions" in Bidyut Chakrabarty and Mohit Bhattacharya eds., *Public Administration: A Reader*, Oxford University Press, Delhi, 2003, pp. 215-30. Earlier published in *International Social Science Journal*, 50(1), 1998, pp.17-58.
4. R. Rhodes, "The New Governance: Governing without Government", *Political Studies* 44, pp. 652-57.
5. Richard C. Box, "Running Government like a Business" in Bidyut Chakrabarty and Mohit Bhattacharya, pp. 231-61.
6. Jan Kooiman, *Governing as Governance*, Sage Publications, London, 2005 (reprint), p.3.
7. *Human Development Report 2002*, UNDP, New York, 2002, p.61.
8. Sakiko Fukuda-Parr, "Democracy for Development: Neither Panacea Nor Luxury", Speech at the Fourth Global Forum: Dialogue and Partnerships for the Promotion of Democracy and Development, Marrakech, Morocco, December, 2002.
9. Stoker, pp. 217-18.
10. Tom Bentley, "Governance as Learning: The Challenge of Democracy",www.opendemocracy.net/debates/article.jsp?id=3&debateId=52&articleId=1314
11. Rajesh Tandon, "The Problem", *Seminar No.* 514, 2002, p.12.

PART - I

1

Democracy and "Governance" in the Wake of Mass Upsurge

Javeed Alam

Dissimilar kinds of mass upsurge have marked democracy in India since the mid 1980s. The popular upsurge among the Backward Castes that got built around the decisions of the V.P. Singh government to implement the recommendations of the Mandal Commission and the reaction to it, best epitomised with Advani's *Rath Yatra* for the construction of *Ram Mandir* on the site where *Babri Masjid* stood before demolition, has been the dialectics of Indian democracy since then. In this paper I will be more concerned with the former. I will look at three important developments that have taken place because of that upsurge in the society and polity, each of which has had far reaching, though contradictory, repercussions for "governance". The first of which has to do with how the Centre and the regions have been forced to deal with each other by a change in the circumstances.

I

Let me start with a commonly observable feature of the present-day politics in India. We are all witness to the development of a pattern in Indian politics since 1996, in which the government of the nation-state called India has been made up as much by the political forces and parties having their base in only one or the other of the various linguistic-cultural regions or "nationalities" that make up India. No all-India party or what in India are called "national party" has been successful in providing a government to the country. Conventionally speaking, it is, on the European example, a coalitional pattern. But given the multi-ethnic or rather the multinational specificity of India, it is, on a deeper analysis, more than a coalition. It is much more a *co-governance* of the country by the nation and the regions that make up the nation. What constitutes the Centre at the level of the nation-state is made up as much of those who speak on behalf of and claim to represent the nation as much as those who do so for the various regions or nationalities. In fact this configuration has been a result of a long contestation, going back to the early years of Independence, between various forces as to how and by whom will the "nation" be represented. What will be the cultural identity marks of the nation(-state). The result is a slow process towards congealing of the respective claims of the diverse forces representing the nation-state and the different forces within the regions and the states. Given the present conjuncture, the nation and the regions cannot do without the other. I am calling it a co-governance in that sense. Now the sense of this will become clear if we compare it with an earlier period in the history of politics in India.

It is quite clear from the above that this period in the 1990's has been marked by a pronounced ascendance of regional parties in a somewhat enduring manner. In the short term (now, it is important to emphasise that there is no long term trend that can be analytically discerned in Indian politics), there seems to be no chance of this trend being reversed. But what informs the ascendance of the regional parties is the absence of any overt conflicts or clashes between the Centre and the state in India however much of differences of opinions can be shown to exist on any number of issues. What seems to be happening between the Centre and states in terms of differences of opinion are in the nature of symbiotic contests. This trend crystallized during the period of the two United Front ministries in 1996-98. Even the BJP with its chauvinistic nationalism, rabid communalism and centralizing zeal has been forced to accept the pattern and pay lip service to the code of behaviour entailed within these patterns, whatever be its efforts to push the hidden agenda on the sly. Barring a region here and there on the borders, the national unity of India seems to be acquiring deeper roots.

On the earlier occasions when the region-based political parties representing the various linguistic-cultural regions of India emerged as a force was in the period 1967-72 (and the pattern repeats itself in the late 1970s as well, though on a relatively smaller scale). Let us only take those occasions for a contrast that is revealing in itself. The entire period was marked by intense (and shrill) struggle between the Centre and the states. There also were constant bickering and mutual accusations. The Central government charged the regional governments of being against the nation-state; in Indian phraseology, of being a threat to national unity. The state governments accused the Centre of becoming authoritarian— both a danger to democratic aspirations and the federal arrangement. Most of the parties ruling in the states—such as, Tamil Nadu, Kerala, Punjab, West Bengal, Tripura, Kashmir and many others— went on to produce documents enumerating measures for the protection of the rights of the States and listing details of how the Centre has gone on encroaching into the sphere of their jurisdiction and has violated the rights of the state.[1] Each of these governments represented diverse ideological views, class preferences, social bases, and so on. It least bothered them as to how this greater power for the states for which they were fighting would be used by the different states, so long as they would have it for their own purposes. What brought them together against the government of the nation-state was, as I have called it in an earlier essay twenty odd years ago, an objective complementarity[2] in spite of different ideological and class preferences as between Tamil Nadu or West Bengal or Punjab and so on.

Today there is no sharp contradiction between the Centre (the nation-state) and the states (regional governments/movements) though there may be many differences of opinion or even conflicts of interests centered around economic and fiscal or monetary policies and on questions of culture and language policies. In the earlier period, the dominant class forces in most of the states— the regionally based, non-big bourgeoisie both in industry and agriculture— also seized the opportunity to use the power of the state governments to better bargain with the Centre for resources and to get better deals for the regionally based dominant classes in the pan-Indian market. The national market with its price mechanisms and terms of trade was, and still is to a relatively lesser extent, controlled by the monopoly sections of the capitalist class; the control by the monopoly section lessened only to the extent of investment choices being determined as well by the imperialist finance capital. The manner of the operation of the pan-Indian market at that time made the entry of the non-big, regionally based bourgeois in the pan-Indian market that much more difficult, through the grant of licenses, input output prices, restrictive trade practices and so on. This in fact intensified the tussle between the Centre and the states.

As an aside, it needs to be mentioned that within this general pattern there was though an exception. The Left forces in general and those states in which it was the dominant partner in the governments were also in the forefront of the struggle against centralization and the "authoritarian" tendencies of the Centre. But it sought the autonomy of the states to curb the power of the ruling classes and to use the autonomy for the state to further the interest of the working classes and the peasantry, pronouncedly in the case of West Bengal.[3] Nevertheless, this tendency operating across the ideological divide and class preferences of the various forces ruling in the different states created, what I have referred to above as, an objective complementarity.

Now no such contradictions seem to operate, at least in a decisive way. Both the Centre and the states (the states hiking stakes vis-a-vis the other states) are competing to attract international finance capital, which itself is getting more and more centralized and therefore as for decisions about investment choices unified.[4] The appeal is to this capital for foreign direct investments (FDIs). All are votaries of Globalisation, barring the Left Front (led by the CPI-M) ruled states, though these too, given the policy imperatives of the Indian state and the class constraints imposed by the big bourgeoisie are keen to get as much foreign capital as possible; the difference being a greater emphasis on public investment and a sharper focus on other components of social democracy like democratisation of agrarian relations, local self-government and all round decentralization and so on. The important point in the espousal of globalisation by most state governments is: a larger share of national market as well as better access to investible resources is seen to be automatically insured by the availability of FDIs in industry and trade and services.

The upshot of the coming together of political and economic forces represented by the Centre and the states has been that the enormous diversity of India is getting mobilized in the shaping of a united India, rather than being a threat to unity as was earlier feared. This is an important stage in the democratisation of national relations in India, something, for which the Left as well as the various regionally based democratic forces have been fighting. But the crucial point is that this has come about not as a result of any alteration in the constitutional scheme due to the pressure exerted by these forces but as a result of a politically emergent constraint on the power of the Centre; the unintended consequence of the compulsions of co-governance.

In rounding off this part of discussion the first major conclusion is the notable change in the functioning of Indian federation. There is a noticeable change in the direction and content of "governance". The polity is free of bickering and tensions. Federal relations seem to be, in relation, to any other period of post Independence history, in better order. There is greater protection, structurally induced, for pluralism and greater tolerance towards regional points of view as well as effective participation of the different states in the decision-making at the level of the Union. National unity is not a much-debated issue from this perspective (even if it faces threats in other ways due to the communal fascism of *Sangh Parivar*). Federalism can function smoothly in India only if the diversity of the plural forms of social life is held in deep respect. Federalism in India is more than a technical matter of division of powers between the centre and the states; it has as much to do with the politics that informs them. It is tied up with the political unity of the nation. This is lesson from the six disastrous years of NDA rule. It could do little with the division of powers but fiddled ruthlessly with the plural forms of social life generating tensions and conflicts between the Centre and many social groups in the states. Gujarat was only the most extreme, gruesome instance of this general trend.[5]

II

The second change has to do with the powerful political currents unleashed by the Mandal politics including the vandalism by the upper caste youths with the connivance of powerful organised forces. These political currents are thoroughly changing the character of the political participation of the oppressed caste and have important implications for the politics of the present phase and consequently for the "governance" as well. Causally, this is due to the internal differentiation and class formation among these castes. The insertion of the causal between the differentiation and the nature of participation requires some careful elaboration.

Two things have been occurring simultaneously within these vulnerable communities. First there was a long period of capitalist development, especially in agriculture, which was followed by land reforms, after Independence.[6] Many of the OBC's became propriety peasants. The long chain of dependence and bondage on the landlords was snapped. Education, employment etc. among the OBC's slowly expanded. New modern classes were slowly emerging among them. Among the Dalits reservations as quotas in education and employment and other meekly implemented affirmative action also led to similar results though on a smaller scale. What thwarted the collective development of Dalits was the nature of land reforms where land often did not go to the direct tiller. Most of the Dalits remained dispossessed of land, having been earlier non-occupancy tenants or agricultural labourers.[7]

As a consequence of all this, class and income differentiation has been taking place, however uneven, among these castes-communities and therefore a dispersal of earlier forms of power with their traditional leadership. Earlier such castes organised as *Jatis* were internally egalitarian because of the same occupation and skill endowment and therefore similar income levels. The breakdown of the inviolable links between the ritual status and occupation had far reaching consequences. It encouraged the movement of people, imperceptible though, among the oppressed, unlike with the Savarnas earlier, into different occupations and the acquisition of varied and dissimilar skills. With all these developments, the *jatis* started becoming internally inegalitarian; the process though has had a different tempo (depending on the possession of prior assets, skills, and status) across the distinct castes leading to the formation of modern classes within the caste communities. Differentiation and dispersion of inherited bases of power, if we go by the global pattern of consequences of capitalist development, also set in process the dissolution of the "primordial" communities. Nothing of the sort has happened in India so far, nor seems likely to in the near future, even with the rapid *individuation* of interests and persons.[8]

Within the class formation hinted above, a middle class as well has been in the process of formation and consolidation within these caste-based communities. Estimates of various surveys indicate that today more than fifty per cent of the middle classes are coming from these oppressed communities; in the colonial period the figure is estimated to be hardly fifteen per cent. A further consequence of this has been the impetus given to a contrary process, or rather opposite to dissolution, of unification of these communities on wider scales. It is in the interest of these newly *emergent* middle classes, as distinct from the established ones who belonged overwhelmingly to Savarna castes, to unify these communities as blocs to compete for power in democratic contestations, especially the electoral competitiveness. We will refer to these emergent middle classes from among the oppressed as a *neo-middle-class* to distinguish it from the earlier *established* one. These two contrary trends, differentiation and undermining of the inherited forms of constitution of castes and that of the process of internal unification, have had a simultaneous run over the last many decades.

To sum up: differentiation and unification form the two opposite poles in the dialectics of caste politics. Therefore the contradiction inherent in the class formation within the communities and the individuation of interests around these manifesting in some sort of class conflict did not fructify. There was thus a negation of the possibilities of the articulation of class tendencies as political positions. Instead what happened has been a consolidation of the caste groups on scales larger than ever before.

To digress here, this development has severely disadvantaged the Left in the entire Indo-Gangetic belt and led to its partial decline in this region, more particularly of Communist Party of India (CPI) in U.P. and Bihar where it had strong popular bases. It is not easy to evolve a strategy to combat or outflank this development among the oppressed castes. The Left to rework its way into the political arena in this region has precisely to work out such a strategy. What we instead have today, on the Left, is the politics of alliances, to contain and defeat fascism. The Left has to continue to go on with the alliances, because these are necessary in the present conjuncture, but a strategy running parallel to the alliances has also to be in place as well; a challenge of a very difficult kind.

To come back to the main argument, a two-way contest has now come about in Indian society with deep repercussions for the democratic process. First, the neo-middle-classes see in white-collar jobs and professional positions the main route to gaining status and prestige in society. Unlike the established middle classes from the *Savarnas* they have no status or other social assets to fall back on. So a breakthrough into these, monopolised by the established middle classes, is crucial for their self-esteem. Hence the clamour for quotas as a necessary aspect of *"social justice."* There is, secondly, a fierce contest on for a share in power. Self- representation, share in power corresponding to the numerical strength, allotment of ministerial berths, and so on are all a part of what is now talked of as "*empowerment*". These two terms sketch out the self-definition of the politics of the oppressed communities.

The struggle today is for recognition and bourgeois equality, without in any way implying a pejorative sense to bourgeois. In the hierarchy of the caste society where status degrading of the lower strata is built-in, the upper caste forces recognition from others without reciprocating, thereby denying equality and dignity to the other. In the situation that prevails in India the struggle for equality therefore becomes shrill and ruthless because recognition often has to be wrested from those who refuse to reciprocate. In a situation where egalitarian values prevail, people achieve recognition together; in other words, mutual recognition is recognition of the other as a human and therefore the moral and bodily integrity of the other is ensured.[9]

In tying up the discussion of this trend, here we can discern the second major change in the mode of "governance". *The system of representation has come into direct contradiction with efficiency and economy in the exercise of state power.* The widespread insistence on the part of the oppressed communities for *self-representation* has led to the decline in the quality of "governance". Given the historical inheritances which work to produce pronounced social disabilities among the lower castes, intrinsic merit, verbal skills, social attainment, intellectual sophistication, and related qualities all are in deficit among the neo-middle-classes who have emerged as the leaders of the oppressed castes. Rise in the din and decline in the decorum in the political debates have also followed this development. Is this something to despair about? I would only like to emphasise that a very important change, spread and expansion of democracy in India, is taking place in a rather *untidy* manner in the Indian politics.[10]

{In parenthesis let us note in passing: talking of the strategy and limits of development in India especially within the agrarian sphere a question needs to be raised here. Imagine a situation of land going to the direct tillers as well, many of whom were agricultural labourers or insecure tenants, and belonging overwhelmingly to the *dalits*. As the land reforms were conceived and implemented most of the land got passed on to the occupancy tenants belonging mostly to the intermediate and backward castes. If it had also gone to other tillers including Dalits, what could have been the consequences? It is obvious that the articulation of interests, the constitution of communities and contestations between and within them, and the formation of classes within these castes and communities would all have been so different. The consolidation of the type that took place and the consequent ascendance of caste based communities like Jats, Yadavs, Kurmis, Marathas, Thevars, Kapus, and so on is inconceivable without the way land reforms got carried out. This question cannot be pursued in any detail here. But it is important to raise it as a counterfactual. It provides a link to the relations of production within the agrarian economy and its influence on the question of democracy in India both its trajectory and inner dynamics. It is just for this reason that I want to add here that what has been said so far, and what will be said henceforth, about Indian democracy is based on this background understanding. There is nothing inexorable about the course of development of Indian democracy being analyzed here. It has been conditioned, quite deeply, by the peculiarity of the surrounding bourgeois condition confronting the Indian agrarian society. Any pre-existing social formation has many possible ways of developing in terms of the transformational strategies adopted and the nature of devel-opment of the popular movements.}

To move off from the parenthesis, first, it hastened the process of this unification of these communities under leadership of the neo-middle-classes within these communities. And if we read this together with the first trend described above, then the Yadavs or the Kurmis or the Dalits are now a caste in only a nominal sense because all the normative markers of what constitutes the *Varna* order are being eroded as well rejected. They have become a *community* in any sense of the term. Communities can be identified when they articulate in a socio-political context. A fixed definition can be a source of mis-specification. Community boundaries vary as per the context. For example, in face of the Hindutva onslaught the entire Muslim community in any specific area would feel like a community. But in a situation of sectarian disputes, Muslims become *Shi'a* or *Sunni* communities. Or, to take another instance, during a village *Mela jatis* act like communities but in case of feud with another village the entire village stands up as a community.

What I want to emphasise is that in the transition to becoming communities, the individual *jatis* survive as identities with caste names, but what made for the caste system was the *varna* ideology. What held this ideology together has been eroded, almost entirely. None among the lower castes anymore subscribe to the notions of purity and pollution (clean and unclean castes) or the ritual hierarchy – the two pillars of *varna* system. It does not matter even if the upper castes hold on to these conceptions, this being simply a case of self-attribution and not that of being held as superiors. The system works only when the subordinate *jatis* were to act according to these prescriptions. This is hardly the case anywhere in India. The individual castes are therefore akin to communities fighting for bourgeois equality.

In spite of all that is positive in politics of the oppressed communities, there is a great infirmity in this battle for bourgeois equality. Each community wants to preserve its own internal relations of power and it is here that they also take recourse to traditional ways of enforcing compliance. The worst result of all this is that the women are systematically excluded from the fight for equality. Women as restricted part of these communities are a segment of this process of egalitarian thrust vis-à-vis the women of the upper castes. But as persons within these communities remain, or are in fact becoming more, unequal in relation to men. Women in the pre-colonial economy performed valuable labour, and in terms of skills their work was comparable to that of men. All this is changing in an adverse way for them. With the development of the forces of production they have suffered a downward mobility. As their work has remained static in relation to the development of skills in society, its value has been going down; in other words it is becoming de -skilled in relation to the work done by men. This is perhaps more pronounced in the case of OBC's as compared to the Dalits. Nevertheless, their work in all the oppressed communities has become marginal and women's economic dependence on men has correspondingly increased.

What makes the matters worse for the oppressed are the moral codes, which define life within these communities. These moral codes militate against equality and gender dignity. This moral code is always *imposed* and never *advocated*. It is here in terms of the criteria of advocacy as against that of imposition that we get a criterial basis to make judgements between modern moral outlooks and traditional moral codes. Any one of the modern moral outlooks seek compliance in terms of advocating a certain way of doing things which in turn involve, many a times, a great deal of persuasion. Quite to the contrary, traditional moral codes are more often imposed with threat of retaliation as the basis for compliance. It is therefore always in terms of the form and not necessarily in the content that the modern moral outlooks can claim certain superiority.

We must therefore be wary of defending identity as *difference* unconditionally on the ground of the rights of the communities to a way of life, as many are doing against the, allegedly, homogenising tendencies of modernity. My question in relation to the concerns of a society seeking to establish a regime of rights as the basis of democracy will be: how much of difference is to be pushed or defended as unconditional, as the votaries of community rights do? My fear is, if too much of difference is to count for too much, then the power of the dominant in the community who uphold the difference becomes the arbiter in the life of the people. In the name of democracy we cannot also allow indignities and atrocities to go on because communities are so constituted or alternatively wait indefinitely for an alternative to emerge from within the community. Given their codes, the dice is loaded against the weak within the vulnerable communities, more against some like the women than the others. While it is important to respect differences of culture and belief, this however must be on two conditions: that any practice which militates against the dignity of person must be forced to defend itself and that the state must be forced to protect the person even it means coercion.

The crucial question therefore is: can a right to a way of life be claimed on behalf of a community when the exercise of the same is denied to the individual? Not unsurprisingly in our struggle for civil liberties we have not properly examined these issues; unsurprisingly because we have not specified which rights can be violated by the State and which rights are under constant threat from communities fighting to hold on to what they think they are. If the rights of the individuals are important as one aspect of the democratisation of society then it is important to distinguish the political-legal rights which can be invoked against the institutions of the state, and those background rights to restrain the powers in the communities from denying choices to the individuals within their fold. So under the circumstances as we are in today, we need a different framework of assumptions to build justifications of what is permissible within the claims of the community.

If a community's right to a way of life cannot be questioned on democratic grounds then this can perhaps be so on the basis that the community justify and defend what it enjoins on the individuals as obligatory. This seems to me to be necessary for the following reasons. A community, first of all, does not live a life of Robinson Crusoe. It lives amidst and surrounded by other communities in society. Its wellbeing is dependent on mutually beneficial material and symbolic exchanges with the others. At issue here is the question of maintaining one's difference from others in the society. The difference that it wants to maintain from others ought not therefore be repugnant to all others in the society or the basis of happy coexistence gets threatened and, in times of the kind we are in, where work and habitations are no more spatially separable as was the case with earlier communities, a potential for violence is created.

It is in order of things that we be careful in saying that it is mandatory to defend difference. Briefly, we ought here to make a distinction between difference in *principle* and differences in the *practice* of treatment. Let me give an illustration. A community may be seen to be justified in asserting that it does not approve of "adultery", but the same justification cannot be granted if it insists on publicly humiliating or brutalising those it holds to be guilty.

To round off the discussion, I want to argue that communities ought to allow the individuals the *right of exit*. In conditions that we are in today *exit* can have many meanings, each of which is specific to the situation that vulnerable people find themselves in. Right to exit in one sense can mean a struggle within a community that is one of principled distance from the prevailing views and practices of the community. The foremost historical instances of these to my mind are the figures of Socrates and Gandhi. From our contemporary scene, we can mention the names of Ashgar Ali Engineer or Swami Agnivesh The principled distance can go to extremes and the communities may go to the extent of physically removing you. But then it leaves us with "exemplars" who then are a source of constant renewal of the urge to greater fairness in society. In a second sense, the exit, let us here consider the case of women, and the right to it can be internationalised; meaning thereby that given the universal structures of patriarchy (for all their variations) women's movements not only have fraternal relations, but build a common struggle cutting across the national frontiers. In a third sense, to consider the Dalits, the right to exit may be absolute; you can simply walk out in the way that one walks out of a filthy joint. The right to exit then from the angle of this argument is quite central in accommodating the claims of the community and the rights of the individual. And to insist that the state protect the individual making the exit is simultaneously to struggle to democratise the state.

So while we recognise the valuable nature of the shift in Indian politics which seemingly is based on castes but we also have to engage in a sustained democratic struggle against the inegalitarian and hide bound outlooks inherent in the emergent communi-ties in India, especially their gender blindness. This means that while we respect the identity of the oppressed communities, we also have to remain suspect of the congealing of these identities. In other words, while we welcome the extension of democracy in India, we simultaneously have to struggle to deepen democracy on this expanding canvas. Deepening of democracy, apart from substantive content, requires two *formal* conditions in the Indian situation. One, Dalits and women have to become bearers of entrenched rights. And, two, these communities must be obliged to embody a condition of rationality; that is, critical scrutiny and reflection as a pre conditions for claims on the members; as happens in the case of self-created communities.

III

The third change has to do with the contradictory responses of the people to their experience of democracy. There is a deepening of commitment to democracy among the ordinary people in India. They have a high sense of "efficacy" or usefulness of their vote. They turn out in much larger numbers compared to the established middle classes or the elite to exercise their vote. This sense of efficacy of vote goes together with their distrust of political leadership including the ones they elect as representatives, parties, the institutions of the state and the other paraphernalia of democratic functioning. The question then is: how did then this commitment to democracy come about?[11]

Governments in India have solved none of the problems of livelihood—work, food, shelter, health, etc.— whether suffered singly or collectively by the people. The point that these problems are less severe, or that fewer people statistically speaking are victims of these problems is a moot point. The point also is not that there has been very little development in building a modern economy in India. Even if it is less than what India was capable of, it is quite considerable looked at from the sheer increase in the size of science and technology, industry, trade, agriculture, infrastructure and so on. But what singularly marks the Indian experience with development even when we compare with it not with east and south east Asia but even countries like Tanzania for instance, is the relative inability of the Indian pattern of development to solve the basic problems of poverty, health, literacy, livelihood, housing, etc. Economic and technological development in India, in other words, has failed to provide solutions to social problems. So obviously the growing acceptance of democracy is not because it has solved the problems of society. Even today half the illiterates of the world are found in India and the number of children at the age of three is close to half of the total. Thus the Indian experience with democracy seems to me to be somewhat unique. It goes contrary to what J.S. Mill theorised and which is taken as the epitome of democratic wisdom.[12] Where then do we look to for such a widespread acceptance of democracy as desirable?

The clue, I would like to suggest, lies in what has happened to the social structure with the working of democracy, in the context of the development of capitalist relations, in India. This has unhinged the rigidity of the mechanism through which social conformity of the most severe kind was conventionally enforced in India. All traditional societies enforce strict conformity; that is, codes both at the level of morals and conventions are not advocated but imposed. It means that force, rather than persuasion and reasoning, is the mode of enforcing compliance. This is important because advocacy implies persuasion whereas imposition is evidently coercive. But in India, in addition to this, much else is involved. With its caste system India has been quite a case by itself. There is a powerful, inbuilt mechanism in it to push people towards a status ridden, hierarchic downgrading and through this process a systematic denial of respect and dignity to people in the lower orders of the caste system. Rather, humiliation is systematically used as a weapon to keep people from developing self-confidence to stand up and speak. Because of the scriptural sanctions that it enjoyed, it has been a self-validating system of authority and traditions associated with it. All this started breaking up, slowly in the beginning but gathering strength as time went by, with the industrialisation and urban growth, increasing penetration of capitalist ways of accumulation of surplus in the country side, subsumption of labour and all else which goes with the development of capitalism. And this ongoing process of capitalist development, since Independence, has all taken place within a framework of a more or less sustained working democracy. This has given a specific flavour to the making of modernity in India.

Modernity may, as it is alleged, enforce normalisation everybody made to live by the same standards and norms but it is not conformist in any sense. Modernity allows for a great deal of autonomy of persons. It does so, first, by giving rise to an objective, historical process of individuation making persons bound up within commu-nities into self-referring individuals and by putting a high premium on individual choices for life styles and self re making. It permits me to become different from my surroundings and to live at a certain distance from the communities out of which I may have emerged. It undermines those conditions, which make life unfree. Democracy, when it functions uninterruptedly in the context of such a change, facilitating and checking its excesses, has a loosening effect on the inherited social structures, which were always seen to be excessively oppressive, especially their hierarchical features, sustaining notions of high and low in terms of purity and pollution. This is what, it seems to me, to have been happening in India over the years of functioning of democracy. Rule of majority, whatever its limitations in India, recognises individual level equality of vote and rights which enable people to wage struggles even when other aspects of equality are regularly denied in practice.

Denials and affirmations are a complex amalgam here in Indian society. As a Dalit I may be denied access to the village well or an upper caste house or even at the barber's shop. As a woman I may not be allowed to regulate my time or work. Nevertheless, as a citizen my vote, whatever I am in social status, is not worth any less as compared to a Brahmin's or that of a patron. Similarly, my evidence as a witness in a judicial process does not count as any less in value. This disjunction between social existence and citizenship does, no doubt, lessen my functioning as a citizen but does not negate it. It in fact opens up a terrain for struggles, and however constrained my struggles, they are means of enhancing my capacity to function as a citizen and to narrow the gap between this and my social existence. With this when people become conscious of group numerical strength, there also comes to them a greater sense of ability to move things in their own favour, a little here and a little there.[13]

Democracy in India is therefore an assertion of the urge for more self respect and a sense of dignity and to be better than what you were made to be. This is a clear manifestation of the secular power of society that is simultaneously the erosion of the self-validating nature of the power of the social structure. All this has conferred an added thrust to and taken forward the radical impulses generated through the powerful popular movements from the time of the Freedom Strug-gle, in spite of the ruling classes acting as a brake on the process. Let us look at this a little closely.

Indian society for ages unforeseen had given an effective voice only to a small stratum made up of what are called the *dwija* castes or the *Savarnas*. It may have, perhaps, been overtly less repressive than the other pre-modern class societies, but its mechanisms of conformity were more ideologically based on the internalisation of direct scriptural sanctions then anywhere else. This stratum called the dwija headed by the Brahmins took the voice of every one else away. The intention here is not to present a very unified picture of pre-modern Indian society. It is simply to draw a contrast, a stark one at that. I am quite aware that Brahminical hegemony was often challenged. This started with Buddhism and continued with Bhakti movements, Islamic Sufism, Sikhism, and similar less known trends among the oppressed. Yet the Brahminical hegemony never got disordered in any sustained way over widespread areas, as any Dalit or woman would vouch for. Alternatively the challenge to Brahminism was often beaten back as Buddhism in 10-12 centuries, or continued as minor trends as happened with much of the Bhakti movements.

Democracy with all the struggles, agitations, mobilisations of all kinds, electoral participation and such other things, broke the rigidity of the enforcement mechanisms of the social structure. The most lowly placed in the Indian society, the worst victims of this, could feel a little less suffocated; in a minimal way they could feel what it means to breath the air of freedom, a sense as well of what all freedom could become. Here both an emphasis and a reiteration are required. The erosion of the inflexibility and hardness of enforcement mechanisms should not be confused with the modernisation of social institutions or the replacement of caste and other traditional institutions with modern ones.

Here we must also be careful and not over read the situation. What the ordinary people have gained, given the conditions of their social existence, is very little. It is important to realise what is the limit on this freedom. It is exercised in a very narrow space. And this space becomes available by the traditional power becoming *loosely regulated and sporadic in its nature*. The power of the traditional institutions has not broken down completely and therefore conditions, which constrain the people from exerting their powers to enhance the realm of choices remains ever present. To put it in another way, it means that reprisals have become *ad hoc* in nature. Ordinary, poor people can go on doing things in their own way, contrary to inherited norms. But then at points unforeseen they may be hit at with varying severity. So reprisals have not gone but have become random and are not systematic like earlier. But then again they now can register a FIR with police and, more importantly, organise more people of their kind to fight back. Nevertheless this, I presume, is the opening they really cherish, in face of deprivations and denials. People have forced their admission, limited though, into the world of social dealings. In defending the democratic system it seems to be this little gain that they cannot think of being deprived of.

From the point made above, an important implication follows. The conditions of social existence being what they are, the inequalities within the society having, without becoming any less severe, changed, seen in a relative sense, their terrain in an important sense. What stared people in the face and which took away their voice were the ritual status inequalities. In their place have come to *fore* the economic inequalities and with this those of power in the secular sphere. Inequalities of income and power in the secular world, unlike those of the ritual world, do not restrain the assertion of civic and political rights. In fact they encour-age these and help bring together, as is happening all over the world, egalitarian values as integral to the democratic princi-ple, for struggle and debate. It is in the very essence of eco-nomic and other secular inequalities to elicit a counter trend of fighting against this. And it is this, which is the basis of all radical consciousness.

IV

Let me conclude this discussion with a conjecture, which seems to me to be the central point of developments in Indian democracy. *The democratic process, or the processes around democracy, has detached itself* from the institutional infirmities surrounding it, whether they be of the parties, representation, leadership, etc. and in the course of this the process has acquired an *autonomy* of its own. The deepening legitimacy for democratic polity inheres here, in the process—the struggles including electoral battles and various others organised and unorganised agitations. The process is the space, which becomes available, contracting now and expanding then, for the range of resistance people are capable of. The invisible incremental advances and "concessions" won are registered here. This happens in spite of the shape that the organised field of politics has acquired. What I want to suggest in passing here is that a radical revision of the theories of legitimacy together with how it comes about and where it resides, as elaborated in academic studies in the West, is called for in relation to other experiences with democracy. With the growing commitments for democracy in India, it is doubtful if the norms of democracy have spread, nor can we be sure if the deference for procedures has grown. Functioning of democracy in India has also not provided for an opportunity for radical solutions to problems of social life. Yet, as we have seen, it has given rise to a new kind of democratic progress, constrained no doubt by the hegemonic bourgeois condition and the remnants of the ritual world.

We thus have a third repercussion for democratic "governance", the disjuncture between the process of politics and the exercise of state power. These have become like horsepowers harnessed in opposite directions but with the balance always tilting in the direction of state power. Given this tilt, the conscience of the state is always in the deficit, giving rise to incongruence between the reason for political participation and governmental outcomes. The defeat of the BJP and the contradictions in the working of the UPA government are clear indications of this severance. This lends a peculiar vibrancy to democracy in India. A silent class backlash is always in the offing. The electoral verdict of the year 2004 clearly tells us this and suggests what democratic "governance" ought to be like.

An End-Word On Governance

All the changes and developments we have talked about are taking place in the era of globalisation, the WTO led liberalisation and structural adjustments. This period of the ascendance of (centralised) international finance capital has targeted the State as an institution of social welfare. It is a period of the decline of State as a benign institution providing small relief to people to make life liveable. This has serious repercussions for people's wellbeing across the world. There are more poor people in the advanced capitalist countries today than ever before after the end of Second World War and a far greater concentration of income and wealth with the capitalists. But the consequences are much worse for the people in the third world.

Ordinary people here, as a routine, live a life of unmet daily needs. They cannot pay for education and health and shelter and so on. The State under the dictates of global capital is withdrawing from these areas and privatising welfare, denying these basic necessities to people in dire need of these. The quality of life of the people in terms of nutrition and health has drastically declined over much of Asia and Africa in the last two decades

Globalisation has also led to the de-ideologisation of politics as can be seen in the position of all parties on the questions of "reform" baring the Left. The main function of politics is no more to tend to people's needs but to facilitate the unfettered growth of capital, both domestic and global but in unregulated competition. How well the

State does this is being referred to as *good governance*. I, therefore, started with and continued using governance in the quotes. My brief was to talk on democracy and governance. So I did not want to begin by picking a tiff with my hosts. Now at the end, when I am re-writing the talk, I want to reflect briefly on this.

Given that the main function of the government is facilitating the unfettered growth of capital, good governance is also dismantling of controls and tariff barriers, low taxes on the proprietors of capital and owners of wealth, privatisation of government assets, and so on; all round de-regulation for unhindered capital flows across the national barriers. The form of State that informs this process is one, which thinks like a corporation. It is, therefore, not surprising that Chandrababu Naidu, the chief protagonist of reform and the monitor-boy of the World Bank crowd, felt proud when he was referred to as CEO rather than as Chief Minister. The state under him became internally akin to a corporation This was the pinnacle of good governance. India was chided to become like Andhra Pradesh under Chanrababu Naidu.

Governance as a descriptive term is quite old and harmless but as a new import from World Bank with its conceptual baggage, it is deeply value-loaded in favour of capital and market. "Corporate Governance", in vogue, is the model for democratic governments. We should, therefore, be aware of implications when take to its use, uncritically use allows the World Bank assumptions to slide in.

It is interesting to note that the government of West Bengal with all its social commitments and democratic initiatives and devolution of powers to people has never been, as far as I am aware, looked upon as providing good governance. Kerala, with a lower per capita income than many states in India but having the highest index for the quality of life, has not had the honour of being called a good governed state. Nor have the governments of some of the Latin American States, where people have revolted against globalisation and forced an alternative agenda on the State, supposed to provide good governance. This is the case with many governments in Latin America and their number is happily growing. But Venezuela under Hugo Chavez is the prime example. The more it does for the basic needs of the people and to build the national economic well being the more it is criticised for irresponsible governance. The manner in which the word has been selectively used for certain types of States makes it deeply suspect, in its current usage.

Notes and References

1. To mention a few of these, the DMK government appointed the Rajamannar Committee to look into this issue and the Tamil Nadu government published Report of the Centre-States Relations Inquiry Committee, (Madras, 1971); the Akali Dal government In Punjab adopted the Anandpur Sahib Resolution, (Amritsar, 1973); and the Left-Front government of West Bengal issued *A Memorandum on Centre State Relations*, (Calcutta, 1977). The Chief Ministers of the opposition ruled states also held regular conclaves for pressuring the Central government for greater state autonomy. See also K.P. Bombwall, (ed.) *National Power and State Autonomy*, New Delhi, 1977.
2. Javeed Alam, "Class, Political and National Dimensions of the State Autonomy Movements In India", *Social Scientist*, No.111, August, 1982.
3. Kerala already had land reforms under the Communist Party led government of EMS Namboodiripad during 1957-59. So the class struggle during this period did look so pronounced here.
4. On the nature and the mode of operation of global finance capital and implications including for theory see from his many writings on this Prabhat Patnaik's "Introduction" to *Lenin—Imperialism: Highest Stage of Capitalism*, LeftWord, New Delhi, 2000.
5. There is a historical coincidence here that makes for an interesting reading and comparison and a possible, though tenuous, connection with the past as antiquity. The reading has to do with, what I consider to be, the manner of the making of Indian plurality and its specificity. As we look at India today, below the nation-state, there are numerous linguistic cultural communities and these are the starting points of Indian diversity or plurality and this diversity, from here, moves down to innumerable smaller communities and groups.

   One important legacy from history has been the fact that what are now the linguistic-cultural communities (evolving as distinct linguistic regions from the time of the Sangam period in the South and from the period of Bhakti movements in the rest of India) could never be kept together into a single State through conquest. This is of quite some consequence. It is quite unlike in the case of China where only a centralized state could create and hold the civilizational belt to-gether. The relatively high degree of civilizational uniformity across the regions that we find and varying degree of cultural unity within the different regions that India achieved before colonialism has not been the result of state induced coercion as happened in China or forced incorporation as in the Czarist Russia which the post-revolutionary multi-national Soviet state inherited. The civilizational uniformity came about imperceptibly and the regions drawn in into patterns in affinity with this uniformity through a single framework of action based mainly on the *Varna* order— ideology and prescriptions or rituals and the slow dissemination of a set of philosophical pre-suppositions like, for example, notions like *karma*, *moksha* and so on (which are common to high tradition and local religious beliefs). These features, both the framework of social action as well as the philosophi-cal pre-suppositions, had come to acquire a deep rooted social accept-ance before the British came. The coming of Muslims and varying large scale presence in different parts of India only added a diversity into the cultural unity of the various linguistic-cultural regions; a diversity unlike other ones in the sense that it could not be assimi-lated into the Hindu world view and which later became problematc with the rise of the national movement.

Suffice it to note here that there neither was an enduring presence of a centralized State (as in China) nor an organized Church (as the Roman Church in Western Europe) to enforce centrally conceived compliance with a belief system and social or ritual norms, important in facilitating the creation of a civilizational belt. Hundreds of locally based, traditionally inherited modes of enforcing compliance do not induce a feeling of being forced by an outside, external power; local chieftains may surely have played a role but these cannot be considered as the key elements in the system of compliance which was the dominant, enduring form in

India.The State as a centralized institution though not absent but was an episodic presence, with very long periods intervening without one such institution. This mode of creation of common or similar cultural complexes and the conceptions and practices embedded in them is very much an Indian inheritance. This inheritance, in multiple reconfigura-tions and constructions, became an important ingredient in the making of modern India, India as a nation state.

All this came about through a peculiar pattern, and this is the second pre-colonial legacy, of Brahminical expansion, an important feature in the evolution of the principles of state-craft. In this mode of social formation and cultural incorporation, the Brahminical or high culture confronted proto-state or insulated sections of society which were in many ways very different from the Brahmanic world-view; various forms and levels of, variations notwithstanding, tribal existence. The Brahminical culture entered into a process of give and take, accommodation, or, to use a more current term, made compromises. Leaving apart the essential features of the social structure the highly hierarchical caste system (with Brahminical supremacy at the one end and at the other end untouchability) and the core philosophical beliefs of *Sanatan Dharam*, everything else was allowed to remain as it was, or was left to itself. [Some of these interpretations are based on works like Romila Thapar, *From Lineage to State: Social Formation in the Mid-First Millenium in the Ganga Valley*, Oxford Paperbacks, New Delhi,1990; and *Ancient Indian Social History*, Orient Longman, New Delhi, 1978, see concluding Ch. for exceptions to this pattern; see also R.S. Sharma, *The State and Varna Formation in the Mid-Ganga Plains: An Ethnoarchaeological View*, Manohar Paperbacks, Delhi, 1996. Although I have drawn on these authors, some of the interpretations are entirely mine and I do not intend to burden them with much of what I am saying here].This provided for an inherent, non-definable plurality of practice in the daily life of the people. This *insulated plurality* was to remain the basis of a great deal of autonomous cultural innovations in the different regions of India. Thus the pre-colonial hegemonic system— civilizational *uniformity across* the regions and cultural *unity within* the regions—

in India was built around core definitions about the world by the literati but the daily routine activity was left to evolve on its own. So we have had the "unique" thing called India with a high degree of unification in the social formation as well as a bewildering variety of diversity.

Now what has all this to do with the argument in the text? My purpose here has been to draw attention to the deep-rooted and highly autonomous nature of Indian "diversity" in the Nehruvian idiom or what I have been calling plurality. The high degree of internal autonomy of the plurality of social forms of life, I presume to think, invites spontaneous resistance when fiddled by an external authority. And this, I again presume, provides a connection, even if tenuous, with the contemporary social reality. Attempts made to homogenise social life by a centralised external force, in the way BJP has been attempting to do, tend to meet with resistance. Nevertheless, it is always a pleasure in the way of knowledge to sometime give in to audacious speculations, if these enrich our imagination.

6. Talking of capitalist development in agriculture I do not want here to enter into the question about the "mode of production in agriculture" debate. I only want to point out that any mode of production can have reference to, methodologically speaking, the entire economy as such and not just to, I believe, this or that sector of the economy. I take it that capitalism has been developing in agriculture in all part of India, much more in some places than in others; whatever the empirical evidence of feudal practices and castes atrocities and gender violence. Anyway for those who are interested in the debate can see Utsa Patnaik ed., *Agrarian Relations and Accumulation-the Mode of Production Debate*, Sameksha Trust Publication, Bombay, 1993.

7. For a general and comprehensive review of land reforms, see P.C. Joshi, *Land Reforms in India,* Allied Publishers, Delhi, 1975; for the strategic implications of various patterns of land reforms contemplated in India and with what political implication these were implemented in different regions of India, a very incisive analysis is in Bhawani Sen, *Evolution of Agrarian Relations in India*, People's Publishing House, New Delhi, 1962.

8. Javeed Alam, "Is Caste Appeal Casteism? Oppressed Castes in Politics", *Economic and Political Weekly*, 27 March 1999; see also mine "Caste, Class and Social Consciousness: Reflections on Contemporary Indian Situation", in K.L. Sharma, *Caste and Class in India*, Rawat, Jaipur & Delhi, 1994.
9. See Hegel's discussion of "Lordship and Bondage" in *Phenomenology of Spirit* for the importance of recognition in the making of the self.
10. For details of this process see my article cited in note 8.
11. For details on each of these like the sense of usefulness of vote, the greater proportion of the poor and oppressed among the voters, the distrust of the leaders, etc. see the chapters 1 & 2 of Javeed Alam, *Who Wants Democracy?* (Tracts for the Times 15), Orient Longman, New Delhi, 2004.
12. In *Representative Government*, Everyman's Library, London, 1960, J.S. Mill is clear that 'universal teaching must precede universal enfranchisement', p. 280. In the following page Mill elaborates how this can be easily ascertained. The ability to read, write, and calculate.... 'should in all cases accompany universal suffrage...", p.281. It is common sense among the western liberal theorist that democracy cannot go along with illiteracy and poverty. Indian experience asks for a different theorising about conditions of democracy.
13. For the importance of small things like these in the fight for equality and for dignifying capability see A.K. Sen, *Inequality Reexamined*, Oxford University Press, New Delhi, 1995.

2

Governance, Social Capital and Democracy: Revisiting the Indian Scenario

Amartya Mukhopadhyay

It is no use decrying concepts just because of their genealogy. For, many of the concepts, terms and phrases that are used daily all over the world have a Western and not wholly immaculate conception. Besides none of the realities encapsulated by these concepts was, once, sometimes, or continuously non-existent in Third World societies. This makes it possible to look at them not only 'etically', but 'emically' too;[1] to not ignore them as 'a breath of politic words' that 'has withered our rose tree'[2] of our lived experience.

But the conscientious scholar who raises such question may falter a bit if s/he is shown the changed atmosphere in which the new breath of 'politic' words is turning into a gale, making any catholicity in their acceptance potentially disastrous. From the beginning of the twentieth century, through the entire history of the Cold War, an alternative repertoire of concepts was always handy to counterbalance the sway of liberal-democratic terms. One might even say that one redeeming feature of the Cold War in hindsight was the absence of the eerie 'oneness' that has overtaken the world ever since. Compared with that time "what stands out about contemporary conceptions of global order is their oneness ... particular doctrines, each with its own constituency and lineage, come together to outline a larger project. Simply to name the discourses tells a story: neoliberalism, democratisation and good governance, civil society, the role of the third sector and the internationalisation of philanthropy, social development and the conditionalities of aid, humanitarian intervention in complex emergencies. A grand narrative if there was one. It holds out the prospect of global management with the promise of popular ratings: elements of a blueprint, yet humanised and often appealing to immediate need. There is also an oneness in another respect: that of one world. Its evangelical appeal meshes neatly with the reassertion of Western leadership."[3]

Darby finds this new project and discourse continuous with the earlier British imperial one that similarly hinged on the alluring wonder of the market economy, of 'the Great Commercial Republic of the World' as a haven of order and prosperity, a similar missionary urge, an identical invocation of military aid in support of civil power, and above all, a meliorism about progress strongly reminiscent of the earlier scheme.[4] So somewhat ignoring the distinction made by some scholars between the "Empire", or the contemporary order, and the earlier Pax Britannica,[5] he warns that "under American leadership after the Cold War, the globalisation of ideas about governmentality has established international benchmarks to which all societies are expected to conform."[6]

This is what is disturbing, not the concepts themselves but the contexts of their origination, not the bullets, but the billets behind them. But even so a saner approach might be to explore if there is anything that is worthy of retrieving from among the terms of the new gospel, do the required amount of conceptual engineering, and re-operationalise them for local purposes in terms not only of their indicators and component processes, but also of their translatability in different settings. It is with the hope of steering this middle course between uncritical, catholic acceptance and mimicry and blind, counterphobic rejection that the present paper seeks in the following sections to evaluate the two concepts of 'governance' and 'social capital', trace their lineage very briefly, point out their conceptual limitations even in the Western setting, zero in on the points of merit in them, comment on their scope and measurability in the Indian context, and then suggest what we can offer to supplement or substitute them.

Governance: Contexts, Meanings and Conceptual Limitations

The concept of governance has had inauspicious birth, namely efforts of the World Bank, in the backdrop of the failure of its structural adjustment initiatives in sub-Saharan Africa, and the safety of its loans, to put an end to the inefficiency and corruption of the local states in these countries. This induced it to equate good governance, in a regime-neutral way, with administrative efficiency, transparency in public institutions, and preservation of law and order.[7] This resulting Washington Consensus pleaded for liberalising reforms in wide areas of fiscal discipline, public expenditure priorities, taxation, financial markets, trade, privatisation and competition policy, deregulation, property rights, foreign direct investment, exchange rates etc. Armed with this neoliberal package, the Bank, the Fund (IMF) and other multilateral agencies wrought deep changes in the economic contours of governance, that have ever since tried to influence global economic policies.[8]

There is nothing surprising in this terminological onslaught. The post-Cold War end to the previous super-power competition had rid the US of the need to humour wily Third World leaders like Mobutu Sese Seko of Zaire, and had obviated the need for gestures like the Brady Plan or the Mexican rescue, in which politics had dominated economics. Still less surprising has been the alacrity with which bilateral donor agencies pounced on the concept;, to link it with democracy, their conception of civil society and other handy concepts, so as to smuggle conditionalities into their aid schemes. What is surprising is the ease with which not only scholars in the West, but in the Third World also desist from attempts to mend the soft boundaries of the concept,[9] before advocating it as the reference point of institutional reform. We are trying to provide below a glimpse of the numerous conceptions of governance in their imaginings.

We begin with two scholars who have distinguished governance from government to free the former from the exclusive control of national governments. By governance they mean the 'the processes and institutions, both formal and informal, that guide and restrain the collective activities of a group.' Government, by contrast, is 'the subset that acts with authority and creates formal obligations.' Since governance need not necessarily be undertaken exclusively by governments and international organisations to which they delegate authority, private firms, associations of firms, NGOs, and associations of them, may engage in it, "sometimes in association with governmental bodies", and "sometimes without governmental authority."[10]

Plotting governance on a global scale, Nye and Donahue proceed to set the terms for project for global governance. Since world government is untenable at present, as the 'nation-state is not about to be replaced as the primary institution of domestic and global governance' (a pity!) and laissez faire might prove 'a recipe for backlash', they profess their search for an 'intermediate solution: a set of practices for governance that improve coordination and create safety valves for political and social pressures, consistent with the maintenance of nation states as the fundamental form of political organisation.' Such arrangements are expected to create a level playing field for a 'heterogeneous array of agents from the private sector and the third sector as well as from governments.' The solution is provided by the principle of 'networked minimalism', 'networked' because globalisation is best conceptualised as such, and 'minimalist' because governance at the global level would find acceptance only if it does not supersede national governance, and if its intrusions into the autonomy of the states and communities, are not easily justified in terms of 'cooperative results'.[11]

Some other scholars, however, suggest leanness of government structures in novel ways and seek to construct a simultaneously lean and strong state to achieve an optimal amount of 'stateness' at the local level. While assuring us that there is nothing wrong with the Washington Consensus per se and that it was for strategic reasons that the relative emphasis in the 1990s was on reduction of state activity, Fukuyama concedes that 'the state building agenda that was at least as important as the state-reducing one, was not given as much thought or emphasis.' He admits that this intellectual myopia had cost the process of liberalising economic reform dearly in terms of delivery of results. So Fukuyama seeks to balance the 'cut back' on states in some sectors and the 'state bloat' in others, with a proper mix of the scope of state functions and the strength of state institutions for different countries. He depends on the *World Development Report* of the World Bank(WB) in 1997 for a list of state functions ranging from 'minimalist' through 'intermediate' to 'activist' categories that provide the X-axis of his stateness graph. For the Y-axis of state capacity and institutional quality he depends on the Corruption Perception Index developed by the Transparency International that uses survey data primarily from the business communities operating in different countries, the privately collected International Country Risk Guide Numbers decomposable into separate measures of corruption, law and order, and bureaucratic quality, and the governance indicators developed by the WB for 199 countries for six aspects of governance. Combining the two dimensions of scope and strength of institutions he constructs a graph with four quadrants. Plotting different states in different quadrants on the basis of their scores in the two axes, he shows how some of them, because of reforms in the two areas, have been moving from one quadrant to a desirable or undesirable other. Unsatisfactory movements are accounted for by the fact that many states have, in the process of reducing state scope, either decreased state strength, or released demands for new types of state capabilities that were either weak or non-existent, to fall on the wrong side of the X-axis. As a result while, according to Fukuyama, the optimum reform path should have been decreasing scope and augmenting strength (Path 1), they chose other routes.

This allegedly convinced Fukuyama of the need to supply institutions across four related aspects of 'stateness', namely: i) organisational design and management; ii) political system design;

iii) basis of legitimisation; and iv) structural and cultural factors. Rightly ordering the transferability of these components of institutional capacity into high (for organisational design and management), medium (for institutional or political system design), medium to low (for basis of legitimisation) and low (for social and cultural factors) zones,[12] Fukuyama has turned his attention to the problem of public administration for weak states.[13] But the morale of the story is that while the amount of transferable knowledge has been greatest for the first component, there has been some transferable know-how for the second and third components as well.[14] But this has depended on the demand for institutions in countries where the state was weak.

Transferability of institutions at any level is, however, admitted to be problematic and not amenable to rational choice analysis. The rise of even good, rational institutions in different countries 'historically out of a host of non-rational, contingent circumstances that could not easily be duplicated in other settings, the utility of exogenous shocks (like currency crisis, recession, hyperinflation, revolution or war)'- all these induce Fukuyama to arrive at a very portentous conclusion. It is that the majority of 'cases of successful state-building and institutional reform have occurred when a society has generated a strong demand for institutions and *has created them out of whole cloth, imported them from the outside, or adapted foreign models to local conditions.*' (Italics mine). The instances of successful creation or adaptation are early modern Europe, the United States after the American Revolution, Germany, Japan, and Turkey in the 19th century, South Korea and Taiwan in the 1960s.

Once the utility of pure or adapted foreign models is thus established, Fukuyama safely turns to the techniques and prospects for generating demand from the outside. Finding aid conditionalities wanting, exertion of political power from countries or consortia of countries as occupation authorities or through a strong direct relationship with the local government doomed to failure, he issues a timely warning. It is that the 'international community is not only simply limited in the amount of capacity it can build; *it is actually complicit in the destruction of institutional capacity in many countries.*'(Italics mine). At least one reason of this inadvertent destruction is the contradictory objectives that international aid agencies seek to serve and their failure to resolve the trade off between capacity building amidst the inefficiencies and corruption of the recipient regimes and providing best services to end users.[15]

Even though Fukuyama's treatment of governance is more sophisticated than most others' and its triumphalism is less marked than in his panegyrics of liberal democracy ten years back, [16]the decadal variation cannot hide the stark reality that governance is more often than not viewed on a global scale, and the *deus ex machina* for it is to be provided by the US whose state-building is near perfect, as it permanently occupies quadrant 1. This is evident from the muffled criticism of European state managers in persisting with quadrant 2.[17] Some other scholars are, however, even less subtle. For example, Manuel Castells starts his plea for global governance and an *emerging network state* on the basis of world-wide surveys of the crisis of political legitimacy in Latin America and sixty other countries including the US and Western Europe, Netherlands and France, as reflected in the disaffection of the majority of their citizens in manifestations ranging from opinion surveys, Gallup polls to voter revolts etc. Then he proceeds by a short series of steps to 'international paternalism'[18] of the worst kind. Castells deciphers the structural underpinnings of the world-wide crisis of political legitimacy and citizen-disillusionment in terms of the 'increasing ability of the political system anchored in the nation state to represent citizens in the effective practice of global governance and the ascendance of global governance as an increasingly essential component of national and local governance.' This helps him itemize different levels of global governance ranging from constitution of a world government on the basis of current international institutions to the 'emerging network state', characterised among other things by 'shared sovereignty and responsibility'. The basis of this re-worlding is of course a synergic relationship between the market, that 'takes care of economic growth and equilibrium with minimal supervision and correction from government', and the 'global civil society, made up of NGOs and other forms of aggregation of interests' that organises popular expression, connecting to the government as the processor of reformist projects and demands in the international system. With the nation states at best suffered as a kind of organisational migraine, even when they toe the line, the monitoring of this civil society is to be done by a multidimensional civil society. The recalcitrant nation states would be made to genuflect in other ways. The following lines are revealing:

> *Granted, it is unlikely that all states will accept this global democracy. Yet such states may well become the new form of failed states. The political outcasts would not be designated by the superpowers, in terms of their own interests, but stigmatized by the global civil society acting on behalf of values of humanity.*[19]

Even when there have been more sophisticated attempts to define governance, they have ultimately come round to the sponsored and certified view of cutting back on state for effective policy implementation. For example, before spelling out her notion of governance, Frischtak [20] churns the existing literature to identify four dominant conceptions of government, each of which refers to ways of preventing the capture of the state by special interests.

The first identifies governance with democratic processes or institutions in its 'classical liberal distrust of government and all things political'. It wants to keep government small, in the idea that the best government is the least government, and that governance is best understood as the exercise of democratic government that maintains the dominance of the rules of economics over those of politics. But in its throwback to the heyday of modernisation theory in the 1950s and 1960s the happy correlation between democracy and growth that this conception restores suffers from a similar desideratum of empirical evidence.

The second conception is implied in analyses that do not refer directly to governance, but locate the prime obstacle to effective promotion of public policy in the institutional capacity of governments, decomposed into such traits as 'insulation, autonomy, rationality, and technocratic qualities, which make both the governmental machinery and its personnel less permeable to the disruptions and corruptions of politics'. Steering clear of any debate between small and big government, this view emphasises on institution building, while eschewing any mechanistic approach to it, but leaves open the question of what conditions would allow countries to develop this capacity.

The third conception points to 'the importance of culture as a code or language'. Borrowing from the development experience of Africa, where development projects imported from abroad, and externally transplanted forms of political organisation, led to maladjustments and to governance crisis and failure, and seeking to learn from countries like Japan and Korea that were able to modernise without losing their cultural moorings, this approach drives home the point that 'governance has to be culturally bound'. Frischtak has no complaint against this conception's cultural relativism, save the revealing reservation that there is no reason to suppose that the 'indigenous community' sustained by it '*will be more congruent with the free public sphere of Western societies* than it has been with the central controls of public agencies' that were transplanted, 'or that this community will be culturally more amenable to the market than to the state as the main resource allocation mechanism.'

The fourth and final conception views governance as 'the provision of universal and abstract rules, the institutions that enforce them and the predictable mechanisms to regulate conflicts over both rules and their enforcement.'

While agreeing more with this conception that with the others, because of its affinity with the Weberian rational- legal ideal type of the state, Frischtak mentions her point of departure. It is that because of the changed contexts of the development of the state in the colonial setting from the original European one in which the liberal state was mandated, the same concept of governance would not apply there. In the non-European context the state is not 'neutral, or contentless, but has to have purposes and directions. By virtue of its anticipatory and creative role, it may be called demiurgic' and the 'behavioural discontinuity between the procedural state of Western democracies and the demiurgic state' makes an alternative conception of governance in developing countries imperative.

Initially we are presented with great expectations when this alternative conception is first spelt out: "positive governance in developing countries depends on the state's capacity to provide a meta goal or meta idea that serves as the organising principle of a changed society and endows the state with the power to withstand capture from private interests. This conception of governance suggests that the capacity to enforce law and order and promote effective policy is contingent on state autonomy, which in turn is contingent on sources of state power distinct from those of the major economic players in society, which, finally, is contingent on the state's ability to project a culturally bound vision of a reorganized society." But after recounting the experiences of Africa, Bolivia, and other Third World countries, Frischtak argues that whenever the states in these countries have expanded the scope of government to enhance government capacity, they have fended off old, vested interests, but become the prisoner of newly created ones. "Expanding capacity by expanding the scope of government, however, and incorporating both old and new interests into the state apparatus , makes the developing state increasingly vulnerable to capture, and in fact mortgages its very autonomy. Because the other face of political incorporation is state penetration, the very logic of behaviour propels the state to expand in order to increase its maneuverability and expand the potential for capture."

From this point on the path is brilliantly simple. Governance as 'the uncoupled dynamic quality of government', the latter understood as 'the norms, processes, instruments, institutions that comprise the state apparatus', has a different shape in the developing countries because of the different nature of the power the developing states exert. While in most western developed countries, the state creates power out of the societal impasse created by the impossibility of any powerful interest kicking, like Punchinello in the puppet show, all out before it, in most developing countries marked by the absence of any similar impasse, state power has typically been generated through the state's espousal of a projected vision of a renewed society.[21]

This vision, however, cannot be anything like a Nehruvian vision applied in India. This is because its parameters have been fixed on the basis of successful examples of 'structural adjustment' in Korea, Turkey, Mexico, and Argentina (of course before the collapse).[22] The details need not delay us. The message is clear that there is no alternative between 'structural adjustment' and total disaster.

The deafening 'silence' in this visionary proposal is on the moving spirit behind the globally operating market, namely, the Bank and the IMF. They need no governance, though very often their doings have wreaked havoc in many countries. And yet the policy package of the Fund and the Bank that has foregrounded governance as the panacea of the administrative ills of the Third World states, have been pilloried by a foremost American economist, who was a key member of President Bill Clinton's Council of Economic Advisers, and later the chief economist of the Bank. He actually went to the length of suggesting governance of the IMF from the vantage point of information economics that earned him the Nobel Prize in 2001. In his opinion the "IMF's policies, in part based on the outworn presumption that markets by themselves lead to efficient outcomes, failed to allow for desirable governmental interventions in the market, measures which can guide economic growth and make everyone better off."[23] Moreover, the reason why IMF's policies were bad was that neither 'good economics ', nor 'good policies' dominated their formulation. "Decisions were made on the basis of what seemed a curious blend of ideology and bad economics, dogma that sometimes seemed to be thinly veiled special interests. When crises hit, the IMF prescribed outmoded, inappropriate, if 'standard' solutions, without considering the effects they would have on the people in the countries told to follow these policies." With breathtaking candor Stiglitz revealed that it was ideology "which guided policy prescription and countries were told to follow the IMF guidelines without debate".[24] Setting out to diagnose why the IMF, the Bank and other international financial institutions (IFIs) did not learn from their mistakes in policies even after the 1997 Asian Crisis, the exacerbation of the crises in Indonesia and Thailand and the collapse in Argentina in 2001, Stiglitz found out that basically it was the 'problem of governance: who decides what they do.' Dominated not merely by the richest industrialised countries, but by the commercial and financial interests of them, the policies of the Fund and the Bank merely reflect their considerations. This could not be otherwise, because the prevailing situation is, according to him, one of 'global governance without global government...'. And the Fund and other IFIs present it 'as received doctrine propositions and policy recommendations for which there is no widespread agreement', rather 'a massive amount of evidence against'. So in his view, the most fundamental change that is required to make globalisation work is the way that it should bring in change in governance. This means nothing more than making these bodies more accessible, not only to Third World states, but to their citizens.[25]

Of course, this view of 'governance' as reining in the IMF and the Bank to put an end to 'market fundamentalism' would not appeal to the new evangelists of the concept. This is because the policies that Stiglitz questioned are not the results of individual quirks of statesmen, or interest-seeking by individual states, but are rather symptomatic of the current phase of a long-drawn strategy of whittling down social democracy of the radical variety. It began with a vision of class harmony administered by welfare states in an expansionary context nurtured by rapid economic growth and relatively autonomous national markets. But as incipient globalisation in the early 1980s started restricting the chances of Keynesianism in one country, the challenges to the national Keynesianism and corporatist orthodoxies started mounting through the 1980s, a number of statesmen and economies began foregrounding an alternative strategy of capital accumulation that would pander to the demands of the new era. The quest for a new corporatism took three distinctive though related and interlinked forms. The *first* type enjoined some sort of productivity pact that linked progressive outcomes to improvements in the competitive capacity of labour and industry and became known as 'supply side corporatism'. The *second* variant went for a new distributional bargain that sought to remould social and income policies in a way that payoffs and sacrifices of economic growth would be spread within international constraints. This option was known as 'open ended corporatism'. The *third* arrangement, however, looked forward to a broader social compromise that wanted simultaneous optimisation of both competitive and distributional scenarios through increasing participation in all spheres of social life, and is labelled as 'corporatist social governance'[25]

Appearing last to remedy or at least attenuate the shortcomings of the first two approaches, the third compromise entailed harnessing available social resources in the shape of institutional networks and community activism, and devised strategies to augment them further. This consisted of 'associative', 'stakeholding' or 'communitarian' forms of social participation across economic, political and cultural spheres. Increased civic engagement was expected to solve the problem of social exclusion to marginalised groups, as also to tap the benefits of increased social dynamism through increasing the flow of information, commitment, and trust within expanding social networks. Seeking to distance themselves from postwar partnership patterns, its proponents chose, as their favourite targets of attacks, a cumbersome bureaucracy, a passive citizenry, and an impoverished group politics that were supposedly definitional of the Keynesian welfare state. In place of big labour, big bourgeoisie and big states they envisioned a more 'porous' state, a more diversified organisational politics and a higher level of political participation. This necessitated a thorough reconceptualisation of civil society that would help the transition from the universal state to a 'mixed economy of care', mediated by private and voluntary sectors. As Zeuge so aptly points out, 'social capital' has been 'one crucial building block of this discourse'.[26]

So this explains not just why the IMF and the Bank not only persisted in its market fundamentalist policies, but pounced a little too readily on the concept of 'social capital' as a twin concept for governance. The contexts of the origination, evolution and seizure of this concept form the subject of our next section.

The Tales of Social Capital and of Its Problems

Social capital, this now-famous term, first originated in the discipline of economics, where it was coined by the economist Glenn C. Loury, to identify the social resources useful for the development of human capital. Imported by James Coleman in social theory it initially meant capital that is distinct from physical or human capital in the following respects. i) It inheres in the structure of relations between persons and among persons, including family relations and community social organisation. ii) It is constituted by social organisation that facilitates the achievement of goals that could not be either achieved in its absence or could be achieved only at a much higher cost. iii) It is created when the relations among persons change in ways that facilitate action. And, iv) it is intangible being embedded in the relations among men.[27]

In what is considered as the 'ur-text' on social capital, Robert Putnam has used the concept to find out the reasons behind the differential performance of Italian regional governments.[28] The distinctiveness of Putnam's analysis lies not just in the emphasis he gives on trust, norms, networks etc for paving the way for coordinated actions in society, because the importance of norms as a social capital resource had been pointed out by Coleman himself. Examining norms from a rational choice perspective, asserting that 'norms do come into existence, that they do constrain behaviour, and that they therefore cannot be ignored in social theory', Coleman had justifiably claimed that he was laying the basis of a different usage of the concept of norms.[29] And he also spoke of the importance of trust in vastly different settings. For example, the trust that is placed in the heads of the state by the electorate, and the trustworthiness that the head in turn seeks in his agents, as also the trust that exists between loving and even lukewarm couples are forms of social capital for Coleman. He also considered concentrations of obligations as a source of social capital, and showed how a cooperative norm such as 'one should forgo one's self-interests to act in the interests of the collectivity', reinforced by social support, status, honour and other rewards, provides the social capital that new nations are built with.[30]

The novelty of Putnam's analysis lies rather in the following: the stress that he lays on historical continuities; the importance that he accords to generalised and impersonal 'thin trust', as distinct from 'thick trust', characteristic of traditional communities, as related to social capital formation; his forceful argument that horizontally organised voluntary associations cutting across social cleavages are more likely to nurture wider social cooperation and strengthen norms of reciprocity than hierarchical segmental organisations or clientelistic structures and make democracy 'work'; the singular importance he attaches to membership in cultural associations as distinct from membership in business groups, unions and parties; and the complex index of institutional performance based on twelve indicators that he has constructed.[31] Actually one signal payoff of the Putnamesque intervention to the concept of social capital is that one can actually measure the level of trust and cooperation and compare these levels across communities/ regions/ countries, and that one can assess empirically the influence of all these measured variables on various micro and macro social phenomena.

Fukuyama, however, regards the abovementioned definitions of 'social capital' as belonging more to the sphere of its manifestations, than to its essence. The different definition of 'social capital' he offers makes the distinction between public and personal social capital nearly evaporate. In his view, 'social capital is an instantiated informal norm that promotes cooperation between two or more individuals.' The constitutive norms can range from one of 'reciprocity between two friends all the way up to complex and elaborately articulated doctrines like Christianity and Confucianism.' They have only to be embedded in an actual human relationship, and facilitate cooperation in groups, through their relation with traditional values like honesty, the keeping of commitments, reliable performance of duties, reciprocities and the like. Besides, to be effective, a group's social capital must create a 'radius of trust'. This can be larger than the group itself if it produces only 'positive externalities', but smaller if 'in-group solidarity reduces the ability of group members to co-operate with outsiders, and ... imposes negative externalities on the latter'. As with Putnam so with Fukuyama, the 'thick' trust characteristic of traditional societies would not qualify as social capital. Traditional societies, suffer from the absence of 'weak ties', or ties among 'heterodox individuals at the periphery of the society's various social networks who are able to move between groups and thereby become bearers of new ideas and information.' Besides, while traditional societies are 'segmentary', modern societies typically compromise 'a large number of overlapping social groups that permit multiple memberships and identities.' Since traditional societies offer fewer opportunities for weak ties among the segments that constitute them, they transfer information, innovation and human resources less easily.[32] Blending this Durkheimian distinction between traditional-segmental and modern societies[33] with the Tocquevillean prescription for associationalism as an antidote to excessive individualism as manifested in American political life,[34] Fukuyama drives home his point that '[a]n abundance of social capital is presumably what produces a dense civil society, which in turn has been almost universally seen as a necessary condition for modern liberal democracy.'[35] Trying to improve on Putnam about new means to measure it, he refers to two broad approaches. The first is Putnamesque, and consists in conducting a census of groups and group memberships in a particular society, and the second in using survey data on levels of trust and civic engagement. They do not, however, reduce the complexities of measurement. The problem regarding the first is that the average size of groups and the number of groups are equally important measures, 'because a small value for group size may limit the range of objectives that a group may realize.' Further, while the total number of groups may by itself provide a separate measure, the number of failed attempts in the US itself to ensure a total count prove the 'near- impossibility of producing a complete census that catalogues the whole range of informal networks and cliques in a modern society'. Speaking of the second measure, since each group has a different level of internal cohesion, and hence of feasible collective action, this necessitates adding a qualitative coefficient that would offer a measure of group cohesion. Yet no accepted method for measuring the internal cohesiveness of groups has yet been devised. As a result each measure of effectiveness has to be calculated by an outside observer keeping in view the peculiarities, problems and constraints the group faces in its activities.

The problem of measurement is compounded by the fact that as social capital is more permeated than other forms of capital by 'negative externalities', any attempt to take stock of a nation's kitty of social capital has to take them into account. This would include judging if a group's 'radius of trust' is optimum, if strong moral bonds of the group are not decreasing the degree of trust of the members toward outsiders and is not harming its capacity to absorb beneficial influences from the outside environment, if group cohesiveness and the radius of trust are positively correlated etc. All these considerations suggest the unavailability of a believable census of a society's stock of social capital.[36] That as a concept 'social capital' is enjoying considerable vogue is only partly due to its appropriation by the World Bank, beyond Coleman's and Putnam's conceptualisation of it.[37] A more important reason might be the veritable growth industry that research on trust, one of its key components, has recently become. As a result trust has become a field for an intellectual 'caucus race'[38] among a self-referential group of scholars. Some scholars plead for 'trusting' it, if only 'because even if people have perfectly adequate motives for cooperation they still need to know about each other's motives and to trust each other, or at least the effectiveness of their motives.' Their reasoning is that if the 'dominant solution' of defection in a 'Prisoner's Dilemma' type situation is to be transcended, then it is 'necessary not only to trust others ... but also to believe that one is trusted by others.'[39] But some other scholars would agree to place trust in 'trust', as it is nothing more than 'encapsulated interest'. For such neo-Smithians who believe that even markets run on trust and are trustworthy because dealers have shared interests between them and other dealers, buyers and consumers, and the public at large, 'the public good of generalized trust ... may not require a moral foundation. It may be little more than an encapsulation of the self-interest of all or most of us.'[40] The real problem with this huge literature on trust[41] is that whether its manifestations are really observed at the 'street level', or in elaborate, sophisticated Bayesian models of learning and measuring estimates in its name,[42] it does not rid 'social capital' of its conceptual and measuring problems. While theorists of trust and confidence test the validity of socio-psychological explanations, social and cultural models, and institutional models of trust in the general context of decline in confidence in government in 'Trilateral democracies', [43] they do not address the problems of how to build up a reservoir of trust in situations where people have completely lost faith not only in the government, but in the political system as well.

But at different generative levels the problem becomes more and more difficult. On one level the relationship between confidence – the epiphenomenal side of public trust – and confidence in government is shown to be problematic. 'Political corruption', like good governance, requires the presence of 'informal norms, reciprocity, and clandestine networks', in one word 'bad social capital. And for a time at least the bad equilibrium may persist. [44] But while one scholar tries to make the crucial connection between public trust and democracy, by positing that '[g]eneralized trust flourishes in democracies, while particularized trust is more typical of authoritarian and totalitarian societies', [45] on a more fundamental level methodological objection to the concept of 'social capital' substituting for civil society itself is raised by Jean Cohen. In his view, Putnam 'reduces civil society to the dimension of voluntary association and construes the latter as the *sole* source of what he calls social capital. The feature of the social context that matters most to the performance of democratic institutions, on Putnam's analysis is the presence or absence of a civic culture.' Cohen's reservation is not simply about taking as the indicators of civicness the ones mentioned in the civic culture studies of the 1950s. He is also unhappy that while providing 'a rich description of the emergence of civicness to take root, at least in the north of Italy', he lapses into reductionism in the concluding theoretical chapter of the book, "Social Capital and Institutional Success". There 'history, tradition, culture, normative orientations and their transmission over time are analyzed in terms of the concept of inherited "social capital"- defined as the social stock of trust, norms and networks that facilitate coordinated actions- whereas the *source* of social capital and of its generalization is narrowed down to involvement in secondary associations. We are left with a weak theoretical framework and an unconvincing analysis. Unfortunately, this framework is greatly influencing the American civil-society debate.' Cohen also questions Putnam's approach to the way how "virtuous circles" generate, generalise, and transmit traditions of civic engagement across centuries of profound social, economic, and political change; his reluctance to squarely face the question of "third party enforcement" to rather rely on trust and generalised reciprocity for the establishment of the institutions in the first place; as also his penchant to move away from 'state structures to "soft" cultural solutions.'[46]

Governance/Social capital: Research in the Wasteland

The research here in India on governance is yet to become a growth industry. This paper is not making any claim of having covered all the major publications in this area. But of the few considered, not all, always maintain the distinction between government and governance, and some expand the concept to absurd limits. While exploring the interface between civil society and governance one commentator thinks that the contribution of civil society should be in the areas of: a) self-governance of civil social institutions including community based organisations, cooperatives, trade unions, sports associations, professional bodies and development NGOs; b) defining public good and prioritising its components keeping in mind the interests of the voiceless; c) influencing public negotiations on policy formulation in important areas; d) ensuring accountability of legislatures, local bodies, elected representatives, the judiciary from the local level to the Supreme Court, the law and order machinery, the public bureaucracies dealing with the citizen's life worlds, the political parties, etc; and e) assuring accountability of the market, i.e. of private enterprises in the profit sector, and other private sector associations.[47] This truly belongs to the defined realm of governance. But the suggestions of another eminent political scientist slightly overstep the limit. He specifies the following four prerequisites of good governance in the Indian context: 'a) informing the process of recruiting the elite with legitimacy; b) facilitating proportionate representation for all segments of the population; c) ensuring respect for the dominated by the dominant; and d) instituting a reward-punishment mechanism.'

While the first entails reforming the electoral process, the second is a catch-all category. This involves reservations for women at the parliamentary, provincial legislatures, and the PRI levels; ensuring proper representation of not only OBCs (the problems of the SCs and the STs having been already largely met) but also of religious minorities in the top political positions as also the higher echelons of the judiciary, to remedy not only the 'democratic deficit in the system but also the 'experiential deficit'. The third seeks to address the ethos of 'Social Darwinism' ingrained in our political system in the name of merit that breeds disrespect for the dalits. And the fourth seeks to institute a subtle system of appraisal that in its astuteness in punishing conformity to obsolescent norms and rewarding the non-conformity of the 'innovator-deviant' would cut through the maze of conformity and deviance that is inevitable in a plural system. Oommen rightly sees the inconsistency and even contradictoriness between the four prerequisites. But remaining undeterred he subsumes in his scheme of governance reform eradication of the three challenges of 'disparity, discrimination, and collective alienation' to participatory democracy in India. While 'disparity' is admitted to be ubiquitous, staggering in even the 'successful' capitalist democracies like the US, and allowed to pervade a vast array of contexts in India, including those of class, gender, rural-urban (Bharat vs. India) and regional (BIMARU states vs. the rest), 'discrimination' is said to be confined to the specific contexts of gender, language, tribe and caste. The logic of inclusion is that all this breeds 'collective alienation'.[48]

Even more ambitious is the scheme proposed by distinguished scholar-bureaucrat and governance specialist Madhav Godbole, who identifies many deficiencies of Indian democratic and parliamentary system that detract from civility, breed inefficiency and opacity, encourage wastefulness and corruption, and reduce the representativeness of the system.[49] The book could really serve as a ready reckoner for anyone searching for the most crucial areas where the government and the political system are to be cleansed. His innumerable proposals belong to wildly divergent levels of analysis. They range from a detailed framework of parliamentary reforms extending to rationalisation of benefits enjoyed by MPs and MLAs; comprehensive legal reform that includes repeal of 1,300 central laws of different categories out of 2,500 laws in force and expeditious amendments to at least 110 laws; extensive reforms in the electoral and representational system; reinvigorating democratic decentralisation; implementing the Right to Information Act; introduction of social audit of public policy implementation; 'sunset' provisions for all governmental schemes and programmes that otherwise do and would continue indefinitely; identification of areas of private sector participation; accepting NGOs as partners in development; comprehensive civil service reforms; downsizing the government; police reforms with accent on human rights while firmly handling secessionist movements 'that no country can tolerate' and that 'are mostly assisted actively by forces from across the borders who are bent on dismembering the country'; making state budgets transparent and user-friendly; evolving a framework for 'auditing the auditors' and providing teeth for the *Lokayukts*; downward to outsourcing of certain municipal functions; and still downward to ending things like Local Area Development schemes for MPs, and ending complimentary railway passes for former MPs. In the sheer extensiveness of these and many other reforms suggested, without any attempt at prioritisation, the initiator of reforms might have to wonder where to start. Besides, in spite of occasional forays into societal areas the dominant focus in the book is on governmentalism.

Still some other scholars dealing with the concept use it in encompassive ways that would leave the originators flabbergasted. One bids *adieu* to the Bank's 'limited', and 'management oriented' use of the term to embrace 'a normative point of view ... particularly from the angle of the most disadvantaged in society', and quite logically gives as much weight in his paradigm to 'economic benefits' as to "dignity" and of being counted in a polity'. In his view this entails two methodological corrections.

The first is that governance 'is best seen within the context of contesting politics and values, as it is often caught in the web of hegemonic and counter-hegemonic politics in societies.' The second, a logical corollary of the first, is that governance 'should be disentangled from the larger, neo-liberal agenda.' This is because of the crucial role that the state plays in the lives of ordinary people in most of the post-colonial societies.' For Mohapatra, however, this step of 'bringing the state back in' is at the most a path-clearing move. Once the need of this is recognized 'reconfiguring society becomes as much an important agenda of good governance as transforming the state.'[50]

Lessons in Retrieval: Governance

I unabashedly endorse Mohapatra's opinion, not just because his theoretical perspective is methodologically in tune with his 'subject' of research of pavement dwellers in a metropolis, nor because of its paradigmatic shift that makes most of the case studies of Section II of this book on governance legitimate entries. It is rather because this reveals how a considerable number of social scientists in India 'interpret' governance. A right-centric approach to government cannot merely subsist on the right to information, however impassionedly propagated. In a consultative meet on 'Democratic Governance in Indian States' at my university, [51] the consensus that emerged not only buttresses Mohapatra's view, but suggests going beyond it to reinterpret governance. With the fond hope that some of the very original ideas from this meet would some day incite new research and beckon us up new paths, I am summarising below a few of the suggestions, not missed by my sieve-like memory. I am doing it in a haphazard way, to preclude any subjective intervention on my part.

- To eradicate Eurocentrism governance reform in India has to learn and utilise the experimentations in non-Western countries like South Africa, China, and South East Asian states, and the East European states reorganising themselves after the fall of their socialist regimes as also embrace Asian values (for example, community-centric versus the right-centric of Europe and America). Besides, the concept of governance evolved in the context of comparative stability of the societies of Europe and America may benefit from a few insights from governance operating in conditions of relative instability in third world societies.[52]

- Contesting notions of governance and its history provide a major problematic of research first because governance has always been viewed from the rulers' perspective that necessitates reviewing it from the perspective of the dominated. Secondly, even the rights framework of governance sometimes ignores people and groups regularly falling outside its purview and reach. Thus a social enquiry on forms and patterns of collective politics and violence that enable some people to enter and force others to fall outside the net of governance is imperative.[53]
- The role of the media in the agenda-setting of governance is to be probed more deeply, not only because of its crucial role of modifying the traditional conception of the public sphere, but also because of its role in mediating in the communication between the individual and the state, creating a false illusion of a participatory democracy, depoliticising the conception of civil society, and maintaining what can be termed as 'democracy by default'. The strategy of mainstreaming adopted by the media has been helpful in not only keeping hunger, unless it has become endemic, out of the agenda of governance, but also in creating a fear-psychosis about strikes and processions that assists in the cause of neo-liberalism. Probing governance of the media is, therefore, necessary.[54]
- From the perspective of social activism, the supply side of governance involving economic, administrative-bureaucratic and political aspects (with panchayati governance occupying the grey area between the last two) should be highlighted. While in rural areas economic governance proceeds from an agro-economic logic, the contours of political governance are determined by the party in power. A case in point is rural tribal communities living in forest settlements, whose view of governance is contingent on the relationship between the three aspects mentioned above. For them, governance basically means the existence of the fair price shop not very far, and protection against legislations (like the Seed Act) that threaten to delink them from their land. Rights as

schemes are not properly understood by them. They do not even understand land tenure in governmental terms. Panchayats do not exist in their consciousness; nor does the police department as protector in cases of infringement of their rights. The nitty-gritty of implementation scenarios of public policies are also nearly inaccessible. The much-touted Right to Information Act does not help. Obstacles in the nature of linguistic barriers, the abstruse offiialese or gobbledy-gook, bureaucratic impediments including the inaccessibility of officials, even the small fees and the difficulties of filling up forms and making sense of the long exemption lists are insurmountable for these outsiders. This underscores the importance of information variables of governance for people in the margins, of the pressing need of not only to provide them more data about policies, but explaining their favourable and unfavourable impacts, and of specifying sections to be adversely affected and available redresses through a balanced 'content analysis'. Another aspect of governance that becomes most relevant in their context is their right to natural community resources as a conflict-space between the state and the non-state sphere (NPS). Awareness campaigns are needed not only for them but also for the government to determine how much governance is allowable for CPRs (Common Pool Resources), in other words, the limits of state rights over CPRs. All this would need a reconfiguration not only of the state but also of the NPS.[55]

In an age in which the role of communications in development is steadily increasing, the importance of images of development and governance among the common people is increasing too. These images have to be collected and collated not only to incorporate the receivers' view of governance in the hegemonic conceptual framework, but also to communicate with the target populations of policies, when endemic misperceptions threaten the effectiveness of their implementation. Examples of some popular perceptions of development in some surveys are that health is not prioritised; neither is a better road, as all these would come 'automatically' with development. Development would rather mean a job for the respondent's child. [56]

Just a glance through these views, coming from people who are considered enlightened, would indicate that governance in India considered in terms of the scope of state functions, the spread of state institutions and relations between the state and society has to be re-thought to make it meaningful in non-Western perspectives.

And Social Capital

Already some serious attempts at working with the concept of social capital in India have been ridden with difficulties. One researcher has shown that although there is plentiful qualitative evidence from India that features such as the level of trust and norms of cooperation crucially impinge on social well-being and on the effectiveness of government actions, the data of the Indian states for the indicators that are normally used to proxy civic behaviour, are hard to identify. Or, the data that already exist cannot be interpreted unambiguously as measures of civicness. The inadequacies not only of aggregate data, but also of high quality survey data of the kind provided by the Centre for the Study of the Developing Societies (CSDS), Delhi, survey, in capturing the Putnamesque indicators of social capital in India induced her to two methodological conclusions and a substantive one. Methodologically, the first suggestion was of reframing survey questions, and using other methods of data collection, including direct field observation, in order to capture the desired characteristics. The second was as pitching the analysis at higher and lower levels than the Indian states that are too 'complex and internally differentiated entities' for comparison at this level to be meaningful. The substantive conclusion was that the dynamics involved in the relationship between social capital and institutional performance is so complicated that intervening variables, operative in the peoples' involvement in public affairs and their civic character, are equally important areas of research. This suggests qualifying conventional policy prescriptions of investing more in social capital.[57]

Another attempt at reforming Putnam's concept of social capital to measure the dynamics of civic- community building in India, even after substituting 'policy outcomes' for Putnam's stress on 'policy outputs', concedes that lack of data incommodes answering the question satisfactorily. [58]

But Mohapatra has shown in a case study of social capital in a village in Orissa that the evidence therefrom 'suggests that trust/social capital alone cannot help people to obtain material benefits from public/state institutions,' though it may well help them to collectively negotiate with their difficulties in a better way.[59] A study on two protest movements in Orissa against projects that threatened displacement of large numbers of people has also shown some use of social capital in collective bargaining.[60]

What do we make of the explanatory inadequacies of social capital, not only at the state level, but at a far lower level, amenable to direct field study? What are their implications for the two concepts? Kothari once showed that public trust, understood as 'institutionalization of objective checks against self-centred behaviour', is 'weak' in India. The 'pervasive skepticism of the Indian mind in regard to the possibilities of achieving something collectively, a basic suspicion of others, suspicion especially of authority and its intentions, and a fear of underhanded and circuitous dealings by others' appeared to him as one of the abiding themes of Indian political culture.[61] But Serra not only deduces from her study that 'the majority of the people in India have some trust in their state and local government', but is so astonished as to wonder if such misplaced trust is to be 'taken as a negative rather than positive element', reflective, sometimes, less of 'a conscious knowledge of government actions and trustworthiness' and more of 'a mechanical and organic compliance, maybe, even the existence of collusion with corrupt behaviour'.[62]

The explanation of all these contrary findings may lie not here but elsewhere. In a different context Partha Chatterjee has made a startling observation that people in post-colonial India resort more to what he terms as 'political society' than to civil society. Even when they are making demands on the state in violation of the law, the people are demanding 'governmental welfare as a matter of "right", that too as 'collective rights', 'on behalf not of individual citizens (since this position is, in any case, unavailable to violators of the law) but of a "community", even if this community is only the product of a recent coming together' on an illegal basis. This induces Chatterjee to reach another startling conclusion that in post-colonial India the most significant transformations are occurring not in the civil society but in the 'political society'.[63] Now the trust in allegedly undeserving governmental institutions, that is troubling Serra, may simply be a reflection of this resort to political society, and may neither be trust nor 'mechanical compliance', but rather a desperate move before resort to anomic violence. This is a situation that panegyrists of a sanitised civil society need carefully to ponder before downgrading welfare and pruning the 'demiurgic' state.

Notes and References

1. Abbreviated from 'phonetically', 'etically' means making use of pre-established categories for organising and interpreting anthropological data, rather then using categories recognised within the culture being studied. 'Emically' (derived from 'phonemically') means, on the contrary, analysing language and behaviour using categories of the people being studied. See dictionary *Encarta*, Chennai, Macmillan, 1999, pp. 615,643.
2. See W.B. Yeats, "The Rose Tree", in *Michael Robartes and the Dancer* (1921), in *The Works of W.B.Yeats*, Hertfordshire, Wordsworth, 1994, pp.154-55.
3. Philip Darby, "Pursuing the Political: A Postcolonial Rethinking of Relations International", in *Millennium Journal of International Relations*, Vol. 33, no.1, 2004, pp. 7-8.
4. Ibid, p. 8.
5. Michael Hardt and Antonio Negri, *Empire*, Cambridge, MA, Harvard University Press, 2000, p.xii, cited in Darby, "Pursuing", p.8.
6. Ibid, p.18.
7. See World Bank, *Sub-Saharan Africa: From Crisis to Sustainable Growth*, Oxford, Oxford University Press, 1989; and also World Bank, *Managing Development: The Governance Dimension*, Washington. D.C., 1991.

8. See Anup Sinha, "Good Governance, Market–Friendly Globalization and the Changing Space of State Intervention: The Case of India", and Daryl Reed, "Good Corporate Governance in the Global Economy: What Is AT Issue?" in (eds.) Surendra Munshi and Biju Paul Abraham, *Democratic Societies and Globalization*, New Delhi, Sage, 2004, pp. 114-16, 292.
9. Leila L. Frischtak, *Governance Capacity and Economic Reform in Developing Countries*, World Bank Technical paper Number 254, The World Bank, Washington, D. C., 1994.
10. Robert O. Keohane and Joseph A. Nye Jr., "Introduction", in (eds.) Joseph S. Nye Jr. and John D. Donahue, *Governance in a Globalizing World*, Harrisonburg, Virginia, Visions of Governance for the 21st Century, Cambridge, MA. and Washington D.C., Brookings Institution Press, 2000, p.12.
11. Ibid, pp.13-14.
12. Francis Fukuyama, *State-Building: Governance and World Order in the 21stCentury*, Ithaca, New York, Cornel University Press, 2004, pp. 3-32.
13. Ibid, pp. 43-91.
14. ibid, p. 31.
15. Ibid, pp. 36-42.
16. See Francis Fukuyama, *The End of History and the Last Man*, Hamish Hamilton, 1992.
17. Fukuyama, *Governance*, p.11.
18. The term, used by Robert H. Jackson in the context of 'situational ethics' toward an 'international society' is used in a pejorative sense by me. See Jackson, "The Political Theory of International Society", in (eds.) Ken Booth and Steve Smith, *International Relations Theory Today*, Cambridge, Polity Press (1995), reprint edition, 1996, p.120.
19. Manuel Castells, "Global Governance and Global Politics", The 2004 Ithiel De Sola Pool Lecture, in *Political Science and Politics*, vol. xxxviii, January 2005, pp. 9-16.
20. For the literature and the survey see Frischtak, *Governance Capacity*, pp.11-16.21.
21. Ibid, pp.17-29.
22. Ibid, pp. 30-36.

23. Joseph Stiglitz, *Globalization and its Discontents*, New Delhi, Penguin Books, 2003, p.xii.
24. Ibid, pp.13-15.
25. Ibid, pp.18-20, 21-22, 220, 226.
26. Alan Zeuge, "The Chimera of the Third Way", in *Necessary and Unnecessary Social Utopias*, in (eds.) Leo Pontich and Colin Leys. *Socialist Register*, First Indian edition, Calcutta, K.P. Bagchi and Sons, 2000, pp.87-114, for here pp.87-92, 94-97.
27. See James C. Coleman, "Social Capital', in Coleman, *Foundations of Social Theory*, Cambridge, Mass., Harvard University Press, 1990, pp.300-21.
28. See James C. Putnam, *Making Democracy Work: Civic Traditions in Modern Italy*, Princeton, N.J., Princeton University Press, 1993.
29. Coleman, "Norms as Social Capital", in (eds.) Gerard Radnitzky and Peter Bernholz, *Economic Imperialism: The Economic Approach applied Outside the Field of Economics*, New York, Paragon House Publishers,1987, p.134.
30. Coleman, "Social Capital", pp.306-11.
31. Putnam, *Making Democracy Work*, pp.154-57, 167-71, 173-75
32. Francis Fukuyama, "Social Capital, Civil Society and Development", *Third World Quarterly*, vol.22, no.1(2001), pp.7-9
33. Durkheim draws the crucial distinction between 'segmental' archaic societies and modern functionally interdependent societies in course of his famous, if ill-fated distinction between 'mechanical solidarity' and 'organic solidarity' and division of labour as the cementing bond of the latter. He also prioritises the creation of 'intermediate', 'occupational' associations that would not block one's vision for the state, and yet provide the necessary social commitment that makes society sustainable. Fukuyama is obviously influenced by this logic to offer his view of the importance of 'weak ties' in non-segmental societies. See Emile Durkheim, *De la division du travail social* (1893), Seventh Edn., 1960, translated and excerpted in Emile Durkheim, *Selected Writings*, ed. with an introduction by Anthony Giddens, Cambridge, Cambridge University Press, 1972, pp.141-46.
34. See Raymond Aron, "Alexis de Tocqueville", in Aron, *Main Currents of Sociological Thought*, vol.1, Harmondsworth, Penguin Books, 1968, pp.192, 205.

35. Fukuyama, "Social Capital", pp. 9-12.
36. Ibid, pp. 10-16.
37. See Ismail Serageldin, 'Foreword' to *Social Capital Initiatives Working Paper* series, World Bank, 1997, cited in (eds.) Dwaipayan Bhattacharyya, Niraja Gopal Jayal, Bishnu N. Mohapatra , Sudha Pai, *Interrogating Social Capital: The Indian Experience*, New Delhi, Sage Publications, 2004, pp. 19-21.
38. The words are quoted from Lewis A. Carol, 'A Caucus Race and a Long Tale', chapter 3, *Alice in the Wonderland and through the Looking Glass*, London, Everyman Paperbacks, 1961, pp.17-24. In the book the term means a race where one could begin and stop running whenever one wanted, for the universal prize of a 'thimble'. Pun on the word 'caucus' is intended.
39. Diego Gambetta, "Can We Trust Trust", in (ed.) Gambetta, *Trust: Making or Breaking Cooperative Relations*, Oxford, Basil Blackwell, 1988, pp.213-39, for present purposes p.216.
40. Russell Hardin, "Trusting People, Trusting Institutions", in Richard J. Zeckhauser (ed.), *Strategy and Choice*, Cambridge, Mass., MIT Press, 1991, pp. 185-209.
41. See, for example, twelve well-researched articles on the trust, trust in government, and its relationship with 'social capital' and democracy, in Mark E. Warren (ed.), *Democracy and Trust*, Cambridge, UK, Cambridge University Press, 1999.
42. Russell Hardin, "A Street Level Epistemology of Trust", *Politics and Society*, vol.21, no.3, December 1993, pp. 505-29.
43. Kenneth Newton and Pippa Norris, "Confidence in Public Institutions: Faith, Culture, or Performance?" in Susan J. Pharr and Robert D Putnam (ed.), *Disaffected Democracies: What's Troubling the Trilateral Countries*?, Princeton, New Jersey, Princeton University Press, 2000, pp. 52-73.
44. Donatella della Porta, 'Social Capital, Beliefs in Government, and Political Corruption', in Pharr and Putnam, *Disaffected Democracies*, pp. 202-28.
45. Eric A. Ulsamer, "Democracy and Social Capital", in Warren, *Democracy and Trust*, pp. 121-28.
46. Jean Cohen, "Trust, Voluntary Association and Workable Democracy: The Contemporary American Discourse on Civil Society", in Warren, *Democracy and Trust*, pp. 209-48, especially pp. 217-19.

47. See Rajesh Tandon, "The Civil Society Governance Interface", in (eds.) Rajesh Tandon and Ranjita Mohanty, *Does Civil Society Matter? : Governance in Contemporary India*, New Delhi, Sage Publications, 2003, pp.59-76.
48. T. K. Oommen, "Civil Society and the Goal of Good Governance", in Tandon and Mohanty, *Does Civil Society Matter?* pp.144.
49. Madhav Godbole, *Public Accountability and Trust: The Imperatives of Good Governance*, Hyderabad, Orient Longman, 2003, chapters 1-4, pp.1-266.
50. Bishnu N. Mohapatra, 'A View from the Subalterns; The Pavement Dwellers of Mumbai", in Tandon and Mohanty, *Does Civil Society Matter*, pp.284-314, especially pp. 290-92.
51. The meeting was held on October 6, 2005 at the Department of Political Science, University of Calcutta. Any deficiency in representing the views of the undermentioned experts is unintentional.
52. S. Datta Gupta, of the Department of Political Science, Calcutta University, pointed this out among many other important ideas.
53. This is part of the observation of Ranabir Samaddar, of the Calcutta Research Group.
54. This is a brief representation of the views of Debashis Chakraborty, News Editor, *Ganashakti* .
55. This is a brief rendering of the views of Subhendu Dasgupta, of the Department of South and South East Asian Studies, Calcutta University, and a social activist.
56. Dipankar Sinha, the co-editor of the volume, pointed this out at the meet.
57. Renata Serra, '"Putnam in India': Is Social Capital a Meaningful Concept at the Indian State Level?" in Bhattacharyya et al, *Interrogating Social Capital*, pp.290-92.
58. Peter Mayer, "Making Democracy Perform: Human Development and Civic Community in India", ibid, pp.236, 250-53.
59. Bishnu N. Mohapatra, 'Social Connectedness and the Fragility of Social Capital; A View from a Village in Orissa', ibid, p.111.
60. Nityananda Barik, *Social Capital and Protest Movements in Orissa: A Comparative Study of Gopalpur and Chilika Movements*, unpublished Ph. D thesis, 2002.

61. Rajni Kothari, *Politics in India* (1970), New Delhi, Orient Longman, 1982, pp.266-68.
62. Serra, "Is Social Capital a Meaningful Concept?", p.276.
63. Partha Chatterjee, "On Civil and Political Society in Postcolonial Democracies", in (eds.) Sudipta Kaviraj and Sunil Khilnani, *Civil Society: History and Possibilities*, Cambridge, UK, Cambridge University Press, 2001, pp. 174-78. By 'political society' Chatterjee means a sphere between the civil society and the state, 'built around the framework of modern political associations such as political parties', revolving round 'the developmental state, which seeks to relate different sections of the population through the governmental function of welfare.' Ibid, p.176.

3

State, Liberalisation and Investment Question: Issues in Corporate Governance

Asish K Bhattacharyya

Introduction

The vast bulk of economic activity occurs within formal, managed organisations rather than through market exchanges. McMillan (2002) estimates that less than one-third of all transactions in the U.S. economy occur through markets and over 70 per cent of transactions occur within firms. Firms occupy a predominant position in any economy, primarily because in many situations market fails to achieve the desired coordination of activities and motivation of people to carry on the needed activities to achieve economic efficiency[1]. Activities are undertaken within the boundaries of a firm to achieve better coordination and motivation and also to reduce transaction costs. In many situations, the productivity of resources increases as a firm grows and achieves economies of scale[2] and economies of scope[3], although the optimal size differs between firms and between industries. This results in the emergence of large corporations. Among the firm structures, 'limited liability company' form is considered as the most appropriate structure to carry out large and complex businesses.

In a limited liability company management of assets rests with promoter managers or professional managers and not with investors. Therefore, the 'State' takes various initiatives to protect investors' wealth from expropriation and to motivate investors to invest in large firms.

A business firm creates value by trading in goods and services or by producing and selling goods and services. The value so created is distributed among stakeholders of the firm, some of whom are internal to the firm (employees and investors) and participate in the process of creating value, while others are external to the firm and trade with the firm - such as buyers of firm products and sellers of inputs to the firm. The community that does not trade with the firm is also external to the firm.

Corporate governance deals with governance of business firms, particularly limited liability companies. Corporate governance refers to mechanisms that aim to achieve economic efficiency and fair distribution of surplus (revenue less boughtout inputs) to those who are internal to the firm and provide resources (e.g. financial capital, knowledge and skills, and labour) to the firm. Distribution of value (created by a firm) to those who trade with the firm is determined by price in market exchanges. The share of the community (which is external to the firm) in the value created by the firm is determined by the 'State', which imposes levy taxes (e.g. income tax) and formulates laws to protect the interest of the community.

There are two approaches to address the problems in corporate governance. One is popularly known as the shareholder theory of corporate governance and the other known as the stakeholder theory of corporate governance. The shareholder theory of corporate governance is based on the assumption that the core objective function of a firm is 'maximisation of firm value'. Therefore, managers are expected to take decisions to 'maximise the firm value'. Firm value is the total of the market value of equity and the market value of debt. The corporate governance system aims to protect interests of financiers by ensuring that managers take decisions to achieve the core objective function of the firm and that the value created (surplus) is distributed among those who are insiders to the firm as per contracts with various participants in the value creating process. The proponents of the stakeholder theory of corporate governance argue that managers should consider interests of all stakeholders (including shareholders) in deciding the mobilisation and allocation of resources to different uses. In other words, managers should balance the interests of all stakeholders, which are often conflicting. The most important weakness of the stakeholder theory is that it fails to provide a single objective function to managers, and thus dilutes accountability. Moreover, it undermines the fact that investors will be motivated to invest in a firm only if, they are assured that the funds provided by them will be used to create value for them. In spite of these weaknesses, the stakeholder theory highlights the fact that the 'firm value' cannot be maximised ignoring the interests of all stakeholders for long. Therefore, managers should take all stakeholders together in achieving the core objective function, that is, 'maximisation of the firm value'.

In this paper we shall focus on the shareholder theory of corporate governance. We shall not deal with issues such as 'corporate social responsibilities', corporate citizenship (e.g. responsibility of companies to behave like good citizens) and ethics.

There is a large literature in economics on the nature of firm. Understanding corporate governance requires understanding the nature of the firm, particularly, limited liability companies. Therefore, sections I and II provide an overview of the nature of a firm and the structure of limited liability companies. Sections III and IV of the paper discuss the concept of corporate governance and corporate governance issues in international joint ventures respectively. Section VI discusses the role of the State in corporate governance.

(I) Nature of Firm

A firm as a nexus of contracts

Alchian and Demsetz (1972) define a firm as a nexus of contracts. A firm may be viewed as a nexus of contracts between stakeholders, including the local community. Some contracts are explicit (e.g. contracts between the manager and financiers, customers, suppliers and employees) and some others are implicit (e.g. contract between the managers and the local community under which the former undertakes not to create negative externalities[4]). According to this definition, corporate governance is governance of a complex network of contracts. The key issue in governance of a contract is how the contracting parties share the 'quasi rent'[5] arising from contingencies. In absence of a complete contract, which covers all contingencies, the distribution of the quasi rent depends upon the ex-post[6] relative bargaining powers of contracting parties. The ex-post relative bargaining powers of contracting parties depend on ex-ante contract between the parties, the institutions in the business environment where the contracting parties operate and alternatives available to contracting parties. We may take an example. B & Co. is looking for a supplier for a special machine to be manufactured specially for it. Until the search for the right supplier is complete, that is, up to the bidding stage, B & Co. operates in the market. Once the search is complete, B & Co. enters into a contract with the supplier (say, S & Co.) specifying the terms and conditions, including the specification of the machine, delivery schedule, the price and payment terms. The manufacturing of the machine takes a significantly long period. Suppose due to change in the business environment (e.g. increase in demand for capital goods) the contract with B & Co. becomes un-profitable (considering the opportunity cost[7]). The probability that S & Co. will execute the order depends on the ex-post relative bargaining powers of B & Co. and S & Co. The relative bargaining powers depend on the ex-ante contract (e.g. penalty clause in the contract), institutions (e.g. the possibility of court's intervention in getting the contract executed, the speed with which the news spreads in the market and adversely affects the future business of S & Co.) and the alternatives available to B & Co. for getting the machine manufactured. As in this example, the distribution of the value created in a firm is determined by relative ex-post bargaining powers of parties participating in the production process. In case of a firm, situations for renegotiation arise continuously. This enhances the importance of relative ex-post bargaining powers of contracting of parties. The power (residual control right[8]) of managing the assets is the prime determinant of the ex-post bargaining powers of different contracting parties.

In the context of transaction costs in trading between two entities, Williams (1991) observes:

'The initial franchise award undergoes a Fundamental Transformation if the assets in question are highly specific, in which event the efficacy of "unassisted" franchise bidding becomes highly problematic at the contract renewal intervals and when adaptations to change are attempted'.

Fundamental transformation occurs when production of the goods by the supplier requires large durable investments, which are specific to the needs of the buyer and are not redeployable. The specificity of the investment or 'lock-in' weakens the ex-post bargaining power of the supplier vis-à-vis that of the buyer. In absence of a complete contract, which takes care of all possible contingencies, the seller builds flexibility in its production process to strengthen its ex-post bargaining position. This increases transaction costs and brings down the economic efficiency. This is one of the reasons why firms go for 'vertical integration'.

Robert (2004a) observes:

'Lock-in is actually inevitable when assets are specialised. An asset is specialised to a particular use when the value it can create in its next-best alternative use is substantially lower than what it yields in the current one. For example, the dies used to shape materials in manufacturing are very specific to that use: If they are not employed for this purpose, they are just scrap material. Firm-specific human capital—the knowledge that is only (or especially) valuable in the context of employment with a particular firm—is another example. When assets are specialized, they are subject to hold-up—attempts by trading partners to appropriate some of the returns that the assets' owners expected when they invested in them. This can lead to a variety of inefficiencies.'

The lock-in, similar to that discussed in the context of trading, arises when an investor invests in equity of a firm because assets that a firm uses are specialized and do not have alternative uses. Therefore, there is a need for a governance system that ensures that managers do not expropriate wealth of investors and that investors get expected return on their investment and get back the principal amount invested in the firm.

Although, the current discourse on corporate governance focus on financiers' interest only, employees' interest should receive due attention by policy makers. The ex-post bargaining power of employees in many industries, particularly in firms that are operating in a matured industry is weaker than suppliers of other inputs. This is so because in absence of new investments in the industry employees face a 'take it or leave it' situation. On the other hand, in a growing industry, which is technology or relationships driven, employees enjoy a significant ex-post bargaining power, because they can threaten to withdraw valuable resources (e.g. knowledge and skills) that they bring to the firm. The position of employees is different from suppliers of other inputs for two reasons. First, the term of contracts with employees is usually longer as compared to term of contracts with suppliers of other inputs. This makes the nature of stake of employees different from the nature of stake of suppliers of other inputs to the firm. Although, it may not be true in all situations, usually a firm has an option to purchase inputs in a spot-transaction. In most situations this option is not available for employee services. Second, and more importantly, the specificity of investment of knowledge and skills, which stays with employees, makes employee services different from other inputs. Roberts (2004b) observes:

'... when a customer "fires" a butcher, the butcher keeps the inventory, tools, shop, and other customers she had previously. When an employee leaves a firm, in contrast, she is typically denied access to the firm's resources. The employee cannot conduct business using the firm's name; she cannot use its machines or patents; and she probably has limited access to the people and networks in the firm, certainly for commercial purposes and perhaps even socially.'

The above observations are more appropriate for employees working in industries in which inanimate assets are significantly more important than capabilities (e.g. abilities to build relationships with buyers and sellers in a banking industry, knowledge and skills to develop complex client-specific software) that individuals carry with them.

Firm as a collection of assets

Grossman and Hart (1986), and Hart and Moore (1990) define a firm as a collection of assets that are jointly owned. For example, in a typical firm, assets are jointly owned by equity holders and debt holders. The ownership is important because it provides rights to control the assets. Equity holders provide the risk capital and undertake business risks, while an investment in the debt capital is exposed to credit risks[9]. The claim of equity holders on the assets is residual in the sense that in a situation of liquidation of the firm, equity holders have claim on assets that are available after payment of the claims of debt holders and other creditors. Therefore, the law gives the ownership rights to equity holders. The conflict of interest between equity holders and debt holders arises in a situation of distress, when the asset of the firm is inadequate to pay creditors, including debt holders. In that situation equity holders tempt to invest in a speculative project. If the actual outcome of the project results in high pay-off, it benefits equity holders, but if it results in huge loss it hurts debt holders. In this context, the ownership right is important. The 'ownership rights' approach suggests that corporate governance system aims to ensure that equity holders take decisions for the benefit of all classes of investors including debt holders.

Firm as a nexus of specific investments

Rajan and Zingales (1998) define a firm as a nexus of specific investments: a combination of mutually specialised assets and people. The definition emphasises the specificity of resources (assets and people) invested in a firm. It also emphasises that the firm is a complex structure that cannot be replicated by the market immediately. According to this definition, corporate governance is concerned with distribution of quasi rent accruing to the firm among mutually specialised parties who have sunk financial and/or human capital in the firm.

Raghuram and Zingales (2000) observe that an individual can derive power from the valuable resources she brings to the production process. In an industry which requires significant investment in tangible assets (e.g. equipment) the power to control stays with the top management, because it brings the knowledge and managerial skills that are required to make the assets productive. It derives the power because it can threaten to withdraw the scarce resources that it brings with it, which will make the investment in tangible assets non-performing because of the specificity of investment. In a large corporation, investors are like absentee landlords. They cannot exercise their ownership rights because the power to control assets rests with the top management whom investors hire to manage the business. In a technology driven company (e.g. bank and software companies), specialised human capital has become equally, if not more, important as inanimate assets. It is not only the top management, but even employees occupying lower positions bring specialised knowledge and skills with them. Therefore, in those companies the power to control is distributed among employees at all levels. From this perspective, corporate governance should address the problem of self dealing by top management and other employees.

All the three definitions of a firm are complementary, although they view a firm from different perspectives. Understanding all the three perspectives is important for understanding different facets of corporate governance.

(II) The Management Structure of Limited Liability Companies

Limited liability company structure is the most commonly used organisation structure to conduct a large business. When a business grows, the entrepreneur needs funds. She promotes a limited liability company to collect equity capital and debt capital from financial intermediaries (e.g. banks and developmental financial institutions), friends, family members and public. A company that does not collect funds from the public is known as private limited company (often called closely held company). A company that collects funds from public is known as public limited company. An investor in the equity of a limited liability company has no liability beyond the amount she agrees to contribute to the capital of the company. In other words, if the value of the assets of a company falls below the aggregate amount of claims of creditors (including debt holders), equity holders are not required to introduce fresh capital in the company to pay creditors. This helps a company to invest in risky projects. A limited liability company is a legal fiction; it has a juridical personality. It can sue and be sued in its own name; it can purchase, sell, and hold assets in its own name; it has perpetual succession in the sense that it continues to exist even if its promoters and other members (investors in the equity capital of the company), who contributed the initial capital, cease to exist because of death or transfer of shares. A limited liability company continues to exist until it is legally wound up voluntarily or otherwise. Shares in a limited liability company are transferable.

A limited liability company (company in the rest of the article) comes into existence by completing formalities required under the law and by submitting, among other documents, a 'memorandum of association' with the appropriate authority. The memorandum of association is a public document which states, among other things, the objectives that the company will pursue. Moreover, a company issues a 'prospectus' while inviting investors to contribute to the capital of the company. The prospectus, among other things, states the purpose for which funds will be used. Thus, there is an implicit contract between investors and the promoter (the entrepreneur who promotes the company) on how the funds will be used and how returns will be divided between the entrepreneur and investors. In addition, a company, at the time of registration files with the appropriate authority a document that sets out the rules for internal management of the company. The document is called 'articles of association'. The Companies Act governs the formation and management of a company and defines the rights and duties of investors in the capital of the company. It also prescribes penalties for different types of violation of the law. The 'memorandum of association', the 'articles of association', the prospectus and provisions of the company law may be deemed to be components of a comprehensive contract between the company and investors.

When an entrepreneur borrows money from a financial institution, she signs a contract with the financial institution explicitly. The ex-ante contract that is entered into between the management and investors, particularly with equity investors, is too broad and does not cover all contingencies because those cannot be foreseen. Therefore, those contracts are subject to interpretations. As a result, courts do not intervene in enforcing those contracts on the ground of 'business judgment' unless there is massive violation of investors' rights. One solution to the problem is the investors retain the rights to take decisions in contingencies. The solution is not feasible because of two reasons. The first and the most important reason is that investors are not qualified and informed enough to take decisions. The second reason is that investors of publicly traded companies[10] are large in number and are dispersed, and therefore, it is impractical, if not impossible, for them to take decisions collectively in every contingent situation that occurs after the investment is made. The free rider problem[11] dissuades small investors acquiring from knowledge and information about the business of the company and actively participating in decision making.

An equity shareholder enjoys many rights, the most important of which is the voting right. Usually, each share has one voting right. An investor can exercise the voting right to elect her nominee to the board of directors. The board of directors acts as a trustee for equity shareholders. The board has a fiduciary[12] relationship with investors. In practice, small investors seldom exercise the right in the general meeting. As a result an investor or a group of investors who hold the majority voting shares or who can organise proxies[13] gets its nominees elected to the board. Therefore, although, theoretically, an individual or group holding more than 51 per cent of the voting rights in a company can get its nominees elected to the board, in practice, in most situations, an individual or a group holding less than 51 per cent of the voting rights (but more than any other individual or group) controls the board of directors of the company. Some decisions can be taken in the general meeting only by a special resolution[14]. Therefore, an investor who holds 26 per cent of the voting rights can block a decision which the law requires to be taken by shareholders by a special resolution.

In practice, the incumbent management gets its nominees elected to the board of directors, unless there is a battle to take over the control of the company between rival groups. In general, the exercise of the voting right in a general meeting is costly for small and dispersed shareholders. Therefore, they prefer selling shares of an under-performing company, rather than changing its board of directors.

The role of the board of directors

The board of directors, elected by shareholders, has the responsibility to oversee the executive management to ensure that it does not expropriate or waste the wealth of investors.

Board of directors has the responsibility to appoint right individuals for top positions, to formulate right incentive contracts to ensure economic efficiency and to renegotiate contracts with the top management in situations not covered in the extant contract. More specifically, the responsibilities of the board include:

(a) To appoint the Chief Executive Officer (CEO) and other senior executives of the company
(b) To terminate the services of the Chief Executive Officer, if required
(c) To ensure that the internal control system is adequate and is operating effectively
(d) To review the vision and mission of the company
(e) To review the strategy of the company
(f) To review financing and operating decisions of the company
(g) To decide compensation (including incentives) of the Chief Executive Officer and other senior executives of the company
(h) To review the performance of the board

The board is in a fiduciary relationship with investors and should take care of their welfare, particularly the welfare of equity holders. In a way the board is accountable to shareholders and the executive management is accountable to the board of directors.

The effectiveness of the board of directors depends on the independence and capabilities of board members, the effectiveness of the board process and the motivation of the board members to effectively contribute to the board process.

(III) The Concept of Corporate Governance

In a limited liability company ownership rights vest with equity shareholders. However, they can seldom exercise those rights because they do not have the technical and managerial skills required to manage the business and also because they are small and dispersed. They invest in the equity of a company because they are ready to take higher risk (than risk in investment in treasury bills or corporate bonds) in expectation of higher return. An investor chooses a security based on her liking for a particular business. An investor selects a security based on the economics of investments. The power to control resources of a company rests with the top management or it is distributed among employees of a company based on the nature of the industry in which the company operates. The residual control rights that the top management enjoys are much more extensive than what it would have been had the courts and shareholders were much more active in enforcing ex-ante contracts between shareholders and managers.

In the context of publicly traded companies equity shareholders are principals and the manager is the agent. The capital market theory establishes that in an economy with a well functioning capital market, managers serve the welfare of investors by 'maximising the firm value'. They need not have to bother about the personal preferences of individual investors. Therefore, a manger should take decisions that will enhance the value of the firm. Although the top management (manager in the rest of the article) is expected to act as the agent of equity shareholders and take decisions for their welfare, it might use its power to control for self dealing.

The promoter manager or the professional manager controls 100 per cent of the assets of the company with less than 100 per cent cash flow right, which is proportional to the shareholding of the manager in the equity capital of the company. Most individuals are selfish and they tend to maximise their own benefits and to pass on the costs that they should bear to others. Managers are no different. A manager is tempted to expropriate investors' funds, because she gets 100 per cent of the fund expropriated, while she gets only a part of the increase in the value of the company, if her shareholding is less than 100 per cent. Expropriation may take many forms, such as:

(a) Absconding with the money;
(b) Selling the output of the firm to other manager-owned businesses below the market prices (transfer pricing);
(c) Selling the assets of the firm to other manager-owned businesses below the market prices;
(d) Diverting funds to themselves (managerial compensation and perquisites); and
(e) Expanding the firm beyond what is rational, reinvesting the free cash, pursuing pet projects, and projects that benefit them rather than investors.

Grossman and Hart (1988) describe these benefits as the 'private benefits of control'. The problem arising from the principal-agent relationship between the manager and equity holders give rise to the agency problem.

Agency problem

Jensen and Meckling (1976) observe:

'We define agency relationship as a contract under which one or more persons [principal(s)] engage another person (the agent) to perform some service on their behalf which involves delegating some decision making authority to the agent. If both parties to the relationship are utility maximizers, there is a good reason to believe that the agent will not always act in the best interest of the principal. The principal can limit divergence from his interest by establishing appropriate incentives for the agent and by incurring monitoring costs designed to limit the aberrant activities of the agent. In addition, in some situations it will pay the agent to expend resources (bonding costs) to guarantee that he will not take certain actions which will harm the principal or to ensure that the principal will be compensated if he does take such actions. However, it is generally impossible for the principal or the agent at zero cost to ensure that the agent will make optimal decisions from the principal's viewpoint. In most agency relationships the principal and the agent will incur positive monitoring and bonding costs (non-pecuniary as well as pecuniary), and in addition there will be some divergence between the agent's decisions and those decisions which would maximize the welfare of the principal. The dollar equivalent of the reduction in the welfare experienced by the principal as a result of this divergence is also a cost of the agency relationship, and we refer to this latter cost as "residual loss". We define agency costs as the sum of:

1. The monitoring expenditures by the principal
2. The bonding expenditures by the agent
3. The residual loss

Shleifer and Vishny (1997) describe the agency problem as follows:

'The agency problem is an essential element of the so-called contractual view of the firm. The essence of the agency problem is the separation of management and finance, or – in more standard terminology– of ownership and control. The agency problem in the context of a publicly traded company refers to the difficulties financiers have in assuring that their funds are not expropriated or wasted on unattractive projects'.

Corporate governance

In a limited liability company, usually, the manager enjoys the power to control and consequently enjoy greater ex-post bargaining power than equity shareholders, who enjoy the ownership rights. Zingles (1998) defines corporate governance as the complex set of constraints that set the ex-post bargaining over the quasi-rent generated by a firm.

Shleifer and Vishny (1997) describe the corporate governance as follows:

'Corporate governance deals with the ways in which suppliers of finance to corporations assure themselves of getting a return on their investment. How do the suppliers of finance get managers to return some of the profits to them? How do they make sure that managers do not steal the capital they supply or invest it in bad projects? How do suppliers of finance control managers?'

In general, corporate governance refers to mechanisms that aim to reduce 'agency costs' primarily by providing right incentive to the manager and by monitoring and controlling her decision.

Incentive contracts

One solution to the agency problem could be to grant a manager highly contingent, long term incentive contract ex-ante to align her interest with those of investors. Incentive contracts are common in practice. Managers are offered variable pay based on the performance of the company. Many companies offer share based payments (e.g. Employees Stock Options) to align their interest with those of investors. However, there are serious problems with high powered incentive contracts. Incentive contracts should reward or punish managers based on objective measures of performance. The optimal contract should take into account, among other things, the risk aversion of the manager and the effect of her decision on the firm. Theoretically, a manager's risk appetite is expected to be lower than equity shareholders. It is difficult to formulate the optimal contracts for different managers and for different contingencies. Moreover, incentive contracts create enormous opportunities for self-dealings to the manager. For example, incentives linked to performance may drive managers to manipulate data, for example, managers may resort to earnings management. Another problem with incentive contracts is that those are to be renegotiated continuously to suit the changed business environment. The manager, who is in a strong bargaining position, may negotiate incentive contracts when they know that earnings or share prices are likely to rise. The opportunities for self-dealing increases manifold when managers negotiate incentive contracts with poorly motivated boards of directors. Literature has found a small sensitivity of executive compensation to the share price.

Passive monitoring

Corporate governance models focus on monitoring and control of the manager. Monitoring and control may be passive or active. Passive monitoring and control (information signals) usually come from the capital market. For example, an institutional investor or pension fund disinvests ("exits") if performance of the firm is poor. Therefore, transparency in and timeliness of corporate financial reporting enhances passive monitoring and control. However, many economists believe that short-termist and bias decisions of institutional investors reduce the effectiveness of passive monitoring and control very significantly. At the worse, it might adversely affect the quality of corporate governance, because it may tempt managers to 'maximize the firm value' in the sort-term rather than pursuing strategies that would maximise the long-term value of the firm.

Active monitoring

The board of directors, a large shareholder, a large creditor, or the market for corporate control actively monitors and controls the manager. Institutional investors often behave like small dispersed investors and do not spend resources for active monitoring and control of the firm, because of the 'free-ride' problem. They prefer to make an exit from an under-performing company rather than spending resources to improve its performance.

Evidence suggests that concentration of ownership improves the control of managers by overcoming the 'free-ride' problem. However, evidence also suggests that a financial institution having large investment intervenes only when the firm is in distress. On the negative side, a large shareholder may indulge in 'self-dealing' and create private benefits. This adversely affects the interest of small shareholders or debt holders.

Evidence points at board of directors dominated by the incumbent management. Therefore, most corporate governance codes prescribe for "balanced board" with adequate number of "independent directors", and separation of the positions of the chairman and the chief executive officer. For example, in India, clause 49[15] of the listing agreement requires that not less than 50 per cent of directors should be non-executive directors; there should be at least 50 per cent independent directors[16] if the chairman is an executive chairman; and in case of non-executive chairman at least one-third should be independent directors. The expectation is that a balanced board would be able to carry on its responsibilities objectively. However, evidence suggests that even a balanced board of directors react very late and mostly under outside pressure.

Holmstrom and Kaplan (2003) observe:

"... the recent events like Enron, Tyco, and WorldCom suggest that the boards of U.S. companies continue to exhibit less than the optimal amount of independence and oversight. The Sewate report on Enron's board is particularly critical in this respect. When a company is not doing well, everyone pays close attention – lenders and investors as well as board members. But when a company appears to be doing well, as was the case with both Enron and Tyco, investors and the board are likely to be less critical."

Debt is another instrument to discipline managers and reduce agency costs. The failure to repay the debt results in transfer of control from the manager to the creditor. Therefore, the manger works hard to avoid default. On the negative side, the debt holder, because of its relatively high bargaining power, may extract rent from the firm. Moreover, excessive debt in the capital structure may cause debt overhang, where the manager does not choose a good project because most returns will go to debt holders.

Presence of a corporate control market helps to improve corporate governance. Proxy contests, friendly mergers, and hostile takeovers are considered complementary with internal control mechanisms. The threat of take over motivates the incumbent management to perform at the optimal level. However, there is scant evidence that operating performance of a firm increases with a takeover.

Board effectiveness

The size of the board of directors is an important variable that determines the effectiveness of the board. With regards to the board size, most experts believe that optimal size should be between 6 to 8 members.

Most corporate governance codes (including clause 49 of the listing agreement) suggest measures for effective functioning of the board of directors. For example, one of the requirements of the corporate governance code is that the board should function through committees, which are constituted of independent directors. Most companies constitute committees (e.g. audit committee, investors' grievance committee, remuneration committee, and nomination committee) that handle sensitive issues and facilitate decision making by the board of directors. Usually corporate governance codes stipulate constitution of committees and scope of work of each committee.

Corporate governance codes also specify the board process to ensure that the board agenda includes important issues that come under the purview of the board. The most important issue that is yet to be resolved is how to motivate independent directors to spend adequate time to understand the business and to contribute effectively to the board process. Usually corporate governance codes limit the number of boards in which an individual can join as a director so that she can do justice to her board positions. However, this is not adequate to motivate an individual to contribute effectively to the board performance. Some argue that a board member should be compensated adequately for the time she spends to serve the board effectively. They believe that the present sitting fee is inadequate. It is difficult to determine what the optimal compensation to a director is. A high compensation might adversely affect the independence of a director. Some others argue that an individual should invest a significant part of her wealth in the equity of the company in which she joins as a board member. They argue that an individual having a stake in the company is expected to have motivation in improving the performance of the company. However, this is not a feasible solution. An individual holds a well diversified portfolio and does not want to expose her investment to undue risks by investing in a single security. Moreover, none prefers to invest in an underperforming company and consequently such a company will find it difficult to get right individuals in its board of directors.

Under the company law, even a non-executive director is liable for the violation of law and other wrongful acts of the company. Although, many argue that the threat of penalty motivates a director to use 'due diligence', but, in practice, penal provisions dissuade individuals from joining board of companies which do not have a track record of good corporate governance. Moreover, usually courts do not intervene and impose penalties for negligence on the ground of 'business judgment' unless there is gross violation of inventors' rights and therefore, seldom penalty is imposed on directors except for the violation of law or for a fraud perpetrated by the company. Therefore, penal provisions fail to motivate independent directors to contribute effectively to the board process. Poorly motivated directors bring down the effectiveness of the board.

V. Corporate Governance in International Joint Ventures

Foreign direct investment (FDI) occurs when a firm undertakes an investment in an overseas enterprise, in which the foreign investor has both the lasting interest and substantial control. FDI implies that that the investor exerts a considerable degree of influence on the management of the overseas enterprise. FDI can be wholly owned (either acquisitions or green field) or joint ventures. With FDI, the investing firm assumes greater risks, compared with licensing or exporting, but has considerably more management control over the overseas operation.

For the host country it is a source of additional external finance (and of risk capital) augmenting fixed investment, potential output and employment. FDI is also seen as a source of technology and management skill, creating tangible and intangible assets in the host country. However, empirical researches show mixed results. Many researchers find that in practice FDI does not create the benefits that are expected to flow to the host country [For example, see Petras (2005)].

Corporate governance in the context of FDI is examined from the point of view of the relationship between the foreign investor and the partner from the host country (local partner) in a joint venture.

Corporate governance in an international joint venture (IJV) needs to focus on certain complex issues, which can be summarised as follows:

(a) control by the foreign partner without majority voting rights because the state puts restrictions on the shareholding of the foreign partner or on the voting power of the foreign partner.

(b) separation of strategic control and operating control.

(c) focus on maximisation of value for the share holders of the foreign partner rather than maximisation of the value of the IJV.

Bargaining Power Approach

The relative bargaining power of the foreign partner is the most important variable that determines the relationship between the foreign partner and the local partner. Usually joint venture partners compete and cooperate at the same time. Negotiations between partners commence from the conceptualisation of the IJV and continue throughout the life of the IJV. Therefore, most researchers analyse the structure and productivity of joint ventures from the 'bargaining power' approach.

A foreign partner enters the host country (e.g. India) through a joint venture with as much equity holding as is permitted by the local government. Child and Yan (1999) observe that there is a strong relationship between the equity shareholding of the foreign partner and its strategic control over the IJV. The motivation of the joint venture partner to participate in strategic decision making comes from the fact that the objectives that the local partner wants to achieve might differ from those of the joint venture partner. Governments in developing countries usually put restrictions on the shareholding of a foreign partner in an IJV. A government determines different limits for FDI for different industries depending on the expected role of different industries in socio-economic development of the country and similar other factors such as security of the country. For example, the Indian government has established 26 percent equity cap for the insurance sector. The low equity cap for the insurance sector reflects the government's concern that if a foreign partner is allowed to have strategic control over an insurance IJV, the firm may undermine its role in socio-economic development of the rural population. A cap on the foreign equity holdings makes a proposal to establish an IJV unattractive to a prospective foreign partner because it restricts the strategic control and reduces the chances that the foreign partner would achieve its objectives.

A foreign partner provides important intangible assets like technology, managerial skills and brand. It is difficult for the foreign partner to write a complete (long term) contract regarding the use of those assets and thus to protect them from misuse. Therefore, it has a motivation to participate in operating decisions significantly.

Although the ownership right of the joint venture partner flows from its equity holding in the joint venture, its ability to control the operations of an IJV depends on its bargaining power. The relative bargaining power of the foreign partner is determined by the relative importance of intangible assets brought by the foreign partner vis-à-vis the intangible assets (e.g. information about the local market, managerial and marketing skills relevant in the host country) provided by the local partner. If the intangible asset provided by the foreign partner is proprietary and the foreign partner's continued commitment to provide access to those intangibles is essential for the success of the joint venture, the foreign partner has a very strong bargaining power. In that situation the percentage of shareholding in the equity of the joint venture is irrelevant in determining the power of the foreign partner to control the operating decisions and some times the strategic decisions of the joint venture. However, the relative bargaining power of the foreign partner and the local partner changes over time due to changes in the business environment (see Nakamura, 2005). The shift in the bargaining power is primarily determined by the extent of learning by both the partners from each other. For example, when the foreign partners acquire the knowledge (e.g. market dynamics, work culture, and the legal environment in the host country), which was originally brought by the local partner, the foreign partner might prefer to go alone and set up a 100 per cent subsidiary in the host country. Similarly, when the local partner acquires the knowledge (e.g. proprietary technology and networking) which was originally brought by the foreign partner, the local partner might not need the support from the foreign partner. Therefore, researchers observe that international joint ventures are typically unstable over time.

Typically, a foreign partner exercises operating control by appointing individuals of its choice in top management positions (e.g. CEO and CFO) in the IJV and by centralising decision making in its office. Therefore, while allowing FDI in particular industry, the government often imposes certain restrictions, including appointment of top management personnel. For example, while the Indian government allows foreign investment up to 74 per cent in telecom firms, it has imposed certain restrictions such as the majority of directors on the board including the chairman, managing director and the chief executive officer have to be resident Indian citizens.

VI. The Role of the State in Corporate Governance

The state plays a very important role in corporate governance because it provides the legal environment in which a firm operates.

While discussing the legal basis for a firm, Scott (1991) observes:

'Ex-ante contracting is a flexible institution. Transactors can, at least in principle, design each relationship to suit their particular needs. In all but the simplest exchanges, however, the process of exploring and stipulating details of a transaction can become expensive very quickly. In addition, many basic terms and conditions are likely to be common across transactions. To minimize the costly duplication of identical provisions in individual contracts, the law provides a set of standard doctrines and remedies to deal with recurring contractual events. Thus, both court-determined penalties for contract breach and common law application of force majeure criteria can be interpreted as substitutes for the redundant stipulation of common provisions by individual Transactors. At the same time, courts recognize the diversity of transactions and give parties wide latitude to augment or modify the terms of the agreement by mutual consent. The existence of a standard set of doctrine to govern contractual exchange and the ability to "contract out of or away from the governance structures of the state by devising private orderings" (Williamson, 1983:520) combine to provide a degree of both economy and flexibility in constructing contractual relationships.'

The law provides standards terms of ex-ante contracts and thus establishes ex-ante bargaining power of contracting parties. For example, labour laws determine the ex-ante bargaining power of employees. Similarly, the company law and regulations governing publicly traded companies significantly influences the ex-ante bargaining power of equity investors and directors. The state also creates various institutions that influence the relative bargaining power of contracting parties in a firm. The ex-post bargaining power of contracting parties is influenced by the approach of the institutions that have the responsibility to enforce the law. For example, the ex-post bargaining power of employees is influenced by the approach of the conciliation authority that arbitrates in a dispute between an employer and its employees and also by the approach of the judiciary which hears the dispute between an employer and its employees. If the conciliation authority considers its responsibility to protect interests of employees, the outcome of arbitration would be different from the outcome of an arbitration in which the conciliation authority takes the position of a facilitator in the negotiation between an employer and its employees. Similarly, the ex-post bargaining power of investors and directors is influenced by the approach of the judiciary in determining the extent to which it should intervene in the internal management of a firm.

Corporate governance from the perspective of the relationship between the foreign investor, the partner from the host country, and the government of the host country should be viewed as the *governance of contracts*. FDI results in a tripartite contract among the state, the foreign partner and the partner from the host country. The government policy and regulation are the instruments that set the contractual terms and conditions from the perspective of the state. The governance issue arises when ex-ante contract is not adequate to take care of contingencies occurring after the initial contract. The sharing of the quasi- rent depends on the relative bargaining power of the contracting agents. The government changes policy and regulations in favour of foreign investors if, they as a group enjoy strong bargaining power or the government is keen to attract foreign investment. For example, the withdrawal of the press note 18, which required 'no objection certificate' form the local partner of an IJV if, the foreign partner wants to establish another firm either as 100 per cent subsidiary or as another IJV, has reduced the bargaining power of the local partner significantly. This reduces the pay off to the host country from the FDI. Therefore, the governance from the point of view of the state requires managing the ex-post bargaining power of the foreign investor.

Conclusions

Corporate governance addresses the agency problems. Corporate governance codes stipulate mechanisms that reduce agency costs. The focus is on monitoring and control of the manager who enjoys the power to control the resources of the firm. In the context of an IJV, corporate governance addresses the issue of the foreign partner appropriating more than the fair share of the value created by the firm. The state plays an important role in corporate governance because it provides the legal environment and creates institutions, which significantly influence ex-post bargaining power of contracting parties. Ex-post bargaining power determines the sharing of quasi-rent between contracting parties.

Notes and References

1. Alchian, A, and Demsetz, H, "Production, information costs and economic organization" in *American Economic Review*, vol., 62, 1972, pp.777-95
2. Child, John and Yan, Yanni, "Investment and control in international joint ventures: the case of China" in *Journal of World Business*, Vol., 34, 1999, pp 3-15
3. Grossman, S and Hart, O, "The costs and the benefits of ownership: A theory of vertical and lateral integration" in *Journal of Political Economy*, Vol., 94, 1986, pp. 691-719
4. Grossman, Stanford and Hart, Oliver, "One Share-One Vote and the Market for Corporate Control" in *Journal of Financial Economics*, Vol., 20, 1988, pp.175-202
5. Hart, O. and Moore, J, "Property rights and the nature of the firm" in *Journal of Political Economy*, Vol., 98, 1990, pp.119-1158
6. Hosmstrom, Bengt, and Kaplan, Steven N, 'The State of U.S. Corporate Governance: What's Right and What's Wrong?', working paper No. 23/2003, European Corporate Governance Institute, 2003, www.ecgi.org/wp.
7. Jensen, Michael C, and Meckling William H, "Theory of the firm: managerial behavior, agency costs and ownership stricture" in *Journal of Financial Economics*, Vol., 3, 1976, pp 305-360
8. Masten, Scotte E, 'A legal basis for the firm' in Williamson, Oliver E, and Winter, Sidney G, (Ed.) *The Nature of the Firm: Origins, Evolution, and Development,* New York, Oxford University press,1991, pp. 197-212

9. McMillan, J, *Reinventing the Bazaar: The Natural History of Markets*, New York, W.W. Norton & Company, 2002, pp 168-169
10. Nakamura, Masao, "Joint venture instability, learning and the relative bargaining power of the parent firms" in *International Business Review*, Vol., 14, 2005, pp 465-493
11. Petras, James, "Six myths about the benefits of foreign investment", 2005, http://www.global policy.org/socecon/ffd/fdi/2005/0702 sixmyths.htm
12. Rajan, Raghuram G, and Zingales, Luigi, 'The Governance of the New Enterprise" in Vives, Xavier, (Ed.), *Corporate Governance-Theoretical and Empirical Perspectives*, Cambridge, Cambridge University Press, 2000
13. Rajan, R. and Zingales, L, "Power in a theory of the firm" in *Quarterly Journal of Economics*, Vol., 113, 1998, pp.387-432
14. Roberts, John, *The Modern Firm*, New York, Oxford University Press, 2004a, pp. 91
15. Roberts, John, *The Modern Firm*, New York, Oxford University Press, 2004b, pp. 104
16. Shleifer,Anderi, and Vishny, Robert W, 1997 "A survey of corporate governance" in *The Journal of Finance*, vol., 52, 1997, pp.737-783
17. Williamson, Oliver E, "The logic of economic organization", in Williamson, Oliver E, and Winter, Sidney G, (Ed.) *The Nature of the Firm: Origins, Evolution, and Development,* New York, Oxford University press,1991, pp. 100
18. Williamson, Oliver E, "Credible commitments: using hostages to support exchange" in *American Economic Review*, Vol., 83, 1983, 519-40
19. Zingales, Luigi, "Corporate Governance" in *The New Palgrave Dictionary of Economics and the Law*,1998, http://ssrn.com/abstract=46906

(i) Economic efficiency is achieved when the value assigned to waste or "friction" or other undesirable economic features in the production process is reduced to the minimum.

(ii) Economies of scale and diseconomies of scale refer to an economic property of production that affects cost if quantity of all input factors by some amount is increased. If costs increase proportionately, there are no economies of scale; if costs increase by a greater amount, there are diseconomies of scale; if costs increase by a lesser amount, there are positive economies of scale. When combined, economies of scale and diseconomies of scale lead to ideal firm size theory, which states that per-unit costs decrease until they reach a certain minimum, then increase as the firm size increases further. The ideal firm size is the theoretically most competitive size for any company, in a given industry, at a given time; which should ideally correspond with the highest possible per-unit profit.

(iii) Economies of scope are conceptually similar to Economies of scale. Whereas economies of scale apply to efficiencies associated with increasing or decreasing the scale of production, economies of scope refer to efficiencies associated with increasing or decreasing the scope of business through diversification, marketing and distribution. Whereas economies of scale refer to changes in the output of a single product type, economies of scope refer to changes in the number of different types of products. Whereas economies of scale refer primarily to supply-side changes (such as level of production), economies of scope refer to demand-side changes (such as marketing and distribution). Economies of scope are one of the main reasons for diversification and such marketing strategies as product bundling, product lining, and family branding. 'Economies of scope' is achieved when a firm leverages resources across business units from a cost perspective.

(iv) In economics, an externality occurs when a decision (for example, to pollute the atmosphere) causes costs or benefits to stakeholders (e.g. local community) other than the person making the decision. In other words, the decision-maker does not bear all of the costs or reap all of the gains from his action. Negative externality is used to refer to external cost or external diseconomy. For example, a firm may create negative externality by producing a product, the use of which pollutes the environment, which in turn creates health hazards for those who do not benefit from the production or consumption of that product.

(v) In economics 'economic rent' refers to the payment to a factor of production (e.g. land) in excess of that which is needed to keep it employed in its current use. Quasi rent refers to the rent that accrues to the superior proprietary assets of a firm which is in the nature of economic rent, similar to the economic rent that accrues to a superior piece of land.

(vi) *Ex ante* is a Latin term meaning "beforehand". The opposite of ex ante is *ex post*, meaning "after the fact". Ex ante contract refers to the contract by which the fund is invested in the company and sunk in the business.

(vii) Opportunity cost is a term used in economics, to mean *the* cost *of something in terms of an opportunity forgone* (and the benefits that could be received from that opportunity), or *the most valuable foregone alternative*.

(viii) Residual control right refers to the discretionary rights to decide the use of assets in contingencies (situations that are not covered by the contract between parties that jointly own the assets). In business, contingent situations arise frequently because a contact cannot cover all contingencies that might arise in a business. In a sense all contracts are incomplete contracts. Residual control right is valuable because it can be used strategically to enhance the bargaining power in negotiating surplus (quasi-rent) arising due to occurrences of contingencies not included in the contract.

(ix) Credit risk refers to the risk that the investor may not get the promised return on her investment and/or may not get back part or full amount invested in the debt capital of the firm.

(x) A publicly traded company is a company equity capital of which is provided by shareholders who are members of the general public and who trade shares publicly, often through a listing on a stock exchange. Ownership of equity shares is open to anyone who has the money and inclination to buy shares in the company. It is differentiated from closely held companies (often called private limited companies) where the shares are held by a small group of individuals often members of one or a small group of families or otherwise related individuals (or other companies). Any entity (e.g. partnership firm and institutional investors), including individuals can hold equity shares in a limited liability company.

(xi) In economics and political science, *free riders* are actors who consume more than their fair share of a resource, or shoulder less than a fair share of the costs of its production. The free rider problem is the question of how to prevent free riding from taking place, or at least limit its negative effects.

(xii) In many common law jurisdictions, fiduciary is a legal term used to describe a relationship between a person who occupies a particular position of trust, power or responsibility with respect to the rights, property or interests of another. Common relationships with this character are those of a guardian and a ward, an attorney and a client, and a trustee and a beneficiary. In general, a fiduciary must act for the benefit of the person to whom she owes fiduciary duties, to the exclusion of any contrary interest. The fiduciary duty is often termed as the 'duty of loyalty'.

(xiii) The corporate law in almost all jurisdictions allows an equity share holder, who does not attend a general meeting in person, to vote through proxy by authorizing some one to vote on her behalf.

(xiv) A resolution in a meeting of the shareholders is a special resolution when the votes cast in favor by shareholders are not less than three-fourth of the total votes cast, either in person or through proxy.

(xv) Clause 49 of the Listing Agreement between a stock exchange and the company which want to list its securities in the said stock exchange incorporates the corporate governance code issued by the Securities and Exchange Board of India (SEBI), which regulates capital markets in India.

(xvi) An independent director is one who apart from receiving director's remuneration, does not have any material pecuniary relationships or transactions with the company, its promoters, its directors, its senior management or its holding company, its subsidiaries or associates which may affect the independence of the director. Clause 49 of the Listing Agreement specifies disqualifications for an independent director.

4

Hesitant Devolution: India's Tryst with Democratic Governance

Asok Kumar Mukhopadhyay

Background

India's tryst with democracy began with the republican constitution coming into force in 1950. Adult franchise was introduced and the first democratic general elections for Parliament and State Legislatures were held in early 1952. Later in the same year the bureaucracy-led Community Development Project was started, followed by the National Extension Service next year. The goal of these efforts was to bring to the people the benefits of democracy and development. However, within three years the high hopes of the political leadership crashed. The National Development Council appointed the Study Team on Community Projects and National Extension Service (Chairman: Balwantray Mehta) in December 1956 to find out what went wrong with the scheme of decentralizing the responsibility of rural development. The Study Team came out with the concept of 'democratic decentralization' for rural development by creating new political units called 'panchayats' at the village, block and district levels. This recommendation was based on the theoretical approach of democratically devolving 'resources, power and authority' to statutory elective local bodies in order to enable the local community to understand its problems, realize its responsibilities, exercise necessary powers through its chosen representatives and maintain constant and intelligent vigilance on local administration.[1]

This recommendation for democratic decentralization, accepted by the Government of India, finally led to the inauguration of Panchayati Raj as the new institutional innovation for devolving powers on elected local bodies to improve democratic governance in India. The Study Team had cogent reasons for recommending devolving powers to democratic institutions at the local level. Identifying the lack of enthusiasm or interest of the local bodies in development work, it commented: "So long as we do not discover or create a representative and democratic institution which will supply the *local interest, supervision and care* necessary to ensure that expenditure of money upon local objects *conforms with_the needs and wishes of the locality*, invest it with *adequate powers* and assign to it *appropriate finances*, we will never be able to evoke *local interest* and excite *local initiatives* in the field of development".[2] (italics added). The Study Team thus very correctly pinpointed the case for democratic decentralization.

Decentralization

Since the Study Team had made the case for decentralization in the mid-1950s, there are now added arguments for decentralization in the era of globalization and liberalization. First of all, decentralization of power and resources to lower-level representative bodies is now viewed as a counteraction to the wrong kind of globalization. It cannot be denied that globalization in economic and financial fields is irreversible today. But one cannot always be sure that such globalization would automatically bring prosperity or good for the country. It would be necessary to examine the moves of global economic and financial agencies and take appropriate decisions. This job can be better performed if decentralized bodies of governance are appropriately empowered, because they are in the right position to know the development needs and interests of local areas. Secondly, decentralization ensures people's participation. When democratically elected decentralized bodies are organised in such a way as to arrange consultation with local people on issues of development, the result in terms of people's satisfaction is far better than when decisions are taken by central or regional governments. Thirdly, decentralization makes it possible to reduce cost of development. If local people could be made adequately interested in local development, they would take interest in collecting information about locally available resources and in mobilizing local resources, both financial and human. Fourthly, decentralization empowers the people and they learn to understand the nature of the different problems confronting development enterprises. Once this is achieved, civil society begins to acquire both power and prestige and becomes vibrant. This is an essential requirement for the success of democratic governance.[3] Fifthly, a vibrant civil society created through adequately empowered decentralized bodies would be a guarantee against centralized and autocratic bureaucracy as well as an incipient syndicalism of organized labour threatening healthy and responsible democratic governance. Decentralization therefore has not only its economic/technical value, but also it has its political/ethical value in protecting the interests and dignity of people and making democratic governance a success.[4]

In the context of globalization, decentralization assumes some special importance and urgency. The nation-state is fast losing its importance as an economic actor, especially in the developing world. The poor and marginalized nations and their marginalized people have been more and more experiencing a sort of shocks generated by the global market forces. The shocks have to be absorbed by local or sub-national system of governance. Decentralization points the way out of this predicament. Joseph Stiglitz has offered an ideological justification of decentralization.[5] He argues that when workers are deprived of the opportunity of meaningful participation in the community by working, when through no fault of their own they simply cannot find work, they lose self-esteem. Social welfare is no substitute for the individual's opportunity to work; and in any case, many developing countries lack even an adequate social safety net, so that the adverse consequences of unemployment are truly dire. The situation becomes desperate with disruptive social consequences. The remedy, as he sees, lies in open, transparent and participatory process of development through adjustment. Devolution of decision-making power is a dependable method for achieving this goal. In the unfriendly ambience of globalization individuals and groups would agree to accept changes if they find that they are convinced that institutions of meaningful participation in decision-making have been created. But, if changes are seen by the people to have been imposed from above and by outsiders, people's resentment would grow, leading to socially destructive outcomes.

Pranab Bardhan has argued in favour of local self-governing institution and community involvement to improve the material conditions and autonomy of the poor in order to mitigate the harshness of globalization.[6]

It is oversimplification to describe the current problem of political economy as "state vs. market". The experience of the Third World shows that withdrawing by the state in favour of the market fails to protect the interests of the poor and vulnerable section of the society. The centralising tendency of the powerful state bureaucracy kills autonomy of the locality and tends to create people's frustration. The state "is to play an activist role in local participatory development, in supra-local support for raising outside finance, in underwriting risk, in supplying training and extension-services, investing in large infrastructure and in coordinating some of the externalities across localities." The state is to pay "attention towards building local institutions and organizations that are more sensitive to the needs of the poor and to their opportunities". [7]

Deepak Nayar has argued that the correctives against the operation of anti-poor market forces under globalisation and anti-people political stances of the nation-states have to be sought in situations "where people are at the center of economic development, not only as its beneficiaries but also as the main actors".[8]

Once this condition could be created, it would be easier to protect the interests of the masses rather than of the classes, and also to frustrate the manipulations of the state apparatus on behalf of groups having vested interests.

That democratic, decentralised governance is superior to authoritarian system of governance is proved by comparing the development experiences of China and India. Since the 1990s China has made some spectacular advances in economic field, but her authoritarian system of governance is likely to be a major economic liability in the long run. The countryside in China has witnessed a number of social unrest at a significant scale in the last decade owing to massive lay-offs in industrial units, arbitrary local levies on farmers, pervasive official corruption and dumping of toxic industrial exhausts. The homogenising tradition of Chinese high culture, language and bureaucracy has not given much scope to pluralism and diversity, and a centralizing, authoritarian Communist Party has carried on with this tradition. Although in recent time the Communist Party of China has adopted programmes of decentralizing economic control, there is always a political tendency to brand dissenting movements and demand for local autonomy as seditious. Experts fear that the refusal to introduce genuine political devolution and local autonomy would create major difficulties in Chinese polity and therefore in the economy.[9]

Rural-Urban inequalities are increasing in China and those who are left behind are getting restive. China's authoritarian system of governance is likely to be the major economic liability in the long run regardless of immediate short-term success in achieving a high growth rate. Income disparity between the urban-rich and the unemployed rural labour has been creating problems of governance in China, the dimension of which is quite serious today.[10]

Political-administrative reforms through decentralisation are now being taken up by the current leadership in China.

Decentralised Planning

Panchayati Raj was introduced in Indian governance in the late 1950s but the idea of 'democratic decentralization' did not catch the imagination of India's power elite. The PRIs remained moribund till the political upheaval of 1977, in which year the Congress Party led by Mrs. Indira Gandhi failed to win a single seat in North India in the Lok Sabha election. The newly- born Janata Party, which was the child of the JP movement against Mrs. Gandhi's autocratic regime in the 1970s, swept the poll and formed the first non-Congress government at the centre. Without wasting any time, the new central government appointed Asoka Mehta committee on PRIs in order to restore democratic governance in India. This committee recommended in 1978 immediate revival of Panchayati Raj in order to lay the foundation of virile democratic governance. [10A]

Till 1979 Panchayati Raj in India was a democratic imposition on the steel frame of bureaucracy. In the wake of the Asoka Mehta Committee's recommendations PR was taken as a serious item of democratic governance in the 1980s. Prime Minister Rajiv Gandhi wanted to revamp the Indian democracy by introducing decentralisation through reformed local government under the 64th and 65th Constitution amendments. But his proposal to revitalize the PRIs by devolving some powers to these grassroots institutions and giving central funds directly to them was frustrated by the state-level political leaders of almost all major political parties. Under the Indian Constitution, local government, including Panchayats, belongs to the State List in the Seventh Schedule, and therefore, the idea of devolving powers and funds directly to the PRIs was not acceptable to the state-level politicians. Later during Narasimha Rao's regime the 73rd and 74th Constitution amendments were brought in as a compromise solution. Throughout the 1970s and 1980s the stalwarts of state politics like Jyoti Basu, N. T. Rama Rao, R. K. Hegde, M. Karunanidhi and others had been demanding more decentralisation for transfering powers to the state government. At the same time, political demands for empowering the people at the grassroots had been made for achieving a higher tempo of rural development not only by local-level politicians but also by the academicians and voluntary agencies concerned with local development.

The 73rd and 74th Constitution amendments (1992) aimed at achieving political stability of the Indian polity as well as ushering in "economic development and social justice" at the grassroots. The elite bias in India's rural development in the form of inequality in the ownership of assets like land was criticised by Hanumanta Rao Committee which suggested the formation of District Planning Committee in order to rectify the elite bias. The suggestion was incorporated in the 73rd and 74th Constitution amendments, which conferred mandatory powers of planning and development to Panchayati Raj. The intended purpose of this empowerment of elected local bodies in planning and development was to reduce the economic disparity between the urban centre and rural hinterland. It was assumed that local plans would reduce social and economic inequality at the grassroots.

Under the 73rd amendment PRIs have been visualised as instruments of planning for economic development and social justice. The state government is required to constitute District Planning Committee (DPC) to facilitate decentralised planning under Art 243 ZD. The idea is that the DPC would consolidate the plans prepared by the Panchayats and Municipalities in the district and produce a draft development plan for the district. Not less than three-fourths of the total number of members of DPC are to be elected by, and from amongst, the elected members of the district level PRIs and of the Municipalities in the district in proportion to the ratio between the rural population and urban population in the district. Under Art 243 ZE the state government is required to constitute Metropolitan Planning Committee (MPC) to prepare a draft development plan for the metropolitan area as a whole. Not less than two-thirds of members of MPC are to be elected by, and from amongst, the elected members of Municipalities and Chairpersons of Panchayats in the metropolitan area in proportion to the ratio between the urban population and rural population in the metropolitan area.

A number of states have not set up DPCs and most of the states have not constituted MPCs. Then again, Haryana and Tamil Nadu have made state government officials the chairpersons of these bodies of decentralized planning. This practice goes against the spirit of the Constitutional amendment seeking to introduce decentralised planning. In some other states the DPC is chaired by the minister. In that case, the DPC/MPC loses significance as the planning body of Panchayati Raj intended to function as " institutions of self-government".

Moreover, some statutory bodies have been constituted in some states as development institutions functioning parallel to PRI. For example, Water User Group in U.P., Gram Vikas Samiti in Haryana, Development Vigilance Committee in H.P., Village Protection Committee in Gujarat and Watershed Committee in Rajasthan.[11]

These bodies have no organic link with PRIs which enjoy Constitutional recognition. Their independent functioning marginalises the PRIs. Side by side, parastatal bodies like District Rural Development Agency (DRDA) bypass the PRIs and handle huge funds meant for rural development.

In addition, the scheme of Member of Parliament Local Area Development (MPLAD) scheme, first introduced by the Narasimha Rao government, gives an annual fund of Rs. 2 crores to each MP of both Lok Sabha and Rajya Sabha to choose his/her own project of local area development in the constituency and allot funds under MPLAD. Since RS members have no territorial constituency, they are free to choose development project anywhere in the state. The implementation of such development schemes is entrusted to the district administration or local government of the area. There is a valid point of criticism against the MPLAD scheme. This development scheme disrupts the process of decentralisation of authority and resources insofar as it bypasses the Constitution-recognised development agencies like panchayats and municipalities. Moreover, the actual experience gained so far shows that MPLAD scheme is irrelevant, even redundant; so also is the LAD scheme for the MLAs. This convoluted exercise in micro-level welfare might have been beneficial for MPs/MLAs and the contractors who have done pretty well for themselves. The reported findings of the Era Sezhiyan committee are an indictment of the scheme that has over the years made a mockery of the founding principle of serving the development needs of the local people. The actual experience is that almost every rule in the book has been violated. Projects worth crores of rupees have been entrusted by MPs/MLAs to private contractors despite directives to the contrary. Then, again, continuity has been disrupted and projects abandoned whenever a constituency has elected a new MP/MLA.

Funds have been diverted for loans and grants and for construction of places of worship. The impact of LAD scheme has been hugely damaging to democratic governance through decentralised planning.

The recent (2004) move by the Union Ministry of Rural Development to constitute District Vigilance and Monitoring Committee (DVMC), a wholly nominated body, to oversee rural development with Members of Parliament as chairpersons also undermine the Constitutional status of Zilla Parishad as a planning and development body. The DVMC was designed as an instrument to improve the efficiency of PRIs, but its functioning would result in political interference and indirect intervention by the higher bureaucracy.

A laudable institutional device of decentralised planning for development has been the 'People's Plan Campaign' started in Kerala in 1995-96. The basic idea was first conceived by E M S Namboodiripad and given a concrete shape by I. S. Gulati, a fiscal expert and vice-president of Kerala State Planning Board, and T. M. Thomas Isaac of Kerala Sastra Sahitya Parishad.

The People's Plan Campaign sought to empower the local bodies to draw up development schemes within their respective areas of responsibility. It aimed at motivating and bringing together various groups of people in every locality in the preparation of development plan. Such groups included people's elected representatives who were to be made aware of their responsibility and equipped for a new style of team work; government officials in the line departments who were to be reoriented to shoulder planning responsibilities under directives of elected local bodies; experts in planning, and retired people available in the locality having technical and professional qualification as well as experience; and lastly, the mass of the people who were to be brought out of the shell of cynicism, and the mass organisations who would successfully mobilise their members for the new development initiatives.[11A]

The Campaign represents an initiative to make use of the legacy of collective social intervention and the strength of mass movements to meet the crisis of development. Apart from power crisis, lack of industrialisation and backwardness in agricultural sector, the development challenges include the persisting pockets of deprivation and poverty among the dalits and socio-economically marginalised people despite the improvement in quality of life of the people at large; dismal performance in literacy campaign as well as primary and secondary education and health sectors despite substantial budgetary allocation; social indifference in achieving gender justice; destruction of the eco system, depletion of natural resources, air and water pollution. Substantial development in agriculture and industry requires initiatives of the central and state government, but on the other fronts local level initiatives with people's participation and mobilisation of local resources hold the key. People's Campaign was designed to help the elected local bodies to use hitherto untapped sources of local resources. Voluntary resource mobilisation from below, primarily through labour enthusiasm, was expected to solve some of the pressing needs of the people. The real agenda of the People's Campaign has been the point that through the Campaign the planning process would hopefully become an instrument of mass conscientisation in regard to the issues in development process.

The Kerala experiment achieved massive popular mobilization and about fifty percent success was achieved in ensuring people's involvement in planning for rural development. This experiment made significant progress towards rural democracy and is considered a great success in micro-planning. But with a change in State government there was a change in the prospect of this institutional device. The budgetary allocations to the PRIs were reduced and the guidelines relating to the People's Campaign for Decentralized Planning was revised to give prominence to the state government officials.

The West Bengal Panchayat (Amendment) Act 2003 has created a new institution viz. Gram Unnayan Samiti (Village Development Committee – VDC) in order to ensure "active participation of the people in implementation, maintenance and equitable distribution of benefits". But its composition has been left for subordinate legislation. Hence informed critics consider it to be a "flawed legislation" on the ground that the substantive matter of VDC's composition should have been clearly stated in the law itself.[12]

The point is that delegation of legislative power should not be excessive in any case of democratic governance. Then, again, VDC would function as planning and development adviser to the Gram Sansad and the recommendation of the Gram Sansad is binding on the Gram Panchayat. Thus, in the name of decentralising planning for development, what is actually happening in West Bengal is indirect transfer of executive power to a deliberative body. Moreover, in case of different Gram Sansads within a Gram Panchayat giving contradictory recommendations, the Gram Panchayat would be stymied in similar way that "gram swaraj" scheme in Madhya Pradesh and "Janmabhumi" scheme in Andhra Pradesh have stymied Gram Panchayat.[13]

When, in addition, the pattern of organisational functioning of the dominating political party in West Bengal is taken into consideration, it is found that important decisions are taken at the level of the Panchayat Sub-Committee of the local party unit.[14] While real authority lies with the appropriate party unit, the elected representatives only endorse and implement the party decision.[15] Thus, the PRIs in West Bengal are controlled through the network of party organisations.[16]

It is one thing to have political panchayats in the sense of recognising the role of political parties in panchayats' elections instead of the concept of 'partyless democracy' in a caste-ridden and class-divided society, but it is another thing to bring the elected PRIs within firm political grip of the ruling party. Democratic decentralisation as a means of improving the quality of democratic governance loses its meaning and significance if the elected panchayat bodies are made to function as the rubber-stamp of the party caucus at the local level in decision-making in development planning as well as implementation of development programmes and projects.

Accountability in a comprehensive sense is the hallmark of democratic governance. It is necessary for guarding against all kinds of non-feasance, mal-feasance and over-feasance of the public functionaries. It is related to achievement of "efficiency" which denotes achieving maximum output with minimum input by making the best use of all kinds of resources – financial, technical and human. This is the essence of good management practice. To achieve 'efficiency' requires accomplishing the programme goals to the satisfaction of the clients (that is, the people for whom development programmes are meant), of the norms of the Constitution and laws within the framework of which development is to be designed and executed, and of the requirements of political morality as well as professional ethics, which would not allow the development administration to be derailed and sunk into corrupt practices detrimental to public interest. The 73rd and 74th Constitution amendments and the laws and rules made in pursuance of these amendments in different states of India, and the political practices adopted in running the elected rural and urban local bodies still leave much to be desired. Accountability and efficiency of elected functionaries are, in the final analysis, more a matter of political culture than of constitutional and administrative law. 'Political Culture' essentially denotes political value judgments of the people, including the media, and their perception of and expectation from the political leaders and administrators. Democratic decentralisation in India till now has not got a political culture conducive to the realisation of its basic spirit of creating self-governing institutions of local government.

Inadequate Devolution

So far as finance of the local bodies is concerned, the 73rd and 74th amendments have made some significant headway towards decentralization by providing for State Finance Commission recommending the principles and determining the amount of funds to be devolved by the State Government to the PRIs and municipal bodies, under the amended Art 280 of the Constitution requiring the Finance Commission to take note of the recommendations made by the State Finance Commission. This amendment has created a Constitutional basis so that the PRIs and municipal bodies can expect to receive regular untied funds for implementing programmes of economic development at their own initiative. The 73rd amendment has added the Eleventh Schedule to the Constitution listing 29 functions concerning issues of rural development, in regard to which the state government may devolve power and responsibilities on the PRIs. Similarly, the 74th amendment has appended the Twelfth Schedule specifying 18 functional areas in regard to which the state government may devolve powers and responsibilities to municipal bodies.

This decentralization scheme, however, has one basic limitation: the local bodies have very little regulatory power. They are generally viewed as agencies of local development under the control of higher-level authority such as the District Magistrate and Departments of the State Government. The local bodies in India are still not "governments" in their own rights. The Constitutional amendments have only ensured that these elected local bodies have a right to exist, that they cannot be superseded or dissolved whimsically by the State Government as was the practice before the enactment of the Constitutional amendments in 1992. As it has been aptly observed: "The Panchayats are horizontal interventions in the vertical jungles of administration. Any hope that they would be able to secure horizontal coordination was doomed because the vertical hierarchies were well entrenched and the Panchayats did not have even minimum administrative weaponry to bring them within the coordinating discipline.[17] The same observation, *mutatis mutandis*, is valid for municipal bodies also.

The key point is that the local bodies in India do not constitute a tier of the Indian federal state. The Eleventh and Twelfth schedules in the Constitution merely indicate the permissible limit of functional areas in which the elected local bodies may be entrusted with development work. There is no Local List in the Seventh Schedule of the Constitution. Governing powers are distributed by the Constitution only between the Union and States.

In the Indian scheme of democratic governance the PRIs and municipal bodies have never been given the real power and financial resources to enable serious development intervention. In reality, their functional scope was confined to mere civic duties and that too under the strict supervision of the state government. The central government also contributed to the process by refusing to devolve more powers to the States and thrusting on them a plethora of centrally sponsored and planned development schemes. Further, numerous autonomous national-level boards and para-statal organisations were formed in whose functioning the elected local bodies had no room. Deprived of powers and resources, the elected local bodies lost credibility and in many States even elections to these bodies were indefinitely postponed. The 73rd and 74th Constitution amendments (1992) constitute an important milestone in the history of decentralisation in India by making the PRIs and municipal bodies a part of the basic structure of the Constitution itself, guaranteeing regular elections to local bodies, and providing for a role for them in the planning process. But these two amendments did not address the important issue of centre-state relations, ignored the need for an integrated self-governing district administration encompassing both rural and urban areas and imposed too rigid a structure uniformly in all the States while giving too much discretion to the state governments as to the devolution of responsibilities, powers and resources.

The 73rd amendment provides for the District Planning Committee to consolidate the plan prepared by the panchayats and municipalities in the district and to prepare a draft development plan for the district as a whole. But it is virtually impossible for the PRIs and municipal bodies to shoulder this task under the real-life circumstances. Even if the elected local bodies are granted real power, decentralised planning might continue to be a mirage for various other reasons such as paucity of reliable local level data, lack of expertise and prior experience, and the widely prevalent cynicism of the people towards development activities.

Fiscal Devolution

Research on the finance of the local bodies in India shows that they spend more funds compared to what they used to spend before the Constitutional amendments of 1992.The total expenditure of the rural and urban bodies, as percentage of GDP, was 12.24 per cent in 1997-98 compared to only 5.53 per cent in 1992-93. But the local bodies do not spend the funds out of their own resources. In fact, their dependence on the respective State Governments and also on the Union Government in financial matters remain as strong as it had been before the 73rd and 74th

Constitution amendments. The fiscal basis of local government autonomy is indeed very weak in India.[18]

The PRIs and the municipal bodies fail to mobilize much resources from their internal sources mainly because their taxing power is limited and they are given such inelastic tax sources as non-agricultural lands and buildings, motor vehicles, and entertainment. Professional Tax which is a Constitutionally sanctioned local duty having revenue potentiality is not assigned to them in any State except in Kerala. User charges for civic services as sources of revenue of the local bodies yield low amount of funds. The local bodies in India cannot expand their own revenue base because the assigned items of tax revenue have least tax buoyancy. Moreover, socio-administrative the tradition of tax compliance by the taxpayers is weak at the village level. There have, however, been some changes since the Constitutional amendments in 1992. It is known that between 1990-91 and 1997-98 there was a doubling in average per capita collection across all the states and across all tiers of Panchayats.[19] The performance is best in Kerala, whereas it is worse in Madhya Pradesh, Orissa, Assam and Tripura; the worst performance is found in Bihar.[20]

It is interesting to note here that the performance of the State Governments in devolving funds to the local bodies in the form of intergovernmental transfer as recommended by the Central Finance Commission and State Finance Commissions has remained poor. Both the State Finance Commissions and the State Governments are responsible for this unhappy situation.[21] Not only the political will of the State Governments but also the shortcomings of the State Panchayat legislations are responsible in this respect. For example, West Bengal's legislation is silent on the point of achieving financial and administrative autonomy of local bodies, whereas Haryana's legislation is vague. Only Kerala legislation is found to have broadened the entitlement of local bodies in respect of financial devolution.

The Eleventh Finance Commission justifiably argued that transfer of duties and functions listed in the Eleventh and Twelfth Schedules of Constitution, from the State Government to the local bodies involve concomitant transfer of staff and resources from the State Government to the local bodies. This measure, if implemented, does not entail any extra financial burden on the State exchequer. The process of transfer should be automatic as it is in the case of transfer of functions and functionaries from the Union to the States.

The annual publication of the Reserve Bank of India on *State Finances: Study of State Budgets* is an important source of quantitative information on financial devolution from the State Government to the local bodies. The data available from this source for the period 1992-93 to 2002-03 show that the average per capita devolution of untied funds and project-tied funds was highest in Tamil Nadu and the lowest in Bihar. The performances of Karnataka, West Bengal and Kerala are not as good as they should have been.[22]

The share of State funds devolved to local bodies in the total revenue expenditure of a State is, however, a better indicator of the relative importance that local bodies get in the disbursement of State funds. The RBI data in this respect show that the percentage of devolved funds as compensation and assignments to local bodies to total expenditure of the State was 1.34 per cent in 1992-93 and 1.87 per cent in 2002-03 (See Table-2). That is, the share of the local bodies has increased after the Constitutional reforms but not at a very high rate. In the entire post-reform period, the best performance in this regard is that of Tamil Nadu, being an average devolution of 3.71 per cent from the State budget to the local bodies. It is followed by good performances of Madhya Pradesh (2.80 per cent), Uttar Pradesh (2.45 per cent), Karnataka (2.41 per cent) and West Bengal (1.80 per cent). Maharashtra (0.94 per cent), Punjab (0.94 per cent), Andhra Pradesh (0.84 per cent) and Orissa (0.67 per cent) are moderate performers. The bad performers are Himanchal Pradesh (0.41 per cent), Assam (0.18 per cent) and Bihar (0.02 per cent) (See Table-3).[23]

The inevitable conclusion is that the fiscal basis of autonomy of local bodies, even after the 73rd and 74th Constitution amendments, remains very weak in India. The PRIs and municipal bodies operate on very weak revenue base. The functions outlined in the Eleventh and Twelfth Schedules of the Constitution have not been adequately devolved to the local bodies. The State governments do not honour the Constitutional provisions of devolution from the Consolidated Fund of the State.

Participatory Governance

Democratic decentralization visualizes people's participation in initiating and implementing policy-decisions. The concrete organizational form of it is local self-government. Development becomes meaningful only with people's participation, which is considered an important aspect of good governance.

In India's Panchayati Raj system people's participation has been institutionalized in *Gram Sabha* (Gram Panchayat level annual meeting of the voters), which signifies rural democracy. It is a mandatory institution under 73rd Cònstitution amendment (1992). On an average, Gram Sabha comprises ten to fifteen thousand voters and is empowered to review the proposed budget for the next year prepared by the Gram Panchayat and the previous year's performance. Because of the sheer number of members, the meeting of the Gram Sabha offers the people limited opportunities to exercise effective control over their elected representatives as well as to provide inputs to the planning process.

Prior to being a mandatory body, this institution had been provided for in Panchayat legislation in some states, but it proved to be ineffective and almost useless mainly because of the fact that its meetings were irregular and thinly attended; even when it met, quorum was hardly achieved.

Since 1994-95, however, the experience of some States like Madhya Pradesh and Karnataka is found to be somewhat encouraging. Heated debate on some local issue and holding the Gram Panchayat functionaries accountable for their omissions and commissions have occurred occasionally. But the overall experience of the Gram Sabha functioning is not at all good. The research team of Participatory Research in Asia (PRIA), which studied the working of Gram Sabha in Gujarat, Haryana, Himachal Pradesh, Kerala and Uttar Pradesh in 1997, has found that although meetings are held almost regularly owing to Constitutional mandate, quorum is hardly achieved yet proceedings are recorded.[24] The team found that there was lack of awareness among the rural voters not only about the time and venue of the meetings but also about its usefulness. Many of them were confused about the Gram Sabha's role (See Table-4).

Broadly speaking, Gram Sabha meetings are political in nature and only the people having some vested interests take pains to attend in order to get some favourable resolutions passed. Except in Kerala and Madhya Pradesh, the Gram Sabha's advice and suggestions are not binding on the Gram Panchayat. Gram Sabha meetings have been seen to have failed in either determining priorities in village development programme or regular monitoring of accountability in respect of the use of resources and examining decisions of the Gram Panchayat. Issues of social justice have rarely been found to be included in the agenda of Gram Sabha meetings. There is party politics and parochial bias in disseminating information. Most often villagers are told about action plans as *fait accompli* by the Gram Panchayat leaders. One reason for this state of affairs is that PRIs in India are generally viewed as development agencies of the state government and they are burdened with the job of implementing central government-sponsored schemes as per conditions attached to development programmes. The fact is that political leadership at the grassroots is mostly concerned with pursuing their party politics or individual interests and not conscientising the rural folk as participants in rural governance.

West Bengal has experimented with a new institution of people's participation in addition to Gram Sabha. Since 1992 (prior to the enforcement of the 73rd Constitution amendment) Gram Sansad has been constituted as constituency-level bi-annual meeting of rural voters. The meeting of a Gram Sansad involve about 700 voters and is held to discuss local needs and new programmes, select beneficiaries of development programmes and examine the budget and accounts of expenditure. Gram Sansad has been designed as an instrument of direct participation of the people in the planning process as well as monitoring the functioning of the elected representatives.

Under the laws, the Gram Sansad is to (i) guide and advise the Gram Panchayat in regard to schemes of economic development and social justice undertaken or proposed to be undertaken in its area; (ii) identify or lay down principles for identification of the beneficiaries for various poverty alleviation programmes; (iii) constitute beneficiary committees for ensuring active participation of the people in implementation, maintenance and equitable distribution of benefits of schemes in the area; (iv) mobilize mass participation for community welfare, programmes for adult education, family planning and child welfare; (v) record its objections to any action of the Gram Panchayat Pradhan or any member of the Gram Panchayat for failure to implement development schemes properly or without active participation of the people of the area.

Since the Gram Sansad enjoys a legal status, Gram Panchayat is under the legal obligation to consider every resolution adopted at the Gram Sansad meeting and decision/action taken on the resolution will have to be reported at the next meeting of the Gram Sansad. Any failure to act in this manner on the part of the Gram Panchayat would be considered a serious lapse and the auditor would declare all expenditures undertaken by the Gram Panchayat as illegal. Thus people's participation in decision-making has been sought to be made effective in West Bengal. However, compared to Kerala's system of People's Plan Campaign, the West Bengal scheme of connecting people's deliberations to actual decisions is more indirect and subject to bureaucratic distortion. Since 1998 Gram Sansad meetings have been regularly held in almost all of the 45,000 constituencies.

The study of some selected Gram Sansads in West Bengal by Maitreesh Ghatak and Maitreya Ghatak brings out interesting conclusions.[25] It has been found that review and monitoring of project implementation receives the highest emphasis, followed by agenda-setting and selection of beneficiaries. Demands for new development projects are raised and project designs are debated, but impact of people's deliberations on project design surfaces very infrequently. Implementation of projects and corruption cases are criticised by villagers, and Gram Panchayat Pradhan and members are compelled to give explanation for their shortcomings. Thus some important changes have been achieved. Earlier the Pradhan was all-in-all in panchayat's development and administration, but now villagers are entitled to obtain information. However, the full benefits of participatory governance are yet to be achieved, because people have little power in influencing allocation of funds and improving the quality of project implementation.

The interstate study of Panchayats by S.P. Jain has put West Bengal not only behind Kerala but also Madhya Pradesh and Karnataka in respect of indicators such as power of preparing local plans, transfer of staff, control over staff, and transfer of funds from the State government to the PRIs.[26] Kerala's People's Plan Campaign has, however, succeeded in directly involving people in the grassroots planning process. The Kerala model of decentralization empowers the people to formulate and implement the plan and thus allows better use of local information and preferences in plan formulation and fixing priorities and also to monitor in a better way to implement development projects. But the problem with this model is that sometimes success eludes the people as they do not always have the expertise needed for plan formulation and implementation. There is also the danger that a pronounced populist and welfare bias may create problems for asset creation. There is always the need for balancing popular participation with expertise in development administration. West Bengal model of using Gram Sansad and Village Development Council in rural development has therefore some plus points in its favour provided, of course, blatant political and administrative corruption can be checked to a reasonable degree.

Both in the Kerala model and the West Bengal model of democratic decentralization there is need for close examination of development plans in regard to their technical soundness and financial viability. This measure is absolutely necessary in order to avoid the very common defect of lack of coordination across different plan units and at different levels. The problem of coordination between village plans, block plans, district plans and the plan of the State government has been successfully solved in practice in Kerala as well as in West Bengal. The Constitution-mandated institutions of District Planning Committee and

Metropolitan Planning Committee have not been set up in all the States of India nor have they been, where already set up, found to have successfully achieved the goal for which they were designed. Duplication of planning activities has been seen in Kerala and critical gaps in planning at various tiers have been noticed in West Bengal and elsewhere.

So far as urban areas are concerned, West Bengal municipal legislations have provided for forming Ward Committees in municipalities and municipal corporations. Each ward committee is to have the ward's elected councillor as its chairperson and two sets of members of the public nominated by the councillor concerned and the municipality/corporation from different walks of life. Such a grassroots institution in municipal governance has been designed to (i) identify the problems of the ward, (ii) fix priority of development projects, (iii) motivate people to pay municipal taxes, (iv) listen to people's grievances, (v) arrest wasteful use of municipal resources, and (vi) organise civic participation. The ward committee is, to some extent, the urban counterpart of Gram Sansad but with less powers. It cannot enforce accountability of municipal leadership, rather it is designed more as an institutional aid to municipal governance by organising and encouraging civic participation.

The State government in West Bengal usually threatens to stop financial assistance to municipalities if they fail to set up ward committees. In most big- and medium-size municipalities in West Bengal, ward committees have been formed and it is known that the ward committees help the councillors in performing their duties as people's representatives. But the biggest urban local body in West Bengal - Kolkata Municipal Corporation - has not taken any initiative for forming ward committees. Left Front councillors maintain that as the party in power has its office in every ward, the formation of ward committees would be of no use. The anti-L.F. councillors oppose the formation of ward committees, as they apprehend that through ward committees the dominating left parties would try to establish their control over the wards represented by non-left councillors and try to malign the non-left parties before the voters. The Left-controlled State government for some reason or other has not taken any punitive move against the KMC in order to enforce the formation of ward committees in Kolkata municipal area.[27] Participatory governance has been very weak in urban India.

Conclusion

Basically the concept of participatory governance is a political design of democratic governance. But the ideological commitment of political parties to democratic decentralization and their electoral compulsion to gain power in competitive politics sometimes prove to be strange bedfellows. The problem assumes critical dimension in both rural and urban India, which are raven by caste conflicts and class antagonism and where mass poverty and islands of 'new rich' are engaged in fierce battle for gaining political power. Social and economic inequality has come to be a permanent feature of the developing scenario in rural and urban India. All political parties pay lip-service to the programme of poverty alleviation and empowerment of grassroots democratic bodies but in no State in India is seen the required degree of political will to decentralise power, responsibility, finances and functionaries to a really meaningful degree to the democratic bodies at the grassroots. The 73rd and 74th Constitution amendments provided for reservation of seats in all local bodies for the scheduled castes, scheduled tribes, other backward castes and women in order to achieve empowerment of the weaker sections of the society, but the extent of devolution of power, functions and finances has been left to the discretion of the State government. A few States have granted considerable functional responsibilities but, except in Karnataka, hardly any serious administrative follow-up of granting adequate powers, staff and financial resources has been made (See Table-1). The kind of State-level politics and electoral compulsions determine, in the final analysis, the extent of devolution. Even the relatively success stories of Kerala, West Bengal, Karnataka and Madhya Pradesh provide testimony to the fact that devolution as a means for improving the extent and quality of democratic governance has been limited because of a deep-rooted hesitancy in the political mind of India. The Indian polity appears to suffer from a sort of Hamletian dilemma: to devolve or not to devolve powers, responsibility and finances from the upper tiers to lower tiers of the polity for the sake of better democratic governance.

Table – 1

Status of devolution of subjects, funds, functions and functionaries

Sl.	*States/UT s*	*No. of departments/subjects transferred to Panchayats with*		
		Funds	*Functions*	*Functionaries*
01.	Andhra Pradesh	05	17	02
02.	Arunachal Pradesh	-	-	-
03.	Assam	-	-	-
04.	Bihar	-	-	-
05.	Jharkhand	-	-	-
06.	Goa	-	-	-
07.	Gujarat	-	-	-
08.	Haryana	-	16	-
09.	Himachal Pradesh	02	23	07
10	Karnataka	29	29	29
11.	Kerala	15	29	15
12.	Madhya Pradesh	10	23	09
13.	Chhattisgarh	10	23	09
14.	Maharashtra	18	18	18
15.	Manipur	-	22	04
16.	Orissa	05	25	03
17	Punjab	-	07	-
18.	Rajasthan	-	29	-
19.	Sikkim	24	24	24
20.	Tamil Nadu	-	29	-
21.	Tripura	-	12	-
22.	Uttar Pradesh	12	13	09
23.	Uttaranchal	12	13	09
24.	West Bengal	12	29	12
25.	A & N Islands	06	06	06
26.	Chandigarh	-	-	-
27.	D & N Haveli	-	03	03
28.	Daman & Diu	05	09	03
29.	NCT of Delhi	Panchayati Raj system is yet to be revived		
30.	Pondicherry	-	-	-
31.	Lakshadweep	-	06	-

Note: Provisions of the Constitution (73rd Amendment) Act, 1992 are not applicable to J & K,, Meghalaya, Mizoram and Nagaland. Source: Ministry of Rural Development,Government of India

Source: Ministry of Rural Development, Government of India, New Delhi.

Table - 2

Compensation and Assignments to Local Bodies as Percentage to Total Expenditure of the State (1992-93 to 2002-03): 16 Major States of India.

State	*1992-93*	*1993-94*	*1994-95*	*1995-96*	*1996-97*	*1997-98*	*1998-99*	*1999-00*	*2000-01*	*2001-02*	*2002-03*
										Revised	*Estimate*
Andhra Pradesh	0.84	0.86	0.81	0.73	0.67	0.88	0.89	0.70	0.71	1.13	0.98
Assam	0.26	0.33	0.18	0.27	0.11	0.00	0.23	0.11	0.14	0.06	0.14
Bihar	0.04	0.04	0.04	0.02	0.02	0.02	0.02	0.02	0.02	0.02	0.02
Gujarat	0.43	0.37	0.46	0.46	0.45	0.43	0.33	0.28	0.23	0.25	0.47
Haryana	0.48	0.17	0.10	0.17	0.11	0.01	0.01	0.01	0.21	0.35	0.17
Himachal Pradesh	0.33	0.27	0.23	0.22	0.22	0.42	0.44	0.50	0.47	0.45	0.99
Karnataka	2.23	2.00	2.02	1.36	1.90	2.52	2.67	2.73	3.19	3.03	2.83
Kerala	1.09	1.40	1.29	1.29	1.71	1.56	0.54	0.68	0.46	0.57	0.51
Madhya Pradesh	2.19	2.15	2.18	2.91	2.87	2.86	2.92	4.01	3.53	2.60	2.65
Maharashtra	0.51	0.33	0.31	0.27	0.42	0.63	0.69	1.90	1.85	1.41	2.04
Orissa	0.44	0.57	0.12	0.27	0.31	0.50	0.35	0.24	1.69	1.51	1.38
Punjab	0.97	1.41	0.79	1.14	0.96	0.90	0.87	0.49	0.76	1.31	0.74
Rajasthan	0.23	0.20	0.22	0.22	0.21	0.21	0.25	0.13	0.11	0.12	0.00
Tamil Nadu	3.42	1.48	1.38	1.95	2.54	5.55	5.85	4.95	4.50	3.32	5.91
Uttar Pradesh	1.91	1.70	1.54	1.56	1.55	2.78	3.35	2.99	3.50	2.92	3.16
West Bengal	2.99	2.53	2.69	2.14	1.72	1.80	1.44	1.25	1.00	1.12	1.12
ALL STATES	**1.34**	**1.12**	**1.06**	**1.11**	**1.20**	**1.67**	**1.69**	**1.84**	**1.79**	**1.56**	**1.87**

Source: *Study of State Budgets,* Reserve Bank of India (various years).

Table – 3

Average Devolution to Local Bodies as percentage to total Revenue Expenditure of the State: 16 Major States in India

State	*Average Period 1*	*Average Period 2*	*Average Entire Period*
Andhra Pradesh	0.81	0.85	0.84
Assam	0.26	0.14	0.18
Bihar	0.03	0.02	0.02
Gujarat	0.43	0.35	0.38
Haryana	0.23	0.12	0.16
Himachal Pradesh	0.26	0.50	0.41
Karnataka	1.90	2.69	2.41
Kerala	1.27	0.86	1.01
Madhya Pradesh	2.36	3.06	2.80
Maharashtra	0.36	1.28	0.94
Orissa	0.35	0.85	0.67
Punjab	1.08	0.86	0.94
Rajasthan	0.22	0.15	0.17
Tamil Nadu	2.06	4.66	3.71
Uttar Pradesh	1.68	2.89	2.45
West Bengal	2.59	1.35	1.80
ALL STATES	**1.16**	**1.66**	**1.48**

Source: *Study of State Budgets*, R. B. I. (various years)

Note: Period 1 = 1992-93 to 1995-96

Period 2 = 1996-97 to 2002-03

Entire Period = 1992-93 to 2002-03

Table - 4

Gram Sabha in Different States: an Overview

Status-Overview Population and Area	*Concerns*
Varies from State to State. It may be * Entire area of Gram Panchayat * One revenue village. * Voters in a single ward or one electoral constiuency of Gram	1. The larger size of Gram Sabha (if it exceeds a few hunderd people) discourages meaningful deliberations. 2. Many times a voter has to

Panchayat.	spend more than an hour
* Spread over few hundred meters to many kilometres.	to reach to the venue of the Gram Sabha.
Meetings-Frequency and Schedule	
1. At least two meetings in a year	1. Gram Sabha members are often not informed about forthcoming Gram Sabha meeting.
2. Gram Panchayat should communicate date, venue and time of meetings to Gram Sabha members	2. A partly among villagers about the outcome of Gram Sabha meeting.
3. Meeting dates fixed in advance, e.g.15th Aug., 2nd Oct., 26th Jan., 13th Apr. etc.	3. Fixed date, timing and venue should be chosen considering harvesting season, availability of villagers in the village and caste dynamics.
	4. Simultaneous Gram Sabha in whole State on a participation of government officials. Many times the meetings of Gram Sabha turn out to a mere formality ones.
Participation, Power and Function	
1. Quorum varies from 5% of voters to one-third of voters to no quorum at all.	1. Gram Sabha has not been enabled to consider subjects of general interest at alllevels of developmental work, line departments.
2. No provision to ensure/enhance participation of women and dalits.	2. No follow-up of Gram Sabha decisions.
3. Status of specifically appointed (in Gram Sabha meeting) government	3. A process of consultation with concerned Gram

officials ambiguous.	Sabhas should be initiated in case of all developmental program -mes across sectors like education, health, agricul-ture, MCH, nutrition etc.
4. Decision of Gram Sabha is not binding on Gram Panchayat.	4. Gram Sabha decisions should be binding.
5. Except few States, Gram Sabha does not have any role in relation to line agencies of government.	

Panchayat Secretary/Government Officials

1. Panchayat Secretary is a village-level official specifically assigned to assist Gram Panchayat.	1. Usually a Panchayat Secretary is assigned to more than one Gram Panchayat making him overburdened to do justice to his work
2. Panchayat Secretary is supposed to assist Gram Panchayat in conducting Gram Sabha meetings.	2. In many States, almost all the Panchayat Secretaries are male only. Gender Problem is easily discerni-ble in case of their inter-action with women memb-ers of Gram Sabha and Gram Panchayat
3. The agenda of Gram Sabha meeting is prepared by Panchayat Secretary in consultation with, and complete supervision of, Gram Panchayat.	3. The Gram Sabhas do not have control over the Panchayat Secretaries. His (rarely her) duties and remuneration are controlled by officials at block level.
4. A Panchayat Secretary acts as a link between Gram Panchayat and government officials.	4. Quite often Panchayat Secretaries create hindrances in proper functioning of the Gram Panchayat

5. Panchayat employees in states like Madhya Pradesh are doing their job more effectively.
6. Gram Panchayats have been empowered to monitor (only) works of many line departments

---

Source: *Panchayati Raj Institutions: A Balance Sheet,* PRIA, New Delhi, 2000.

Notes and References

1. Report of the Team for the Study of Community Projects and National Extension Service, Committee on Plan Projects, Government of India, November 1957, Vol. I, Sec. 2, p. 23. See also, Asok Mukhopadhyay, *The Panchayat Administration in West Bengal,* Calcutta, World Press, (3rd edn.)1991, Ch. 2.
2. Report, p. 5.
3. For further discussion on decentralisation in the era of globalisation, see UNDP's *Human Development Report* (1993).
4. For a very good discussion on this point, see L. J. Sharp, "Values of Local Government", *Political Studies* (Oxford), XVIII(2), 1970.
5. Joseph Stiglitz, *Participation and Development: Perspectives from the Comprehensive Development Paradigm*, 1999.
6. P. Bardhan, 'Research on Poverty and Development', in Annual World Bank Conference on Development Economics, 1995.
7. Ibid.
8. Deepak Nayyar, 'Globalization: What Does It Mean', in S. Jomo and K. S. Nagaraj (eds), *Globalization versus Development*, New York, Palgrave, 2001.
9. Pranab Bardhan, 'Giants with Feet of Clay', Yale Global Online (a publication of the Yale Center for the Study of Globalization), quoted in *The Statesman,* Kolkata, 28th Oct. 2005.
10. Anirban Chattopadhyay, 'China at the Zenith of Development or on the top of a Volcano' (in Bengali), *Ananda Bazar Patrika* (Kolkata), 1st Nov. 2005.

10(A). See Asok Mukhopadhyay, op.cit., pp.166-68.

11. Prabhat Datta, 'The Third Generation Panchayati Raj: Old Issues and New Challenges' (unpublished memographed paper).

11(A). T. M. Thomas Isaac and K. N. Harilal, 'Planning for Empowerment: People's Campaign for Decentralised Planning in Kerala', *Economic and Political Weekly,*, January 4-11, 1997.

12. D. Bandyopadhyay, 'The Caucus and the Masses', *Economic and Political Weekly*, 15th Nov. 2003.

13. *Ibid.*

14. Harihar Bhattacharyya, *Micro Foundations of Bengal Communism*, New Delhi, Ajanta, 1998.

15. Maitree Bhattacharyya, *Panchayati Raj in West Bengal: Democratic Decentralization or Democratic Centralism*?, New Delhi, Manak Publication, 2002.

16. B. Ghosh and G. Kumar, *State Politics and Panchayats in India*, New Delhi, Manohar, 2003.

17. N. Mukarji and D. Bandyopadhyay, *New Horizons for West Bengal's Panchayats*, Calcutta, Govt. of West Bengal, 1992, p. 9.

18. Ratan Khasnobis, 'Financing the Urban and Rural Local Bodies in India', *The Calcutta Journal of Political Studies* (New Series), vol.3 & 4,Nos. 1 &2, April 2003 – March 2005.

19. I. Rajaraman, 'Revenue Incentives at the Third Tier' (2004), quoted in Ratan Khasnobis, op.cit.

20. I. Rajaraman, *A Fiscal Domain for Panchayats*, Oxford Univ. Press, 2003.

21. This information is available in the Report of the Eleventh Finance Commission.

22. For a detailed discussion on this and other related points of financial devolution, see Ratan Khasnobis, *op.cit.*

23. Source: Reserve Bank of India, *Study of State Budgets* (1992-93 to 2002-03).

24. The observations of PRIA have been referred in Prabhat Datta, *Panchayats, Rural Development and Local Autonomy*, Kolkata, Dasgupta & Co., 2001, p.117.

25. Maitreesh Ghatak and Maitreya Ghatak, 'Recent Reforms in the Panchayat System in West Bengal: Toward Greater Participatory Governance?', *Economic and Political Weekly*, 05 January 2002.

26. S. P. Jain, 'Devolution of Power, Functions and Authority to Panchayats in Different States', Working Paper of National Institute of Rural Development, Hyderabad.
27. *The Statesman* (Kolkata Plus), 05 December 2005.

PART - II

5

The Law and the Field : Citizen Participation and Urban Governance in West Bengal

Prabhat Datta

One of the most popular State-enunciated reforms that has opened spaces for a wider and deeper participation of citizens at the local level is the decentralisation process. Decentralisation has a number of merits having political and administrative implications. In the first place, it decongests government at the centre making the national leaders free from the onerous details and unnecessary involvement in local issues. In this way co-ordination is facilitated and action at the local level is expedited. Second, it helps increase people's understanding and support of social and economic development activities and in this way, people can contribute to their own activities. Third, social and economic development programmes at the local level become more realistic and target group oriented. Fourth, decentralisation plays a meaningful role in training the people in the art of self-government, and thus acts as an instrument of political education of the citizens. Fifth, it not only increases popular capacity to ensure responsibility and accountability but also improves delivery of services by allowing careful consideration of local needs and creating conditions for innovations. Sixth, it makes local development plan more responsive to local conditions and helps implementation by facilitating local resource mobilisation. Seventh, it helps achieve flexible implementation through quicker decision-making.

Most developing countries have implemented some form of decentralisation, with varying degrees of financial and political power. Parallel to these developments, enabling legal frameworks and institutional channels for citizens' participation at the local level have been developed in many of these countries. The essay, in this background, has a special focus on West Bengal. In the first section it enumerates the legal provisions relating to the urban governance in the state. In the second section it specifically focuses on two prominent municipalities to critically assess the field-level reality.

The Seventy Fourth Amendment of the Constitution

The Seventy Fourth Amendment of the Constitution seeks to institutionalise citizens' participation through the formation of ward/ Ward Committees (WCs) in all urban local bodies with a population of more than three lakhs to ensure the participation of the citizens in civic affairs at the grassroots level. The amendment breaks a new ground by providing for an institutional framework for the citizens to actively participate in their own administration and development through a two-tier system of local governance – the municipality and the WC. The former is an elective body at the level of the municipality consisting of the elected representatives of the people (councillors) and the latter is a nominated body at the level of the Ward.

The Seventy Fourth Amendment authorises the state governments to decide on the composition,territorial area and manner in which the seats of the WCs will be filled. The state governments have also been given the power to decide how the members of the WCs would be nominated. It is argued that such nomination will encourage the experts who do not like to be involved in partisan politics, to join the WCs giving them necessary vigor, vitality and relevance. One may question the logic on the ground

Table- I

Status of Ward Committees in Some Major Corporations as on 31.7.2003

Sl. No.	*Name of States*	*No. of ULBs with 3 lakh & above M. Corp.*	*Other ULBs*	*Composition of Ward Committees*	*Whether Functional*
1.	Andhra Pradesh	7	1	For group of wards (not less than 5 wards in Municipalities and not less than 10 words in Corporations)	Constitution and functioning
2.	Assam	1	-	One or more wards (not more than 4 wards)	Not yet constituted /Rules not framed
3.	Bihar	4	-	Group of wards	Not yet constituted/Rules not framed
4.	Chattisgarh	3	-	One or more wards	Not yet constituted
5.	Gujarat	5	1	Group of wards	Not yet constituted/Rules not framed
6.	Haryana	1	-	One or more wards	Not yet constituted/ Rules not framed
7.	Karnataka	6	2	For group of wards	Only in Bangalore Municipal Corporation
8.	Kerala*	5	53 MCL	For each ward	Constituted in all ULBs

(Contd.)

(Contd. Table 1)

Sl. No.	*Name of States*	*No. of ULBs with 3 lakh & above M. Corp.*	*Other ULBs*	*Composition of Ward Committees*	*Whether Functional*
9.	Madhya Pradesh	5	-	One or more wards	Constituted in all Corporations
10.	Maharashtra	22	-	Group of wards (Municipal Corporation 3 to 25 WCs & Municipal Council 3 WCs)	Constituted and Functional in 16 Municipal Corporations
11.	Orissa	2	-	For each ward	Not yet constituted/Rules not framed
12.	Punjab	4	-	Not less than five wards	Not yet constituted
13.	Rajasthan	3	3	One or more wards	Not yet constituted/Rules not framed
14.	Tamil Nadu	6	2	Group of Wards (10-12 wards)	Constituted but only with councillors
15.	Uttar Pradesh	11	3	Group of wards (not less than 5 wards for Municipalities and not less than 10 wards in Corporations)	Constituted in all Corporations

(Contd.)

(Contd. Table 1)

Sl. No.	*Name of States*	*No. of ULBs with 3 lakh & above M. Corp.*	*Other ULBs*	*Composition of Ward Committees*	*Whether Functional*
16.	Uttaranchal	1	-	Group of wards (not less than 10 wards in Corporations)	Not yet constituted/Rules not framed
17.	West Bengal*	6	112 MCL + 4 NP	For each ward	Constituted (partly in Kolkata Corporation)
18.	Chandigarh	1	-	One or more wards	Not yet constituted/Draft Rules framed
19.	Delhi	1	-	Group of wards(10-12)	Constituted

Note : (a) No ULBs exist in Lakshadweep, D & N Haveli and Arunachal Pradesh, (b) 74th Amendment has not been applied in Meghalaya, Mizoram and Nagaland; (c) No election has been held in Pondicherry, Sikkim, Jharkhand and Jammu & Kashmir, (d) No ULBs having more than 3 lakh population in Goa, Tripura, Manipur, Himachal Pradesh, Andaman & Nicobar Island, Daman and Diu.

Abbreviations: M. Corp.- Municipal Corporation; MCL— Municipal Council; ULB-Urban Local Body.

*Total number of ULBs irrespective of the size

that there is lack of democratic element in the process of nomination. While accepting the argument it needs to be emphasised that given the nature and degree of political development and political culture in our country the functioning of the two sets of elected bodies at the local level may cause conflict and confrontation leading to an unhealthy situation. It would ultimately impede development.

Ward Committees in State Legislations.

While the elected councillors are automatically members of these committees, the state governments have made different arrangements for the members of the public to be included in the WCs. Table provides a view of the status of WCs in some major city corporations of India as on 31.07.2003.

It is found from the table that WCs have not been constituted in states like Gujarat, Haryana, Assam. Rules with regard to the formation of the Ward Committees in some urban local bodies have not yet been framed in states like Gujarat, Assam, Haryana and Bihar. In Chennai and Delhi, WCs are actually zonal committees. Large size cannot ensure people's participation. In Maharashtra, there is distinction between municipal wards and administrative wards. Administrative ward is the geographical unit of the WCs and 3-4 municipal wards constitute an administrative unit. Elections are due in many corporations. Where they are not held regularly it becomes a violation of the mandatory provision of the Constitution. There seems to be lack of political will to institutionalise citizens' participation through the WCs.

The Ward Committee System in West Bengal

West Bengal has taken a step further by making the constitution of WC mandatory for all municipalities irrespective of size of the population. The WC is a municipality in miniature, a sort of 'friend, philosopher and guide' of the municipality concerned. The local councillor chairs it. It consists of elected councillors and such other members as may be nominated by the elected councillors of the ward and the municipality/Notified Area Authority (NAA) from amongst the residents of the ward. The nomination of the members will be made in the following manner:

Table II

Total number of other members of the Ward Committee	*To be nominated by the Councillor elected from the ward*	*To be nominated by the Municipality*
7	5	2
8	5	3
9	6	3
10	7	3
11	8	3
12	9	3
13	10	3
14	11	3
15	11	4
16	12	4
17	13	4

While making the nomination care has to be taken to ensure proper representation of engineers, physicians, educationists, social workers, sportspersons, women, persons from economically backward sections of the society or any other persons from among the residents of the ward. Among the total number of members, the councillor shall nominate at least two representatives of the Community Development Society (CDS) in which there are 7-9 members, and three representatives where there are more than 9 members. In case of nonavailability of CDS members, the councillor shall nominate women members from below-poverty-line families in the ward.

It has to be constituted within one month from the date of the first meeting of the Board of Councillors after a general election. After the formation of the committee, the councillor of the municipality/Notified Area Authority (NAA) concerned is required to place the names of the members of the committee in the next general meeting of the residents of the ward. The proposals, if any, from any resident of the ward regarding change of any name or any other matter relating to constitution of the committee will be considered by the councillors or the municipality/NAA, as the case may be. The councillors or the municipality/NAA, as the case may be, may replace any of the members of the committee. The tenure of the committee is the same as that of the Board of Councillors of the municipality/NAA. In the case of any casual vacancy caused by the factors mentioned in the *West Bengal Municipal (Ward Committee) Rules 2001*, it would be filled up by the councillors of the municipality/N.A.A. as the case may be, either in the annual general meeting or in an ordinary meeting of the ward convened for that purpose.

Rules of Business

The first meeting of the committee will be convened by its Chairperson within 15 days from the date of its constitution. Apart from the normal business, the committee is required, at its first meeting, to select a member-secretary from among the members. The member-secretary is authorised to convene the subsequent meetings of the committee in consultation with the Chairperson apart from performing the secretarial functions of the committee. The committee must meet at least once in every month, the date, place and time being is fixed by the Chairperson. It is clearly laid down that no meeting shall be held unless at least seven clear days. Before the day of the meeting a notice specifying the date, place and time of such meeting and the business to be transacted there has to be given to the members. One of the important tasks of the committee is to convene one half-yearly and one annual general meeting of the residents of the ward by intimating every resident of the ward and also by public proclamation specifying the time and venue of the meeting. The half-yearly meeting will be held in October-November each year to apprise the residents of the activities of the municipality/N.A.A. in general and the ward in particular. This meeting will discuss the proposals for preparation of the development plan for the next year. The annual general meeting will be held within 30 June every year to apprise them of the activities of the municipality/NAA in general, and the ward in particular, during the preceding year and to assess the popular needs of the ward for the current year. In order to make the meetings meaningful and effective, it is clearly mentioned in the rule that it is a duty of the municipality/NAA to furnish the following documents to the committee for public information and deliberation thereon:

(a) a detailed report about the activities of the municipality/NAA in the ward during the preceding year;

(b) a copy of the annual administration report along with the annual financial statement of the municipality/NAA for the preceding year.

The committee has to maintain a minute book to record the proceedings of the meetings. The minute book will contain the names of the members who attended the meeting, the business transacted, the decision of the committee on each item of business, the date of meeting and the time of commencement and closing of the meeting.

General Powers/Functions of the Ward Committee

The Chairperson of the Ward Committee has been authorised to:

(a) call for any information insofar as it relates to any matter within the ward;

(b) call for and consider all periodical statements relating to the receipts and disbursement

Any member of the committee is entitled to draw the attention of the Chairperson to any requirement of the locality or to any lapse in execution of the work or to any waste of municipal fund or municipal property and may suggest any improvement, which he considers desirable. It is laid down in the *West Bengal Municipal (Ward Committee) Rules 2001* that the committee may require, with the permission of the municipality, any officer of the municipality, to attend a meeting at which any matter dealt with by such officer in course of his duties, is being discussed. When any officer is thus required to attend any such meeting he may be called upon to make a statement of facts or furnish such information in his possession relating to any matter dealt with by him or produce a report as the committee may require.

The committee has been given a wide range of supervisory and monitoring powers within the ward, subject to the general supervision of the Borough Committee of the municipality. Such powers include, *inter alia,* detection of violation of the various provisions of the Act such as unlawful construction, public nuisance, tax evasion, arresting wasteful use of various municipal services such as tap water, street hydrant, street lights, parks, playgrounds etc., collection and removal of garbage, removal of the accumulated water in streets, health immunisation services, improvement of slums including its clearance wherever necessary etc. The committee is also required, as per direction of the Borough Committee or the municipality/NAA, as the case may be, to monitor and supervise within the ward a good deal of activities such as:

(a) work of assessment, collection of property tax, other taxes, fees and other sums due to the municipality/ NAA.
(b) maintenance and repair of roads and drains;
(c) execution of public works;
(d) maintenance of sanitation and public health;
(e) generation of internal resources.

The WC has also been given specific role with regard to participatory planning. Within three months from the date of the constitution, the committee is required to prepare a list of schemes for development of the ward during the next five years and also annual priority of the schemes in the ward area.

Supervision of the Development Schemes

The Ward Committee has to monitor and supervise the execution of the development schemes in the ward area. In order to ensure client participation there is a provision for the constitution of beneficiary committee consisting of the citizens of the ward by the ward committee, which under the supervision of the former, looks after the development work being conducted in the concerned ward and may offer any suggestion relating to the work. It is also the duty of the ward committee to make the work schedule of any development scheme available to the beneficiary committee.

The Municipality has some duty towards the Ward Committee in order to enable the committee to work effectively. The Rule lays down that the municipality has to make available the following information:

(a) decisions of the Standing Committees;
(b) decisions or resolutions of the Municipality;
(c) ward-wise budgetary allocation made by the Municipality;

(d) copy of the ward map;
(e) details of municipal properties ward-wise;
(f) Annual Financial Statement and Annual Administration Report;
(g) demand and collection figures of tax and non-tax revenue of the ward; and,
(h) such other information as required by the Committee.

The WC has also been involved in the disaster management programmes. The municipality, on a written requisition from the Chairperson of the Committee, is required to make available an advance amount to meet the emergent needs of natural calamity, accident and the like.

The Committee has been given a major role in respect of resource mobilisation. It is required to consider the opportunities for creation of new sources to augment municipal income through a number of ways. For example, it can suggest using lands vested in the government or municipality/NAA and any land belonging to any government department subject to permission of such department for:

(a) tree plantation on long term and short term basis; or
(b) constructing market complexes, shops and buildings for commercial use; or
(c) for such other purposes as mentioned in the relevant rule.

The Committee has to submit a detailed proposal for creation of internal resources to the municipality/NAA. It is authorised to interact with the members of the other Ward Committees for this purpose, if necessary. It is obligatory on the part of the municipality/ NAA, to spend 60 per cent of the income from the newly created internal resources, as per proposal of the committee, in the ward/ wards, where such new internal resources have been created, after deducting the cost for implementation of such project, if any.

II

Rajpur- Sonarpur Municipality

The author conducted a study sponsored by the UNICEF in Rajpur-Sonarpur. The former is a municipality located within the

Kolkata Metropolitan Development Area (KMDA) and the latter is located outside the KMDA area. Rajpur was a part of the south suburban municipality till 1876. A municipality of more than hundred years old, it has a long tradition in governance. Sonarpur spreading over 10 Gram Panchayat areas became part of the present Rajpur-Sonarpur Municipality on December 16, 1993. Having been located close to Kolkata it is one of the fast-expanding ULBs in West Bengal. With a geographical area of 45 square kms, the population in the ULB has been on the rise ever since its inception. The present population is little over 3 lakh with holdings being 1 lakh. All these have resulted in the construction of multi-storied buildings. Drainage is one of the major problems of the municipality. The ULB is divided into 5 boroughs each one of which has independent offices. There are 33 wards in it.

The supply of drinking water has received top most priority in the municipality as is evident from its Annual Development Plan. The citizens are engaged in various kinds of activities. Apart from service holders, there are artisans, daily wage labourers, small traders, self-employed professionals. Agriculture continues to be the mainstay of people living in one or two wards. In the poverty pockets education is still to make a dent.

It has had the benefit of Calcutta Urban Development Project III and Indian Population Project VIII. These two projects have benefited many people in the below-poverty- line category. Health services reach out to a large section of them, although it is inadequate compared to the needs of the people. Roads are good. WCs supervise road construction and repair work, which has led to the improvement in the quality of construction and repair. The ULB has made it mandatory to involve the beneficiary committee for all development work. The WCs keep watch on the working of the beneficiary committees.

We interacted with 43 members belonging to different WCs in Rajpur-Sonarpur municipality. It is found that middle-aged members predominate the Committees in terms of composition. They constitute more than 70 per cent of the members. The members belong to diverse occupational groups. The caste background of members also bears it out. However, only 13.95

per cent of members were women. This is not desirable after the reservation of seats for women in all ULBs in terms of the Seventy Fourth Amendment. The Board does not seem to have taken the gender component into account while making nomination. At least one third of the members in the WCs should have been women. Is it due to lack of political will to empower women through the WCs or there is reluctance on the part of women themselves to take up this kind of work? While talking to the political functionaries we have not received any satisfactory answer. Our impression is that the patriarchal values are still very strong among political leaders and this is not absolutely unexpected in a society like ours.

The formation of the WC started in 1997. Most of them were formed in 2000. Almost all the members (93.4 per cent) are first timers. As a result they are yet to perceive their roles appropriately. It is evident from the analysis of data about their reactions to the objectives of the WC. Although many of them are aware of the legal status of the WC as a constitutional body, a good number of them do not know the role of the ULBs in terms of the Constitution of India. This merits serious consideration because they will not be able to play their role properly if they suffer from such deficiency. The traditional role of the ULBs as providers of municipal services continues to remain ingrained in the minds of the WC members. It underscores the need for imparting suitable training to them at the ULB level. For this purpose the Institute of Local Government and Urban Studies (ILGUS) may be helpful in organising training programmes.

It is found that 86.05 per cent of the WC members have reported that they are aware about the rules of the WC. Such awareness however implies that they have only heard about them. While interacting with them intensively it was noticed that most of them have not read the rules. It will adversely affect the working of ULBs. The state government has laid down detailed rules and it is the declared policy of the government to involve the WCs in the working of the ULBs as much as possible. The vibrant WCs with the clear perception of the role of the members can be effective in a situation like this because they are in regular touch with the people. It is good that most members seem to be aware of the major problems in their areas. They have fair degree of knowledge about the categories of residents and their occupations in their respective wards.

We have tried to tap the perception of the members about the issues calling for attention and we wanted them to prioritise their issues. Interestingly, the drainage problem has been identified as a problem to be attended to with top most priority. It is true that this is a very acute problem in this ULB. Most of the streets get flooded during rainy season. What strikes us is the lack of adequate concern for education and health, which receive priority in the agenda of the Government of West Bengal. There is a consensus in the state that the earlier Left Front Government (LFG) could not address the issue effectively. Now the government seeks to improve the situation through the modality of decentralised development. This calls for an effective role of the WCs.

It is found that only 23.26 per cent members of the Ward Committees have their independent offices. It is not desirable because without a permanent office the WCs cannot be expected to function effectively. The WCs are required to interact with the people, which is possible only when there is an office where the citizens would come to discuss their problems. It has to be kept open during specified hours. The recent revision of the Ward Committee rules has laid down that the ULB concerned has to make provision for it. The WCs cannot be citizens' committees in the true sense if the citizens are denied a place for interaction. Again, the WCs have to meet at regular intervals. It is gathered that meetings are held in the house of the Chairperson or Secretary or members. However, there is no budgetary allocation of the WC on this purpose, as a result of which small expenses incurred in holding meetings are borne by the Chairman/ Secretary or members. This practice cannot be encouraged. Some funds need to be placed at their disposal; otherwise the concept of participatory governance and development will turn into a mere formality, if not mockery.

We tried to ascertain from the respondents if there has ever been any issue of serious debate in the meeting leading to sharp differences of opinion. The answer has largely been in the negative indicating that there is consensus among the members on matters pertaining to development. The annual general meetings are regularly held in all the wards. The date and venue of the meetings are communicated to the citizens through notices. In some wards the WC members are asked to make door-to-door campaign for the meetings. As expected, meetings in such wards are comparatively well attended. In most of the meetings, as reported, the attendance has not been beyond 25 per cent of the total citizens. Attendance of women has not gone up beyond 10 per cent. In the meetings two reports, one on annual administration and the other on the present budget are generally placed. The degree of effective participation has not generally been encouraging. Only few people participate and almost all the participants refer to the problems relating to drainage, sewerage and sweeping and the like. Major human development issues hardly figure in the discussion.

In Rajpur-Sonarpur there is a unique feature of the Ward Committees. Apart from the annual general meeting the municipality organises Ward Conventions where all the members of the WCs assemble and interact on the issues concerning their wards. Such Conventions are held once a year. It is chaired by the Chairman himself. In the annual Ward Conventions they identify the schemes and prioritise them and examine how to fund the programmes. They discuss the question of mobilization of resources and promise help to the municipalities in resource mobilisation. The Conventions try to locate areas where more resources can be mobilised. This is an important event and will be very useful for the purpose of participatory decentralised planning. It is interesting to note that about 79.07 per cent of the members of the WCs visit municipality offices regularly. They discuss the problems of their ward with the authorities and try to collect information about the schemes, which can be implemented in their wards. This indicates that the members take active interest in their work. The proceedings of the WC and those of the Ward Conventions are transmitted to the municipality for the perusal of the latter. The reactions of the municipality are not, however, made known to the WC. We have been told that the proceedings of the conventions are carefully considered by the municipality. In order to examine the extent and level of interaction between the municipality and the WC we wanted to know if the representative of the municipality, other than the local councillor, visits their wards. 74.42 per cent of the respondents have replied in the affirmative. We also wanted to find out from the respondents if the municipality seeks their help. 86.05 of the respondents have told us that the municipality seeks their help.

One of the problems of the municipality being located close to Kolkata is the tendency to use lands and buildings illegally because land prices are very high. There is a widespread tendency to encroach upon the public space, if available. It is difficult to prevent this kind of illegal construction without involving the WC. In Rajpur-Sonarpur Municipality the WCs appear to be active in dealing with the situation. 81 per cent of the members draw the attention of the municipality and discuss it in the meeting of the WCs.

As is the case in other states the slums form part of the urban areas. Now there is a comprehensive centrally-sponsored slum development programme called Swarna Jayanti Sahari Rozgar Yojana (SJSRY). This programme is implemented by the Community Development Societies (CDS) created for that purpose. Formally speaking, earlier there was no specific role of the councillor not to speak of the WC, other than the general role of the ULB. The recent revision of the WC rules as noted above has sought to develop a linkage between the WCs and the CDSs. In West Bengal there is Urban Poverty Eradication Cell (UPE) in each ULB, which is supposed to supervise the implementation of all anti-poverty programmes. Insofar as the implementation of the SJSRY programme is concerned the councillor has not much to do because he is not a member of the community structures in terms of the guidelines for the programmes. In West Bengal an attempt has been made to involve the councillor. This arrangement seems to be working well here. The WC discusses the poverty issue and 93.02 per cent of them participate in the implementation of the SJSRY programme.

In order to encourage savings among the poor people in the slum areas there is a provision of self- help programme called

Thrift and Credit Group. We wanted to know from the members if they are aware of the scheme. 83.72 per cent of them proved their awareness. To go deeper into the matter we asked them about the problems of implementation of the programme, if any. A little more than 60 per cent of the respondents have told us that the major handicap is the attitude of the banks, which are supposed to provide loan to the BPL families. 23.26 of them have, however, pleaded ignorance. This is a cause for concern.

In Rajpur-Sonarpur Municipality beneficiary committees are functioning in each ward. It is gathered from the discussion with the members that the young citizens have been inducted into the committees. They keep watch on the activities being undertaken by the municipality. They keep the WC posted about how the schemes are implemented. The members mention that they discuss about the developmental activities being undertaken by the municipality in their wards. They do not, however, seem to be aware of all the programmes.

Berhampore Municipality

Berhampore Municipality was established on 1 July, 1876, following the merger of the cantonment area with other areas like Saidabad, Kashimbazar, Kalikapur, Khagra, Gar Berhampore, Gorabazar. In 1932 the Bengal Municipal Act was enacted. At that time Berhampore was divided into 30 zones covering an area of 15.65 square kms. The West Bengal Municipal Act was enacted in 1993. The number of zones was reduced to 23 out of which 7 were reserved for women and 1 for women belonging to the Scheduled Caste.

It is found from the data that more than one third of the Ward Committee members have been drawn from sectors other then teaching and service, including small traders, retired persons and the like. Unlike the Rajpur-Sonarpur municipality the professionals like doctors are absent here. It is not that they are not available. Either they are reluctant to join or the ruling party does not want them in. The number of service holders is insignificant unlike the situation in Rajpur-Sonarpur. It may be attributed to the location of the municipality. Rajpur-Sonarpur having been located close to the capital of the state, many people are service holders. The general caste members far outweigh the members belonging to SC/ST. In fact, the general caste members have overwhelming domination in the ULB area. The younger members dominate the WCs. In terms of the age-group 34.15 per cent of the members belong to the age group 31-40, almost double the percentage of the members in Rajpur-Sonarpur municipality. Nearly 30 per cent of the members belong to the age-group 18-30, thus a little more than 63 per cent of the members are below 40 years. The Chairperson and the elected members mention that they have given special consideration to this factor while nominating members in the WCs. Most of them are, however, unemployed and insist that some payment should be made to them for doing the work of the WC. It is good that the municipality has been able to motivate them. There is a general feeling in Kolkata Metropolitan Area that the young members do not take much interest in this kind of local governmental activity. This seems to be reflected in the age-group distribution of the members of the WCs in Rajpur-Sonarpur municipality. However, the gender-wise distribution of members indicates that there is lesser representation of women in Berhampore WCs. In Rajpur-Sonarpur their number in the WCs is double the numbers in Berhampore. There is nearly absolute predominance of the male members. Even in respect of reserved constituencies the female members are numerically insignificant.

It does not provide a positive image of the municipality. It reinforces the assumption that there should be reservation of seats for women even in the WCs. The informal discussions brought out that there is lack of interest on the part of women insofar as joining the WC is concerned. Women do not consider themselves properly suited for this kind of job due to their heavy domestic commitment. The women representatives should take special care in this regard. Women need to be motivated and roped in. The WCs can be turned into a training ground for the future women councillors.

Nearly 20 per cent of the WC members in Berhampore do not know the exact legal status of the body they are attached to as members. In course of informal interaction with many of them it has become clear that they do not have any knowledge about the distinction between a constitutional body and a non-constitutional body. They cannot be held responsible for the lack of awareness. The ULB has not tried to make them realise the legal significance of the body. In fact, some of the councillors we could interact with, are ignorant about it. When the state government has been emphasising on strengthening this body and developing them as nurseries of genuine democracy it is high time to generate awareness among the WC members about the legal status of this body. It is one of the ways of creating respect for the grassroots participatory body.

What causes greater concern is the lack of awareness among 41.46 per cent of the members about the rules of the WC. None of them has seen the copy of the rules. Only a few of them have come to know about them from the councillors. We wanted to find out if they did not have time to read the rules. The answer was that they did not know about it. They evinced interest but they did not have any information. It is, again, a failure on the part of the ULB. We tried to tap their perception about the priority of issues in their agenda. Nearly 40 per cent of the members could not respond as they do not have any idea about it. Amongst those who responded, nearly one third laid stress on drinking water and road. Education is not a priority agenda item. They seem to be aware of the problem of massive unemployment in their wards but do not know what to do. All of them are sure that employment has to be generated, otherwise there would be youth unrest. But that is the end of it. They seem to believe that it is the task of the government, not that of the ULB.

Not all the members visit the municipal office for the work of the WC. About one fourth of them have reported that they do not go to the municipal office. They have told us that they interact with the councillors, attend meetings and take part in the discussions. They have never felt it necessary to visit the municipal office. On further investigation it became evident that two such wards belong to the councillors who are members of the Chairman-in-Council. Presumably, the WC members do not experience any difficulty in getting their work done.

The situation is not really substantively different from that obtaining in Rajpur-Sonarpur municipality. Clearly, the linkage between the WC and the municipality is yet to be firmly established. It may be suggested that the municipality should take initiative in this regard for establishing an organic linkage between the WC and the municipality.

According to the revised rules, the WCs are authorised to look into the matters pertaining to illegal construction in their wards by drawing attention of the municipality to the matter. We tried to elicit reactions of the WC members on this issue. The data in **Table II** demonstrates that 63.41 per cent of the members have reported that they do not take any initiative in this regard. It shows that the WC members are failing in their duty. It is definitely not an encouraging phenomenon. The WC members of Rajpur-Sonarpur are more alert in this regard and a large number of them play their role. It may be due to the fact that there has, of late, been construction boom around Kolkata. The promoters in the real estate business connive with the 'influential people' to carry on illegal construction. Although not widespread, real estate business has started picking up in Berhampore. If it is left uncontrolled, it may play havoc in near future causing immense harm to the town.

One of the basic problems that the urban local bodies have been facing in India since the days of the British rule, is the lack of necessary financial resources. It was one of the basic reasons why the institutions failed to work effectively during the days of the colonial rule. The same problem recurs in post-colonial India. The Seventy Fourth Amendment of the Constitution has sought to solve the issue by appointing the State Finance Commission. The local bodies also get a share of allocation from the Central Finance Commission. Still the local bodies are starved of funds. In West Bengal the performance of the local body in this regard is not satisfactory. The data collected by the Department of International Development, Government of the United Kingdom show that West Bengal lags significantly behind the other major states. While the 'own sources of revenue' constitute about 89 per cent of the total revenue for ULBs in Gujarat, 88 per cent for ULBs in Punjab, 77 per cent for ULBs in Kerala, 71 per cent for ULBs in Assam, the share is as low as 28 per cent for ULBs in West Bengal. Similarly, in West Bengal the per capita revenue collection is a mere Rs.36 as compared to Rs.441 in Gujarat and Rs. 252 in Punjab, Rs.132 in Kerala. It needs to be mentioned that the abolition of octroi duty, the proceeds of which were earlier shared by the urban local bodies under the Kolkata Metropolitan Development Authority, has led to a significant shrinkage in the "own sources of revenue". The Government of West Bengal has of late given special emphasis on resource mobilisation by the ULBs and there are indications that it has started yielding results.

As a result, the municipalities have become usually dependent on the state government. A comprehensive study of the receipts of different municipal bodies from own source and Government Grants (non-plan) during 1997-98 to 1999-2000 tends to show that during 1997-98, out of 96 municipalities 81 were dependent on the state government to the extent of more than 51 per cent, in 1998-99 out of 98 municipalities, 80 were similarly dependent. In 1999-2000 the number of dependent municipalities rose to 90 out of 100.[1] The recent data on the resources of the ULBs however indicate that the dependence of the local bodies on the state government has been reducing.

All the data make a strong case for more resource mobilisation by the municipalities. It should also be stressed here that the constitutional concept of municipalities as the institutions of self -government loses its significance in a situation of increasing dependence of the municipalities on the state government. The state government has revised the WC rules empowering them to play an important role in this regard. In response to the question of whether the WC members are aware about their role in this regard it has been found that one third of them is not aware. It is a matter of concern and the municipality should be in touch with the members of the WC to discuss their roles and responsibilities in this matter.

In West Bengal there are good numbers of tax defaulters as a result of which arrears keep on accumulating. The WCs are supposed to help the municipality in this regard. In Berhampore, the WCs extend help in this regard as the reactions of the members show. It may be mentioned that Berhampore's performance in respect of resource mobilisation is commendable. There is, however, no study to measure the performance of the WCs in this regard. In our estimate the performance of the WCs of Berhampore municipality appears to be better than that of Rajpur-Sonarpur municipality in some respects. It could be due to the inclusion of large number of younger members in the WCs or greater political attention to the problems.

As in Rajpur-Sonarpur municipality we wanted to know from the respondents about their role in the SJSRY programme, although formally speaking, it is a matter under the charge of the three-tiered slum committees set up for that purpose. Roughly, one third of them take interest in the programme. On the question of awareness about the Thrift and Credit Society in the slum areas, more than 50 per cent of them have responded in the negative. It is difficult to explain this variation. The second programme, however, involves greater involvement. A recent study[2] on the working of the WCs in Siliguri and Bidhannagar Municipal Corporations has shown that women representation in the WC is very poor. There are functional sub-committees within the WCs. Beneficiary Committees have been formed in many wards. The general functions performed by the WCs are the following:

- Preparation of schemes for development work at ward level.
- Supervision of the developmental work in the respective wards.
- Redressal of complaints regarding civic amenities in the ward.
- Organising Annual Sports and Cultural Functions at the ward level.
- Identification of the beneficiaries for schemes for the poor like old age pension, widow pension.
- Supervision of poverty alleviation programmes and other state and central government sponsored programmes like *Sarvya Shiksha Abhiyan*.

In Siliguri the WCs play important role in monitoring the payment of taxes, particularly property tax. In both the ULBs the WCs get some money from the fund placed at the disposal of the concerned councillors. The meetings of the WCs are held regularly and they are usually attended by three-fourth of the members. The issues discussed relate primarily to the services and developmental activities in the wards. There is a remarkable interface between the Community Development Society and the WCs.

The study, however, brings out the lack of interest of the ordinary citizens about the WCs particularly in wards where there is concentration of the middle class and high income group people. There is a general tendency to select citizens who either belong to or are 'close' to the political party to which the councillor belongs. There is no financial allocation for the WCs to take up developmental works. The performance of the WCs depends largely on the interest and initiative taken by the councillors.

Concluding Observations

Participation is about power, and its exercise and denial by the different social strata call for a space for the interaction between the citizens and the local government. There are, at the same time, certain structures for participation. WC is one such structure. To make it effective we need to take two kinds of steps, namely, creation of necessary objective and subjective conditions and identification of barriers to participation. In Tanzania it has been found that decisions over who should participate in the Ward Development Committee hinder effectiveness in achieving high level of participation. In India, Manor and Crook[3] have shown that the participatory procedures affect the opportunity of citizens to participate.

To ensure genuine participation of the citizens what appears to be very important is political determination and motivation of the wielders of powers at the local institutional level. They have to create both objective and subjective conditions for participation. It may so happen that there is reasonably adequate will and motivation at the top but at the bottom, where participation takes place, the local leaders may be reluctant to take the people into confidence and to share power with them. There should be penal provision in the legislation in line with the *West Bengal Panchayat*

Act, 1973 to compel the recalcitrant local leaders, if any. If an ULB does not constitute WC for which the concerned municipal body is responsible, the government should have power to dissolve the ULB after giving necessary hearing. If the councillor concerned is found responsible, the government should be authorised to dismiss him after giving necessary hearing.

There is also the need for developing accountability mechanisms. In Bolivia, for instance, there is provision for Vigilance Committees in the legislation. In Kerala also, there are local Vigilance Committees which scrutinise local projects before making payments to the contractors. It enables the citizens to realise that their opinion has value. It will encourage them to participate.The media, both print and electronic, have to be utilised for generating awareness of the citizens. Materials have to be developed for popular education. The citizens have the right to information. Incidentally, the right to information campaign organised by the non-government organisations in Rajasthan has been helpful by and large in raising awareness of the rural people although there is reluctance on the part of the political leaders to transmit information to the people despite clear legal provision. Legal guarantee of the right to information does not always prove effective unless there is a demand from the people backed up by organised strength. The non-government organisations can play effective role in this regard.

The findings of the study clearly indicate that although the WCs have started working, the members are still to perceive their roles properly. The lack of infrastructures and funds often create problems. It is good that the recently revised rules of the WC have taken note of the problem and have made it a duty of the ULBs to provide for office space of the WCs. In fact, institutionalisation of citizens' participation will not make much sense if an office is not provided for the institution.

There seems to be lack of awareness on the part of the ordinary citizens about the WC. The concept of WC as a constitutional body for grassroots participation is yet to be popular among them. It is, therefore, necessary to make awareness campaign for this purpose. The annual general meetings, wherever held, have become a ritual. Rule has been amended to provide for two meetings in a year. The government, it seems, is making efforts to ensure that citizens will decide on the priorities for development planning in their wards. But the holding of annual general meetings should be preceded by widespread publicity campaigns through house-to-house contact, posters, leaflets etc. The meeting notice may be given individually to generate interest of the members. The way the general meetings are held does not create necessary conditions for participation. It has been noticed that this kind of meetings takes the shape of election meetings. A podium is built. The WC members and the councillors sit on the dais and the ordinary citizens sit on the floor. Thus, a distance is created between the members of the WC and the citizens of the ward. The way the meeting is arranged and conducted often discourages the members to participate.

To ensure better participation the following steps may be suggested.

- Attempt should be made to bridge the distance between the ULB and the citizens as far as possible. It would be good if podium is not erected at all and all sit together at the same level.
- As there is lack of awareness among the citizens the meeting should start with a briefing of what needs to be done in the meeting itself in terms of the legal provisions to enable the members to play their roles effectively. It would be better if the relevant sections of the Act and rules are photocopied and distributed among the members along with the meeting notices.

Note

The percentage used in the text of the article is based on an UNICEF-sponsored project on *Participatory Urban Governance in West Bengal : A Case Study* , UNICEF, 2003.

References

1. Source: Institute of Local Government and Urban Studies, Govt. of West Bengal.

2. Archana Ghosh and Madhulika Mitra, 'Decentralisation of Urban Governance in West Bengal: Role and Importance of Ward Committees,' *Urban Management*, September, 2004.
3. R.C. Crook and James Manor, *Democracy and Decentralisation in South Asia and West Africa: Participation, Accountability and Performance*, Cambridge, Cambridge University Press, 1998.

6

Evolution of the Panchayati Raj System in West Bengal: Political and Legislative Initiatives of a State Government

Manabi Majumdar and Indrashis Banerjee

I. Introduction

"I am sitting on a throne of nails and wearing a crown of thorns", said the former Chief Minister of Tamil Nadu, referring to her 'unenviable' task of rebuilding the state in the wake of a crippling financial crunch (The Hindu, March 11, Tuesday, 2003).[1] Ignoring the imperial allegories of the 'throne' and the 'crown', it is quite possible that the Chief Executives of most other state governments of the Indian Union would share her anguish, as they all face a similar financial crisis. Recent hikes in public sector salaries and escalating defence budget have made a major contribution to this near-bankruptcy of state governments. The poverty of the state governments, in its turn, poses new challenges to the eradication of the poverty of the people, as it diminishes the state's capacity to provide welfare. To put it conversely, to achieve redistributive gains through pro-poor policies, we need to address the prior question of 'resourcing' the state. Economic growth may enrich state coffers, as one would expect that with greater economic growth more will be available for public expenditure. But a more direct route toward augmenting public resources would be to mobilise resources from the people. The latter will have a straight bearing, as the thesis of 'revenue source and presumed responsiveness of government agencies' would suggest, on whether and how the public money is spent for public purposes, and by extension, on the larger issue of the relationship between public institutions and citizens.[2]

Within this larger analytical framework of fiscal sociology (the description of which remains quite crude and in-exhaustive at this juncture), this paper examines the experience of rural decentralisation in West Bengal.[3] Three brief comments are apposite here vis-à-vis our focus on: a) decentralisation, b) inter-state variations in this respect, and c) the choice of the study state.

Decentralisation as Democratisation?

Support for decentralisation, both in India as well as in different parts of the globe, has come from diverse quarters – from statists, protagonists of the market, and communitarians, and for varied reasons – of market failure, government failure or of the bankruptcy of both. One prominent group of advocates – theorists as well as practitioners – suggest decentralisation as a way of improving public service delivery; they delineate the *information* and *incentive* advantages that local level organisations enjoy over their central counterparts. In making such an *economic case* for decentralisation, some protagonists, however, neglect what is arguably the basic spirit of decentralisation, namely, people's participation (especially participation of the underprivileged) in decision-making and implementation processes. But decentralisation does not automatically enhance people's participation. In other words, decentralisation cannot be treated as synonymous with local democracy (Dreze and Sen, 2002). In fact, in situations of sharp local inequalities (situations far from uncommon in a segmented society like ours) decentralisation sometimes reinforces existing biases in the local power structure and discourages participation among the disprivileged sections of the population. Simply put, 'decentralisation is a double-edged sword' (Webster, 1996).[4]

To be sure, the 73rd and 74th Constitutional Amendment Acts are examples of the strengthening of democratic institutions, but how these institutions perform is a matter of democratic *practice*, influenced in its turn by a wide range of social conditions (Dreze and Sen,2002). This contingent and contextual nature of democratic decentralisation makes it a prime candidate for further enquiry, especially as part of a larger project which aims to examine the relationship between the legitimacy and performance of public institutions on the one hand, and the participation of the people on the other – people as beneficiaries of local public services, as tax payers, as providers of information on local preferences, costs and needs, as social auditors demanding information from local authorities on past accounts and future spending priorities. Simply put, our principal aim continues to be an enquiry into how the state can be influenced to adopt a pro-poor policy stance and the extent to which decentralisation can further this.

The top-down decentralisation initiatives stand in need of close scrutiny for another related reason. Both central and state-level authorities display an ambivalent position vis-à-vis decentralising efforts. For example, speaking in general, the state-level leadership in India has thus far shown little willingness to share power with the local leadership. The 'conformity' legislations remain highly wanting in this respect in many Indian states. If decentralisation is a problematic proposition for the central or state governments, the question then is why it occupies a place of prominence in the current reform initiatives in the country (as a matter of fact in so many countries).

Weiler (1993) provides an interesting clue to this puzzle when he observes that in exercising its power the State has dual, mutually contradictory interest: to maintain control on the one hand, and to enhance legitimacy on the other. The decentralisation measure has its political utility; when overcentralised systems tend to lose legitimacy, decentralisation may act as a useful strategy for ensuring legitimacy. But coincidentally it poses a challenge to State's control over power, hence the dilemma. What we may, therefore, expect to see are cycles of decentralising and recentralising reforms. Hence, the political purposes and motives behind State-sponsored decentralisation initiatives become focal variables here.[5] We, of course, do not wish to suggest that the 'politics from above' fully determines the 'politics from below'. In other words, what goes on at the grassroots level may differ from the political calculus, which originally motivates the process; the 'subaltern politics of panchayats' expectedly differs from what is envisaged at the supra-local policy plane. Simply put, interactions, negotiations and manoeuvring both at the local level as also between the top and the bottom assume a dialogical character.[6] Therefore, our aim here is to examine forces underlying reforms and reciprocally, those unleashed by political and legislative reforms. All these constitute parts of our enquiry of whether decentralisation makes government more responsive to the needs of the poor.

Differently Decentralised

Our focus on varieties of decentralisation is inspired by the fact that the states in India are larger than most countries in the world in terms of geographical territory and population. Understandably different regions of the country are 'differently democratic' and 'differently decentralised'. Consequently, we need to adopt a disaggregated approach that captures the diversity and complexity of Indian social, political and economic reality. Several scholars focus on ways in which the historical-social context has shaped the democratic institutions in different parts of India and reciprocally how social realities have been affected by such widely divergent patterns of democratisation.[7] As we try to demonstrate through our collaborative research in the three selected states of Karnataka, Tamil Nadu and West Bengal , inter-state variations in decentralised reforms reveal themselves in at least three distinct ways : a) legislative reforms have followed very different courses in the selected states; b) political motives behind such initiatives have been quite distinct, as has been the nature of social/historical forces that have either helped or hindered the reform process; and c) practical results of state initiatives have varied a great deal depending on social and economic conditions, the nature of political parties, social inequalities, the educational and political awareness of the public and so on. All this has surely influenced the local features of respective Panchayati Raj Institutions (PRIs).

The political/legislative narrative of decentralisation in West Bengal

The selection of West Bengal as one of the case studies is prompted by the obvious reason of its being in the national forefront of decentralisation efforts for nearly three decades. Such a long and secure tenure of the decentralised regime, that too under the tutelage of the same ruling coalition throughout the entire reform period, provides us with a rare opportunity for studying the 'evolution of devolution' in a meaningful way. Indeed, to mention it somewhat simplistically and prematurely, as the process of decentralisation has unfolded over the years in the state, PRIs have grown out of their role as 'development' panchayats (as mere appendage to the development bureaucracy) to assume the character of 'political' panchayats (spearheading, in concert with the CPI(M), the programme of agrarian reforms launched by the state government). But with decelerating agricultural productivity growth in the 1990s in the state, an imminent policy shift from land reforms to contract farming, and growing austerity in state-level spending, the 'third' generation panchayats are envisaged to play a new role. That is to say, they are expected to become more active in generating their own resources.[8] Tied to this new imperative of panchayats raising funds are issues of fiscal autonomy and fiscal responsibility and their possible effects on redistributive goals. These are the sets of issues that constitute the themes of our subsequent research.

At this point, however, we push back our enquiry to focus on the political as well as legislative initiatives in decentralisation reforms, undertaken by the ruling coalition in West Bengal during the period between the late 1970s and the mid-1990s. Based upon the analysis of relevant documents and Acts, Legislative Assembly debates and proceedings, and interviews with academics, senior administrators and politicians, we summarise below our findings regarding the constellation of forces that has made the decentralisation experiment happen in the state, the sweep of state legislative measures, the concerns and conflicts of major political parties evinced through Assembly debates, the nature of party-PRI relationship and relationship between 'local power' and state-level politics.[9] While the literature on decentralisation reforms in India is quite vast now, varieties of decentralisation within the nation, their varying contexts and implications remain a relatively understudied area. A comparative account of the 'politics of Panchayati Raj' in the three selected states – the larger objective of our research - will hopefully shed some light on these not-so-well-understood issues. To put it another way, there is a great deal of scope to learn from 'within' India (Dreze and Sen, 2002). Comparisons are always difficult within, leave alone, between nations. Still, nations share some common problems which persist despite their contextual specificities. Hence, results of this study will likely have some implications beyond national borders, as they will hopefully throw light on international understanding of both democratic institutions and democratic practice. Arguments in the rest of the paper are developed in three parts. In section II, we attempt to build up a political narrative of the PR system in West Bengal. Section III discusses the relevant PR legislations in the state, the core issues that emerged during Legislative Assembly debates around these legislative initiatives and then undertakes a thematic analysis of the Panchayat Act of 1973. In section IV, we revert back, although very briefly, to the question of fiscal devolution and look for some pointers for future research.

(II) The Politics of Panchayats West Bengal

The panchayat system in West Bengal has been acclaimed as a 'pioneering model of participatory governance' in India, with maximum stability and longevity (Ghatak and Ghatak, 2002). Interestingly, however, scholarly assessments of this model span a wide spectrum, ranging from highly laudatory to highly critical. This indicates a scope as well as a need to trace back the evolution of PRIs in the state, especially at its present juncture of agrarian transition. In the following, necessarily inexhaustive overview of the political history of panchayats in West Bengal, our aim is to straightforwardly narrate what happened in the realm of decentralisation, offer some plausible explanations for it and dwell upon some of the implications for policy outcomes.[10]

The Centre and the state

Before embarking on this historical journey and deviating for a moment, it is useful to consider here, albeit in a limited manner, the motives of the central government for mandating decentralisation in the states of the Union through constitutional amendments during the 1990s. We may recall that Panchayati Raj as a model of village self-government was strongly supported by Mahatma Gandhi. But his idea of 'village republics' did not receive much attention in the initial stages of constitution making and was dropped into the Directive Principles of State Policy – 'the Constitution's basket of ineffectual good intentions', as Kaviraj (1996) puts it. The Constitution Assembly Debates are replete with bitter arguments that raged on this issue, with the chief architect of the draft constitution, Dr. B.R. Ambedkar describing these village republics as a 'sink of localism'. In the post-independence period, early initiatives in decentralisation emerged in the context of India's state-led development strategy, especially in the wake of the launching of the Community Development Programme. In 1957, in response to complaints of misuse of resources of the massive rural development programme and in search for an efficient delivery system, the Balwantrai Mehta Committee recommended the creation of local bodies responsible for the implementation of development programmes. While these recommendations were not binding on state governments, by 1959 all states in the Union had passed Panchayat Acts. However, these first-generation 'development' panchayats never took firm roots in the Indian soil either as an engine of development or as the third tier of government within the federation.[11]

Efforts to promote rural decentralisation through constitutional amendment were revived through the 73rd Amendment Bill in the early 1990s and entered into force in 1993, after an abortive attempt four years earlier under the rule of Rajiv Gandhi (the 64th Panchayat Amendment Bill of 1989). What are the possible motives that prompted Rajiv Gandhi to constitutionalise decentralisation reforms in the late 1980s and early 1990s? The reasons behind such moves were both manifest and subtle. As Bandyopadhyay (1999) analyses incisively, initially Rajiv Gandhi was looking for some efficiency-enhancing administrative reforms that would address the problem of widespread inefficiency and callousness among administrators toward their developmental tasks at the district level. But soon it became clear to him that "..if our district administration is not sufficiently responsive, the basic reason is that it is not sufficiently representative" (Rajiv Gandhi's remarks at a workshop on 'Responsive Administration', as quoted in Bandyopadhyay, 1999, p.71). Therefore, some mildly reformist tinkering with the system would no longer suffice; a more fundamental change was in order at the district and sub-district levels – from a bureaucratic administration to a 'representative and responsive elected system of governance'.[12]

But beneath these overtly reformist concerns of the then Prime Minister lay, Bandyopadhyay (1999) helpfully speculates, another set of reasons shaped by his crafty political calculations. These were the turbulent periods for India, rocked by militant movements in different parts of the country. This was also the time when in the wake of the rise of non-Congress political forces, the so-called 'opposition' Chief Ministers (for example, the puissant leaders like Jyoti Basu, Ramakrishna Hegde and N. T. Rama Rao) were clamouring for greater devolution of power from the Centre to the states. Faced with growing challenges from sub-national power centres, Rajiv Gandhi pushed forward the plan of creating new constitutionally-mandated power centres at the sub-state level, that would in their turn make similar demands on chief ministers for a greater share of state powers. In other words, the Centre wanted to strengthen PRIs so that state governments would find themselves in the same position vis-à-vis the panchayats as the Central government is vis-à-vis the states.

Many other respected commentators on the subject corroborate this line of analysis, by affirming that the constitutional amendment was intended to bypass state governments and introduce direct links between the Central government and 300 odd districts. One senior bureaucrat suggests in an interview[13] that there was indeed a charge against Rajiv Gandhi that he wanted to reduce powers of Chief Ministers through panchayats – otherwise known as the 'PM to DM' (from the Prime Minister to the District Magistrate) strategy. The latter would remain loyal to the PM, Rajiv Gandhi surmised, through the network of centrally sponsored schemes. A former influential minister from the state of West Bengal alludes to similar political intentions when he notes that the centrally-sponsored decentralisation programme is part of a legacy of centralism begun by Indira Gandhi which sought to 'chop up stste governments and pass on power to districts', as a way of maintaining a strong centre.[14]

The Left Front politics and revival of the PR system

It is time to turn our attention towards the state's own reasons for introducing decentralisation reforms. The history of decentralisation in West Bengal (as in the rest of the country) pre-dates independence; yet many accounts of decentralised governance in the state focus on the decentralisation reforms initiated in 1978 by the Left Front government.[15] Why did decentralisation begin in West Bengal in 1978 under the tutelage of a party [i.e., the CPI(M)] committed to democratic centralism?[16] The Centre-State relations prevailing in the late 1970s are very much germane to an understanding of this issue. The Left Front came to power closely on the heels of the Emergency; there was serious concern in the state political circle at that time that the Centre might dismiss the new government (as it had removed the previous United Front government on two occasions – in 1967 and 1970). The revival of the PR system may be seen in this context as part of the Left Front's [especially CPI(M)'s] political strategy or a protective mechanism, whereby the party would expand its power base in rural areas and so counter the power of the Centre. Until then its support base was predominantly urban. As Bandyopadhyay perceptively notes, under the leadership of Jyoti Basu, the Left Front decided to reinvigorate panchayats with the ostensible political purpose of penetrating the countryside and expanding their power base such that even if they lose power at the state level due to predatory central interference, at the grassroots level the influence of the party will continue. 'It was sort of an anticipatory bail against the onslaught of centralised eviction'.

The point to be seized here is that although the then Central and state governments were being driven by almost diametrically opposite political intentions, both the parties chose a very similar reform strategy to secure their respective interests, namely, decentralisation reforms. It is this ambiguous nature of decentralisation that makes the need for analysis of its implications so urgent.

To be sure, apart from catering to the survival needs of the party, on a more positive side of the register, the Left Front showed some genuine interest in protecting the interests of the poor. Indeed, the PRI reforms were not taken up in isolation but in concert with fairly progressive agrarian reforms. The Left coalition's agenda of panchayat reforms is closely intertwined with its programme of agrarian reforms. And the 'politics of Left panchayats' is very much a product of this association. To have a fleeting glance at this linkage, we step back a little to look at the first phase of land reform programme during the United Front (UF) government in the late 1960s. Under the charismatic leadership of Harekrishna Konar, the *Kisan Sabha* – the mass peasant front – called for mass participation in the seizure of *benami* (illegally held) land. The UF government resorted to a direct approach with regard to land distribution. Under the famous 'land-grab' movement, *benami* lands were identified and distributed by peasant organisations.

In contrast, the Left Front coalition adopted a more institutional approach to land distribution in the late 1970s and early 1980s. While peasant organisations continued to be involved in the reform process, panchayats were the chief machinery for identification as well as distribution of *benami* lands (Sengupta and Gazdar, 1996). The key pillars of this programme were the redistribution of ceiling-surplus land to landless and marginal farmers and the registration of *bargadaars* (i.e., sharecroppers). The latter programme, termed *Operation Barga*, accorded legal rights to share croppers, reduced the share of crop due to land owners, and provided the former with tenure security (Seshiah,

2003). The spectacular growth in agricultural products in West Bengal in the 1980s may be attributed, at least in part, to the programme of land reforms, launched by the Left Front government in the late 1970s and early 1980s (Bandyopadhyay, 2003a). Another significant effect was the atrophy of the class of rentier, the landed gentry. 'The space they vacated was gradually occupied by middle and upper peasantry who were productive agents' (Bandyopadhyay, op cit, p. 881).

It may be noted here that part of the support for the implementation of the reform programme came from an unexpected quarter, that is to say, from some reform-oriented bureaucrats. In a recent interview (November 9, 2002), a senior bureaucrat incisively suggests that the implementation of the programme was relatively easy as many of the government officials directly entrusted with this task came from the then East Bengal, having no vested interests in land and therefore carried out their responsibilities with enthusiasm and commitment. Bureaucrats, however, were less enthusiastic about the PR reforms, at least during the initial phase.[17]

Both these sets of reforms were based on Acts passed by the previous Congress state government; but these were never implemented. The CPI(M) took up the PR legislation, recognising that it was deficient. But developing new legislation would be too time-consuming; hence the party decided to implement the PR and agrarian reforms, based upon legislations that had come into existence prior to the arrival of the Left Front government.[18] The 1973 Panchayat Act which constituted the basis for decentralisation reforms, in its turn, had been designed after the original panchayat acts passed in West Bengal in 1957 and 1963, as we elaborate in the next section.[19] Suffice it to state here that earlier acts had created a four-tier system of panchayats including the *Zilla Parishad* (at the district level), the *Anchalik* Panchayat (at the block level), the *Anchal* Panchayat (roughly similar to the old Union Board which covered approximately ten villages) and the *Gram* Panchayat (at the village level). The system functioned with minimal participation by the people, few powers and meagre financial resources. A substantial change in the nature of PRIs occurred in 1978. The four tiers were reduced to three. The earlier Anchal panchayat became the basis for the new Gram panchayat and the former Anchalik panchayat now became the Panchayat Samiti. The Zilla Parishad retained its position as the apex body covering the whole district. Previously direct elections had been held only for the gram panchayats. Under the new model, party-based direct elections are held for all three levels of panchayats every five years (Webster, 1996).

Role of a committed party

The Left Front coalition has continued to be in power throughout the entire reform period under review. Indeed, the close relationship between the CPI(M) and the panchayats is a focal issue here. To quote Bandyopadhyay (1999, p. 70), "The Panchayat system has survived because of the Left Front, which introduced it, continued in power through subsequent elections... Similarly, the Left Front has rooted itself strongly in the rural areas through panchayats... In a way both the Left Front and the panchayats have been supporting each other in retaining power through the election process." This synergistic relationship between the Front and panchayats and their complementarity can be reconceptualised, following Crook and Sverrisson (2001), as 'the politics of centre-local relations', taking the state government to be the central party here. They suggest it to be a crucial variable in accounting for differential success of decentralisation experiments across the globe. More elaborately, the authors argue and we quote them extensively (2001, p. 48):

> "It is highly significant that the most successful cases were the ones where central government not only had an ideological commitment to pro-poor policies, but was prepared to engage actively with local politics (even for its own politically self-serving reasons) to challenge local elite resistance if necessary and to ensure implementation of policies. In India (West Bengal) and Brazil pro-poor outcomes were in fact a product of the synergy between local and central factors: centrally funded, poverty-relevant programmes implemented in cooperation with local

governments and given a strong ideological and organisational impetus at the local level from the commitment of local employees and political activists."

Surely, the CPI(M) came to power in 1977 with an ideological commitment to decentralised governance and to encourage increased political participation in institutions of local government (Webster, 1996). And its readiness to engage with local politics has been beneficial in at least three ways: a) it has challenged the entrenched traditional power structure at the local level, b) it has brought about pro-poor development outcomes, and c) it has encouraged the involvement of the underprivileged in local government and development. That the intervention of the long arm of the 'central' government in local affairs sometimes yields positive results is increasingly appreciated in scholarly works (Bardhan, 2001). Kohli (1987), for instance, argues that the organisational arrangements of the CPI(M) have allowed it to penetrate the countryside without being captured by the propertied groups. Similarly, Webster vividly describes how direct party-based elections, often drawing upon external (read supra-local) political resources and thus remaining fairly insulated from localised pressures, have broken the parochialism of the earlier system, in which the traditional village leadership could mobilise blocks of votes by invoking the dependency ties of loans, networks of kinship and caste and other patron-client ties that prevailed.

As for their performance records in implementing rural development programmes, PRIs had an early success. They did a magnificent job in flood relief operations in the late 1970s that made PRIs a 'living thing for the people'.[20] Also, panchayats hold laudable records, as Sengupta and Gazdar (1996) demonstrate, for the implementation of poverty-alleviation programmes when compared to other states. Of course, there exist inter-district variations in development outcomes. Some districts have progressed more than others. One interviewee helpfully notes that in the districts where the *Kisan Sabha* movement was strong initially PRIs have experienced success. In contrast, in the areas where the *Sabha* was weak, PRIs have performed relatively weakly. But on the whole, the outcomes of decentralisation have been positive.

West Bengal's record for implementation of poverty alleviation programmes owes, in part at least, to greater popular participation in implementation that has the advantage of directly providing information on local needs and conditions (Sengupta and Gazdar, 1996). In many parts of West Bengal there is now significant representation in gram panchayats from among the underprivileged sections of the society. Based upon his field work in the district of Bardhaman, Webster (1996, p.246) unequivocally states, "They [the underdogs] have a presence and involvement in local government and development that they had never previously possessed. This is a direct consequence of the CPI(M)-led implementation of the Panchayati Raj in the district."

In passing, we wish to note that while the organisational character and strength of the CPI(M) can be hardly ignored in the entire decentralisation project of the state, we can neither afford to lose sight of the visionary role played by some key charismatic leaders in this endeavour, namely, Harekrishna Konar, Benoy Chowdhury, Pramod Dasgupta and Satyabrata Sen among a handful of others. It is their vision of participatory local self-government ('So long we have wielded sticks, now let the rustics do it for all') that was subsequently internalised into the party agenda. A rough parallel can be drawn with the decentralisation experience in the state of Karnataka where a similar constellation of reform-minded bureaucrats (this time not political leaders) was instrumental in pushing the decentralisation agenda forward in the late 1980s, without underestimating, of course, the political leadership provided by the then Chief Minister Ranmakrishna Hegde.Satish Chandran (the then Chief Secretary),S.S. Meenakshisundaram (the then Secretary to the Department of Rural Development) and P.R. Naik (the then Development Commissioner) all felt committed to decentralisation reforms in Karnataka during that time, partly explaining the initial success of the project in the state. Their values were internalised gradually and later on the mass of bureaucracy got adjusted to the programme.[21] Thus, the history of individual leadership, of associations of bureaucrats with particular departments and their professional and personal equations with ministers all have important bearing on the success or otherwise of decentralisation, over and above crucial variables such as the nature and functions of party organisations.[22]

This is acknowledged, on the whole, that in West Bengal it is the 'party' panchayats that have acted as the chief instrument in developing power structures that '*function under the state government*' (Sengupta and Gazdar, 1996, emphasis added). But in so doing, is the CPI(M) entrenching itself in local politics in a manner that robs itself of dynamism and creates a tendency toward a 'political ossification'? To probe along these lines would require us to focus on two important features of the contemporary Left Front politics, namely, (a) the 'politics of middleness' and (b) 'state-level centralisation'. Bhattacharya (1999) forcefully argues how the CPI(M) has been modifying its agrarian policies and politics to achieve electoral success over time. The party's electoral pragmatism has had the effect of it safeguarding the interests of the rural middle class – hence the characterisation of the 'politics of middleness'. The author further argues that a clear shift has been taking place in the ideological stance of the *Kisan Sabha* as well, indicating an urge to broaden its support base. Consequently, the theme of 'peasant unity' has become the dominant party line effecting, in its turn, a realignment of its class position. It is important for the party now to make use of middle peasants and in this project school teachers play a vital role.

Analyses corroborating this line of reasoning can be found in the writings of several other scholars. Webster(1996), for example, echoes similar views when he observes that over time the CPI(M) party has succeeded in winning over sections of the middle peasantry, including those with more landholding, small businesses or those employed in government such as teaching. Gazdar and Sengupta (1999) talk about similar alteration in the character of panchayats that has resulted, according to the authors, from the Left Front's strategic shift from radical class mobilisation approach to a more conciliatory approach in more recent times, under the compulsion of consolidating its support base in the countryside. Again, Ghatak and Ghatak (2002) assert that the rural middle strata comprising middle peasants and white-collar employees have emerged as a new political force at the grassroots level in West Bengal. They resist further devolution of power on two grounds : a) they feel threatened about their position and b) a significant number of them employ wage labour. The shifting ideological radar of the party thus raises uncertainties about the future course of the PR movement in the state. To quote Webster once again (1996, p.238), "What is less certain is whether the principal reason for promoting panchayats remains that of a radical approach towards rural development with a political commitment to the poor, or it has shifted to the more instrumentalist purpose of securing the party's electoral strength in order to remain in government, *with all the compromises and alliances which that might require*." (emphasis added)

As the ruling party comes closer to the 'median voter' to ensure its electoral durability and correspondingly modifies its previous radical ideological posture, the engagement of the 'centre' in local politics and development does no longer appear so benign as the thesis of 'central-local relations' seems to suggest. On the contrary, fresh concerns emerge about state-level centralisation, that is to say, about recentralising tendencies on the part of the state government. As mentioned above, there is a view among scholars which attributes, for justified reasons, much importance to the role of political parties, of party competition and the pro-poor commitment of the ruling party in democratic decentralisation (see the literature cited in Seshiah, 2003). Some also justify the need for a disciplined party that would impose 'party diktat' and some degree of ideological integrity on local institutions against tendencies towards corruption and other abuses of power. But one must recognise both the radical as well as the hegemonic potential of a highly organised political party, enjoying not just dominance but predominance over a long stretch of time.

Admittedly, whether or not limits are imposed on the PR system due to the fact of their working under a rigid party structure will depend on factors like the nature of the party system, the extent of party competition, inner party democracy and so on. Some scholars hold that the CPI(M) has increasingly organised itself along strong democratic centralist lines (Bandyopadhyay 1999,

Webster 1996). The party asserts a strong control over its members and supporters, including the members of the panchayats. "The *gram panchayat's* affairs are discussed by the local party members in closed meetings and the elected supporters are then advised as to how party policy should be carried out through the *gram panchayat*" (Webster, 1996, p. 237). The overwhelming presence of the party in the management of local politics and local development, combined with a noticeable dilution of its radical ideological commitment, poses a challenge to the autonomous functioning of local democratic institutions as well as the local public, especially the poor.[23]

Moreover, factional quarrels within the party have become more and more manifest. The Left Front alliance has grown so wide that as if conflicting class interests are getting internalised and erupting occasionally as intra-party rivalries. Indeed, opposition to further reforms now come from within the party.[24] The party is caught between the new beneficiaries who are fearful of losing their newly acquired property through more radical land reforms and the landless demanding their share (also see Bandyopadhyay, 2003a). Finally, a quick comment is in order here regarding the nature of party competition in the state. Here, Local Body (LB) offices are filled by multi-party elections; moreover, there are no exceptional allegations of fraud or repression. Yet the same party has controlled, with unfailing regularity, an overwhelming majority in the LBs for over nearly three decades. Following Przeworski's dictum (Przeworski et al. 2000), democracy is a system in which incumbent parties should lose elections and opposition parties have some chance of winning office as a consequence of election. Stated otherwise, it is not the least of democracy's attraction that it is a government, which makes dominance strictly impermanent (Kaviraj, 1996). Yet in the state of West Bengal no serious contestation or competition among political parties seems to be taking place and accordingly no alternation in office happens. We are inadequately equipped to comment on this any further. But the implications of all this for decentralisation as well as for the responsiveness of the LBs to the poor stand in need of close scrutiny.

From administration Raj to Panchayati Raj?

Before we close this section, we wish to touch upon the subject of PRI-administration relationship, as it has unfolded over the years in the state of West Bengal. Prior to 1978, the District Magistrate was the ultimate authority at the district level and the BDO was in command at the block level. After 1978 they were required to work alongside elected members of PRIs and to implement the decisions passed by them. It is worth examining how the relationship between these two sets of actors has evolved during the long, uninterrupted, rule by the Left Front coalition in the state.[25] At the initial stages of decentralisation reforms, some conflicts and tensions remained between bureaucrats and locally elected politicians. A former minister for finance, for example, notes that during this time problems developed if a 'haughty politician' came to power or an 'egotistical IAS officer' was placed in the local administration (Seshiah, 2003). Also, during the initial years of the Left Front rule, the bureaucracy did not think that the government would last long in power. But now after five consecutive panchayat elections, politicians and administrators have accepted each other. Moreover, tension or friction is not uniform; instances of synergy of action and mutual cooperation are also visible, as one experienced bureaucrat observes.[26] Several interviewees concur that the present relationship of bureaucrats and politicians may be described as one of 'grudging respect' and 'mutual learning'. They further argue that the bureaucracy has accepted its place as 'second in command, 'as their wings are clipped'. Some express concern that the relationship at times is too close for comfort. For example, there is an excessive readiness among some young administrators to 'toe the line' of local political bosses. These comments indicate the intricacies of the relationship between politicians on the one hand and bureaucrats on the other. Also, just as politicians constitute a motley group, bureaucrats also are not a homogeneous category. The IAS officers have very different equations with their political bosses, as compared to those between local politicians and the BDO or the 'street-level' bureaucracy. In short, at different layers of government there exist different sorts and shades of the 'Neta-Babu' relationship.

III. The Evolution of Panchayat Acts in West Bengal: A Legislative History

In this section our goal is to develop a somewhat descriptive account of the major legislative initiatives undertaken over the years in the state to further decentralisation. We then highlight the core issues that dominated the Legislative Assembly debates, which took place around these legislations (including the conformity legislation of 1992). Finally, we attempt a thematic analysis of the Panchayat Act of 1973, which constitutes the main legislative pillar on which the present PR system in West Bengal stands. The significance of this legislative narrative lies, we believe, in the light this will hopefully shed on the way the state legislature responded to the political developments (both at the national and state levels) at particular historical moments, what views and concerns different political parties expressed vis-à-vis these legislations on the floor of the Legislative Assembly and finally the content and depth of decentralisation in the state, measured through a set of specific criteria embodied in panchayat legislations. We feel, all this supplies a very useful backdrop to our understanding of how the PR system unfolds after the legislative reforms are introduced.

The major legislations on decentralisation in West Bengal

Legislative initiatives in decentralisation have a history that predates independence in 1947, indeed it predates the colonial period. For example, in medieval India, under Sher Shah, village councils were given legal recognition; the headman was a semi-government official who acted as a coordinator between the village elders' council and the higher administrative authority.Under the Mughals, especially under Akbar, village administration by the elders' council was made an indispensable part of the civil administration – each was autonomous in its own sphere, and exercised powers of local taxation, administrative control, dispensed justice and meted out punishment. Hence, the 'Panchayat Raj', literally meaning the rule of five persons, has its moorings in ancient and medieval social practices of the country. However, the pre-British Indian panchayats were dominated, often monopolised by the high-ups in the caste hierarchy in the villages.

During the colonial period, the British used decentralisation as a tool of 'regime maintenance, entrenchment, consolidation and legitimation', and also to augment the 'Raj resources'. The Bengal Village Chowkidari Act of 1870 and the Bengal Village Self-government Act of 1919 are instances of such centralising tendencies. A landmark in the history of British Indian panchayats is Lord Ripon's famous Resolution (18 May, 1882): 'the smallest administrative unit, the sub-division or the *taluka* or *tehsil* - shall ordinarily be placed under a local board, which would further be controlled by the District boards'. Taking a leaf from such recommendations, the first important enactments found shape in the Madras Local Boards Act, 1884, and the Bengal Local Self Government Act in 1885. The rural local administration thus came to have the District Boards (DBs) at the District level, the Local Boards (LBs) at the sub divisional level, and the Union Boards (UBs) at the village level. The UBs had powers of taxation, and most of this came from the Chowkidari Cess.

Ironically, even after independence the Colonial district administration was retained and the DMs, SPs, and District Courts reigned supreme. The District Boards and Union Boards continued to function, and there was no initiative at ensuring a people-led developmental effort. Instead, the early efforts at developmental planning, under the Community Development Programme (CDP), were sought to be coordinated at the level of a new administrative unit, termed Block, to be headed by a Block Development Officer (BDO). Such a bureaucratised developmental effort soon languished. Castigating the CDP for failing to evoke popular initiative, the Balwantrai Mehta Committee Report, 1957, strongly advocated a popularly elected three-tier system of rural local self-government. 'State governments were free to devise their own panchayats which would suit their local conditions, retaining a uniformity in the broad pattern...'. The Report set the ball rolling; the country saw a spate of PR legislations. It is useful to trace the evolution of panchayat acts in the state of West Bengal against this broader historical backdrop.

While many analyses of decentralisation in post-independence West Bengal take 1978 as their starting point when the Left Front government came to power, the history of decentralisation in the state is much longer. Like many state governments, the West Bengal government responded to the recommendations of the Balwantrai Mehta Committee through enacting the West Bengal Panchayats Act in 1957, followed by the West Bengal Zilla Parishads Act in 1963. Under these two Acts, a four-tier structure of Panchayati Raj came into effect in West Bengal in 1964, with the Zilla Parishad (ZP) at the District level, the Anchalik Panchayat (AKP) at the Block level, the Anchal Panchayat (AP) at the Union level, and the Gram Panchayat (GP) at the village level.

The elections of 1969 installed the second United Front Government (UFG), which took up its unfinished job of overhauling the PR system. On 23rd April 1969, just four and a half years after their inception, all 15 ZPs and 325 AKPs were superseded. The APs and GPs remained moribund, and the UFG sought to bring about a truly comprehensive piece of PR legislation. This found shape in the WBP Bill (Bill No.42) of 1969. Introduced on 9th September, 1969 in the Forty-ninth session of the West Bengal Legislative Assembly, the Member-in-charge (MIC) of the Bill, Bibhuti Bhusan Dasgupta, sought to refer the Bill to a 19-member Select Committee. In stating the objects and reasons for initiating the Bill, the MIC lashed out at the earlier Acts of 1957 and 1963; these denied the right to suffrage to the village folk, he maintained, and the working of these Acts failed to implement the Directive, as enshrined in Act 40, of the Indian Constitution.

It called for a three tier structure of PRIs, stating that 'the long and persistent demand from the people of West Bengal has been to abolish the existing PRIs by repealing wholly the existing Panchayat Acts and to substitute them by real democratic structure..'. The Bill remained un-enacted, for, the Second UFG fell in 1970 and President's Rule was re-imposed in West Bengal.

The WB panchayat Act of 1973 is the basis for rural decentralisation in West Bengal today, but echoes of the basic outlook and philosophy with which the Left Front government in the state has been going along with its project of reforms can be traced back to the Bill of 1969. To a large extent, this Bill also influenced the Congress ministry which enacted the West Bengal Panchayat Act , 1973, after coming to power in the polls of 1972. The Communist Party of India (CPI), with 36 seats, was the main opposition party in the House, when the Congress introduced the West Bengal Panchayat Bill, 1973. An interesting observation may be made here about the political motive of the Congress-dominated state government in initiating this legislation. The point to be seized is that though the Congress had a large number of seats, both in the WBLA and the Parliament, the Left representation was very much palpable, spanning the tea plantations of Jalpaiguri to the seas of Sagar, from the industrial belt of Ranigunj-Asansol to the urban settings of Chandanagar, Behala and Jadavpur. In 1972, West Bengal's Parliamentarians numbered 40, of whom only 5 were from the Congress; the CPI(M) had 21 seats, the CPI 2, and the RSP 2. Thus, in terms of numbers and geographical spread, the left consolidation was in the air.

One may speculate that the Congress perhaps felt threatened, and as a step towards ensuring a support base for itself and warding off the Left challenge, it tried to effect changes that would ensure support from the grassroots into which the Left was steadily making inroads. Some observers contend that the West Bengal Panchayat Act 1973, was an attempt in this direction. On May 3, 1973, Santosh Kumar Ray, Member-in-charge (MIC) presented the Bill, indicating that the Acts of 1957 and 1963 had failed to actualise the spirit of decentralisation and accordingly voicing the intention of the Congress government to replace the two Acts by a comprehensive legislation. In keeping with the all-India perspective, the Bill proposed to introduce a three-tier structure of PRIs from the village to the district level, with direct elections of members.

The MIC stressed that the chief objectives of the Bill were to:

(i) structurally reorganise the PR system.

(ii) provide for a direct election at the newly created three -tier PR system.

(iii) ensure coordination between the PR bodies and the District and State Planning Boards in the overall backdrop of the planned economy of India.

(iv) create conditions to augment resources of PRIs and instilling a sense of social responsibility to ensure proper utilisaiton of scarce resources.

Dissenting notes in the Select Committee

Certain members of the Select Committee came up with several reservations, which were recorded in the 'Minutes of Dissent'. For instance, the CPI members, Ajit Kumar Basu and Ajit Kumar Ganguly observed:

(i) Powers of PRIs are to be interpreted as powers of the bureaucracy, for the former were subject to approval by the 'prescribed authority' - an euphemism for the bureaucracy.

(ii) Non-performing Panchayats could be easily earmarked by a vindictive government; therefore supersession of such bodies or removal of PR functionaries are defective provisions.

(iii) The 1957 Act provided for a Gram Sabha; it had a supervisory role. This role under the new Bill has been earmarked for the government. This strengthens the bureaucracy.

(iv) The Bill empowers government officials to be in charge of Panchayat bodies. Panchayats must be consulted when such officials are recruited, (esp. the GP Secretary). Such officials must be made responsible to the panchayat bodies, and not to the government.

(v) The government should provide sufficient funds to PRIs.

(vi) By retaining total control over PR matters, the government has paid only lip service to 'devolution of powers'.

The RSP MLA from Beldanga, Murshidabad, Timir Baran Bhaduri dissented on the following points:

(i) The enhanced role of MPs and MLAs proposed in the Bill of 1973 would choke local leadership from emerging.

(ii) An ill-financed PRI under total governmental control will not be able to perform satisfactorily. This will have a negative impression upon the village folk. They would view with suspicion and cynicism the very notion of democratic institutions.

(iii) *Pradhans* and *Upapradhans* of GPs should be directly elected by the people so as to avoid factional feuds.

(iv) The provision that any matter can be taken up for discussion even if it is not in the agenda if the members present agree to it by a majority decision can have serious consequences.Any and every matter can be then decided upon by taking advantage of an opportune moment when progressive and opposing members are absent from the meetings.

(v) The state government must provide for funds.

(vi) Panchayat tax has to be so fixed that the rural rich are taxed at higher rates and the poor at lower rates, ensuring exemption for the poorest.

A Congress(O) legislator, Pradyot Kumar Mahanti, was eloquent in scripting his dissent:

(i) A fundamental principle of people's participation has been disregarded; power has been concentrated in the government, for use through its bureaucratic apparatus. Thus, it seeks to tie the hands of Panchayat bodies with different controlling measures that act as brakes at every step.

(ii) No commitment for adequate resources has been made available to Panchayat bodies to enable them to discharge their responsibilities. Thus, there is ample scope for the government either to squeeze the power of Panchayat bodies in the name of granting financial assistance or to make them tools of the party in power.

(iii) There has been no move to place the Block staff at the disposal of the Panchayat Samiti.

(iv) Under Clause 216, the state may appoint administrators for PRIs; in such cases, the members of PRIs shali vacate their offices. It can reasonably be apprehended that if the panchayat bodies fail to satisfy the party in power in spite of their capability, sincerity and good work, they will be ousted from office. Such provisions are denial of democratic rights to elected bodies.

Debates in the Legislative Assembly

The West Bengal Panchayat Bill, 1973 was tabled in the Assembly's 55th session by Subrata Mukherjee, MLA, for consideration by the House. Highlighting the main differences with the earlier two Acts and the new Bill, Mukherjee focused on the following:

(i) A three tier, not four tier-system of PR.

(ii) Direct elections at all the three tiers not like the earlier Acts that provided for direct elections at only the lowest tier.

(iii) The earlier Acts provided for reservation of seats for two members of the SC, STs and two women members at the ZP and AKP level, whereas the new Bill secures the provision at all the three levels.

(iv) MPs and MLAs, as members of ZPs and AKPs, could also become elected as Chairmen, Presidents etc. under the earlier Acts. Under the new Bill, they would not have such rights. This will encourage local leadership to emerge.

(v) The new Bill seeks to augment the resources of PRIs by enhancing the rate of taxes on land, buildings, trades, businesses, etc. as also for charging additional stamp duty for any transfer deed relating to immovable property in the GP area.

(vi) ZPs are to be given matching grants for road and public works cess collected by it.

(vii) The Bill provides for a State Development Board and District Development Boards to supervise and evaluate the working of PRIs. This is an improvement over the earlier Acts for if the Accountant/Auditor finds and reports any illegal work performed by any PRI, its members will be liable to pay a surcharge. Thus PRIs will work legally, and within their jurisdiction.

A perusal of the debates in the WBLA proceedings pertaining to the WB Panchayat Bill, 1973 shows that opinions were sharply divided among the protagonists and the opposition members. We may recall that in the 281-member Seventh WBLA, the Congress had 215 seats, the CPI(M) 13. The latter charged that the elections of 1972 were rigged and therefore it boycotted the House. The CPI, with 36 seats, was the main opposition party in the House when the Congress introduced the Bill in 1973. It is possible to argue that the nature of the Assembly debates on the Bill was shaped in no small degrees by the fact that the CPI(M) members could not lend their voice of support to their CPI peers.

The following core issues were highlighted during the course of debates:

(i) Direct elections to the posts of office bearers of the PRIs.
(ii) Nomination of members from the backward classes and women in the PRIs.
(iii) Bureaucratisation and government control of PRIs.
(iv) Resources of/for Panchayats.
(v) MLAs and MPs as members of PRIs.
(vi) The apprehensions that the promised panchayat elections of 1974 would *not* be held.
(vii) Training of PRI personnel.
(viii) Infrastructure development for PRIs.

Several opposition members, including Sish Mohammed (RSP) and Ajit Kumar Basu (CPI), were doubtful about whether the promised PR elections of 1974 would be held at all.

The Bill was an attempt, they pointed out, to falsely create an impression on people's minds that they were soon going to be masters of their own destiny!

The skeptics also felt that the PRIs have been given only nominal powers and much important matters intrinsic to rural life such as water, irrigation, health, land reform cooperatives etc. have been left out of their purview.

Prodyot Kumar Mohanti of the Congress (O) stressed the importance of proper training for PR personnel. He also noted that the mistrust and suspicious attitude of the government was palpable, or why else would PRIs not be given adequate finances? He also raised concerns about the relationship between elected members and bureaucrats, pointing out that Executive Officers (E.O.s) of Zilla Parishads belong to the IAS, and the E.O.s of Panchayat Samitis belong to the WBCS (Exe) cadre. Their parent department being the Home (P&AR), their loyalty lies there, not with the Department of Panchayats. Only officials from the Panchayat department should be attached to PRIs, so that responsibility can be fixed, and accountability ensured. Their promotion prospects must be linked to their services under the Department of Panchayats. Many other opposition members echoed similar scepticism about the role of the bureaucracy in the PR system. In their view, unless faith in the bureaucracy is shed, not much can be achieved. Similarly, the CPI member, Ajit Kumar Ganguly felt that there was too much government control over PRIs for, in his words, 'one who pays the piper calls the tune. We must remember that the bureaucrat is a paid patriot – his patriotism is expressed because he is remunerated for it. This practice can lead to nowhere'.

Subrata Mukherjee summed up the discussion by saying that for a socialistic pattern of society, people's participation is a must. Hence after the 1974 PR election, more than one *lakh* representatives will be directly involved in governance. The Bill was assented by the President on 17th January 1974 and became the West Bengal Panchayat Act, 1973. But the promised panchayat elections of 1974 did not take place!

Under the new legal regime, the four tier PR system of 1957-64 was no longer in existence. The ZPs and AKPs had been superseded, and the state government managed these bodies by appointing administrators to replace all members. Though the APs and GPs did not encounter anything as dramatic as the supersession faced by the upper most two tiers, they remained sterile. This remained till 1978.

The Janata phase in Indian politics at the Centre ushered in the Ashoke Mehta Committee Report on decentralisation in 1978. Assuming office for the first time in June, 1977, the Left Front Government in West Bengal adopted one of its major recommendations, namely, the participation of political parties in the panchayat polls. The Left Front Government seemed to be in a great hurry and brought about the necessary technical changes in the relevant Act and WB Panchayat election rules, needed for conducting the panchayat elections in1978.

The decade between the 1980s and the early 1990s was witness to the regular holdings of panchayat elections in the state, as per the Act of 1973, until it was amended as the Conformity Legislation in 1994 (amended again in 1997 and 2003).

Debates around the Conformity Act[27]

The 73rd Constitution Amendment Act, 1992, comprises two sets of provisions – mandatory and optional. The states were free to accept, reject or modify the provisions in the latter category. Some of these provisions include the mode of election (direct or indirect) of the chairperson of the *Gram Panchayat*, reservation of seats for backward classes, reservation of seats for SCs, STs and women on a rotational basis or otherwise, representation of chairpersons of panchayats to the immediately superior body and representation of MPS and MLAs (also MLCs) in *Panchayat Samitis* and *Zilla Parishads*. Some important issues are, however, included in both mandatory and optional categories.

The state government initially declined to ratify the act. It was strongly critical of the fact that several mandatory provisions were being imposed on states by the Centre, thereby usurping the autonomy of the former in deciding how much they should or should not devolve to the panchayats. As the Minister-in-Charge for Panchayats and Land Reforms, Dr. Surja Kanta Mishra, remarked on the floor of the Assembly, the Centre is 'steamrolling' the states in the name of uniformity (as quoted in Kumar, 2002).[28] On April 13, 1994 he presented the Bill in the Assembly for consideration.

Interestingly, there was not much debate on the substantive aspects of the Bill *per se*. Rather the Opposition, mainly the Congress legislators, focussed on what was left out of the proposed Bill, namely, modification of the procedure for counting votes at the polling stations. Indeed, the whole tenor of the debates was dominated by arguments and counter-arguments on this issue. Several opposition members, for instance, Atish Sinha and Saugata Roy, alluded to electoral malpractices in course of counting at polling-cum-counting centres. Expressing deep reservations about electoral irregularities, Roy stated, "Counting starts late, by then CPI(M) *armed guards* (emphasis added) literally take over the polling booths. They...quite often prevail upon the presiding officers to declare results in favour of their candidates. There are hundreds of such instances in the State..." (as quoted in Kumar, 2002). A mention was made by him of the evaluation report on panchayats by Nirmal Mukarji and D. Bandyopadhyay that takes note of this problem by stating that "the counting of votes in the polling stations creates problems, especially if the contest is a close one. Under pressure, irregularities tend to be committed while counting and in the declaration of results" (Mukarji and Bandyopadhyay, 1993, pp.20-21). Leaving this issue un-addressed, the Opposition felt, constituted one major lacuna of the amendment bill. As a remedial measure, it would be more appropriate, they suggested, if the booth-wise counting procedure is replaced by centralised counting of votes at the block or sub-divisional level. In response, the Minister noted that the proposal for modification, if accepted, would amount to 'setting up a bad precedent' and therefore could not be accepted. Instead, the State Election Commission in consultation with the state government could make some alternative arrangements.

Similarly, the Minister-in-Charge did not accept the proposal for direct election of the *Gram Panchayat Pradhan* by stating that, "If he is directly elected then he cannot be removed by any other means". Thus, electoral procedures, and by extension the alleged nexus between panchayats and the CPI(M), invited the most vociferous responses from the opposition. The opposition members expressed concern about some other provisions in the State Panchayat Act pertaining, for example, to the size of the Gram Panchayat (the oversized GP would be like a small *Vidhan Sabha*, that too in the absence of its own panchayat '*Ghar*' in many cases), the difficulty of holding a *Gram Sabha* meeting after nearly a dozen meetings of the *Gram Sansad* at the ward/constituency level etc.

In contrast, barring comments from one or two members from the ruling party, there was very little discussion about the proposal for a District Council to be headed by the leader of the opposition party in the *Zilla Parishad* or the proposal for prohibition of the tabling of the no-confidence motion against the *Pradhan* and *Upapradhan* during the first year in office. Similarly, not much attention was paid to provisions regarding the 'quorum' required for both the *Gram Sabha* and *Gram Sansad* meetings or provisions addressing practical problems of identification, reservation and rotation of seats for SCs and STs or problems of making annual plans for the village by involving all the members of the *Gram Sabha*. Again, only a couple of legislators commented on the new taxation power given to the GP under the Amended Act. Saugata Roy, for example, questioned the logic of proposing, for taxation or fees, items such as unlicensed dogs, birds or other pet animals, grazing cattle on GP lands, or cremation *ghats* etc. Birendra Kumar Maitra, on the other hand, gave an useful suggestion for including tractors that are frequently used for commercial purposes and cause damage to rural roads as one of the taxable items.

The West Bengal Panchayat (Amendment) Act, 2003

As a proclaimed move away from the bureaucratic district administration and allegedly bureaucratic gram panchayats and as a step toward greater democratic governance, the Left Front Government has amended the core legislation on panchayats once again through the passage of the West Bengal Panchayat (Amendment) Act in July, 2003. The amending act tries to establish, among other things, linkages among various tiers of panchayats and creates a Block Sansad and a Zilla Sansad where the representation of the lower tiers is ensured. It also provides for the constitution of sub-committees at the GP level, in line with standing committees at the upper tiers. But the most important provision of the Act pertains to the constitution of the Gram Unnayan Samiti (GUS - Village Development Council) at the Gram Sansad level ostensibly to facilitate the task of local development planning. In all, there will be 49000 GUSs for the same number of Sansads in the state (Chatterjee, 2003). The capacious and ostensibly inclusivist GUS will consist of (nominated or elected) members from the GP, the person or persons securing the second highest votes in the preceding panchayat election (that is to say, members from the opposition party), members from NGOs and other community based organisations, from self-help groups functioning in the area, serving or retired government employees in the area, serving or retired teachers. At least 40 percent of the members shall be women. Far from being a politically settled issue, the constitution, composition and functions of the GUS are still very much at the centre of public debate. Only recently some government orders have been issued to facilitate the operationalisation of the project of planning from below, involving local development experts and the people at large.

Three distinct responses to the current drive for creating the GUS are in circulation now in the state, ranging from a laudatory, to sceptical, to an overtly critical overtone. Some commentators view this recent legislative initiative as a welcome extension of the lowest tier of self-governance in order to ensure greater transparency and accountability in developmental activities – 'as a bold step towards open direct participatory democracy'. The idea is, so the laudatory view holds, not to create another 'mini panchayat' and thereby substitute 'people's representation' for 'people', but to move away from representation-based democracy to people-centred direct democracy. A more sceptical reading of the latest legislative initiative invites us to recall the experience of the programme of the Convergent Community Action (CCA) – introduced by the Government of West Bengal in 1986 in the district of Medinipur. The current proposal, some argue, is just a new 'avatar' of the old CCA movement – village planning by the villagers, with an accent on mobilisation and utilisation of local productive forces, the achievement record of which is mixed at best. Hence the question, "Why is it being revived by giving it some other name?" (Chatterjee, 2003, p. 4091).

A stronger critique is waged against the latest Amendment Act on the ground that additional rounds of decentralising exercise often lead to unnecessary institutional proliferation, which leaves new institutional vestiges without making any substantive difference to the functioning of the existing regime. Bandyopadhyay (2003b), for example, argues forcefully that legislation is creating tier after tier of non-functional PR bodies, without funds, functions, and functionaries. Instead of empowering the GP, he continues, the amending act makes it more 'dysfunctional'. Indeed, the Act is not very clear about the kind of relationship that it envisages between the GP and the GUS, or for that matter with the state government. Is there any overarching authority that can supersede the GUS? The Act only stipulates, without any further elaboration, that 'The State Government may, in the interest of public service, issue any direction in the matter of functioning of the GUS'. What irks someone like Bandyopadhyay more is that the law is silent about the manner in which the GUS would be constituted except to vaguely suggest 'in such manner as may be prescribed'. "This is far too important an issue", Bandyopadhyay (op. cit., p. 4825) remarks, "to be left for subordinate legislation. Leaving it to the rule-making power of the government makes the intention suspect." Moreover, he sees a more crafty design in the proposal than just an act of omission or silence. In his words (op cit., p. 4827), "One can only infer two possible reasons for such a retrograde step in the name of 'mass participation'. First, to create a front organisation under law in the shape of VDC to legalise the illegitimate exercise of power by the party local committee. Second, to appease the rank and file who had lost the election by making them members of the VDC either through manipulative 'limited' election or by nomination."

How the opposing perceptions of the promises and perils of the GUS will materialise in actual practice only time can tell. Meanwhile, it is useful to look at some of the substantive contents of the Panchayati Act of West Bengal.

A thematic understanding of the Act of 1973

Necessary amendments have been made to the WBP Act of 1973 from time to time; in fact there have been twenty one Amendment Acts since 1978. We focus below on some of the major features of this Act, as it stands now, in 2003. In particular, we focus on various provisions enshrined in the Act under the following thematic heads:

(a) (State) government control over PRIs.
(b) Control over lower tiers by the upper tiers.
(c) Institutionalised participation.
(d) Developmental Schemes and PRIs.
(e) Electoral constituencies, reservations, and rotation.
(f) Fiscal devolution.

Government control over PRIs

The Act provides for varying degrees of governmental control over all the layers of PRIs. This control may be further classified into administrative and financial control. The state government is authorised to supervise and inspect all the activity of PRIs. The

PRI activity is supervised by the government through its bureaucratic apparatus, that is to say, through the Divisional commissioners, DMs, BDOs, Joint BDOs and government staff. They report to the government, and the government can take steps. Similarly, all work of GPs, PSs, and ZPs may be inspected by the Director of Panchayats and officers appointed by the government not below the rank of Deputy magistrates/Collectors. For the purpose of their examination, the PRIs would be required to produce any books, recordS, documents, plans, and accounts for the perusal of inspecting authorities. Also, the State Planning Board and the DPC have been authorised to supervise and evaluate the activity of any PRI.

But although the state government retains powers to inspect and supervise functions of PRIs, concerned officials are very careful about taking any action in this regard. An unsympathetic characterisation of this cautious behaviour, according to one senior administrator, could be one of collusion and mutual understanding between administrators and locally elected politicians.

Again, the Act permits the state-level authorities and the higher echelons of the bureaucracy to suspend and supersede panchayats. More specifically, the Act entrusts the state government to supersede a PRI on account of proven cases of incompetence or abuse of power, to rescind or suspend a PR resolution, suspend any elected member of any GP, PS or ZP on proven charges of gross financial irregularity or remove office bearers of PRIs (i.e., any *Pardhan* or *Upapradhan*, any *Sabhapati* or *Sahakari Sabhapati*, or any *Sabhadhipati* or *Sahakari Sabhadhipati*) for failure to carry out the provisions of the Act or misuse of power and gross negligence of duties.

But as one respected senior bureaucrat notes, these powers are used carefully (mostly in proven cases of corruption or embezzlement of funds).[29] Though individual resolutions have been suspended, instances of panchayat suspensions are indeed rare. Corroborative statements come from ministerial quarters, indicating that while the state retains these powers it does not frequently use them.[30] Some are not happy with this provision, it is further noted, but just like Article 356 of the Constitution, there is a time when this has to be used. More interestingly, informal mechanisms come up around formal rules, whereby attempts are made to 'sort out' matters before extreme measures are used.

In general, the state government holds the purse strings and exercises various degrees of financial control over PRIs. For example, in order to raise loans and borrow money the PRIs need to secure approval of the state government; also the state government is authorised to appoint an auditor to examine and audit the accounts of funds of PRIs. Moreover, PRIs, especially the GPs, may levy fees and tolls, the upper limit of which is fixed by the state government.

Control of lower tiers by upper tiers

The WBP Act of 1973, with certain subsequent Amendments, enshrines legal provisions so that in the three tier PR system, the ZP, the uppermost tier, can supervise, direct and control activities of the PS and GP and likewise, the PS has certain powers to control the GPs, that lie within the block area. A sort of hierarchy exists in the functioning of the PR system such that when a ZP takes any action or issues new direction in respect of any GP, this has to be routed through the PS having jurisdiction over the concerned GP.

The PS is required to prepare in the prescribed manner a report on the work done during the previous year and the work proposed to be done during the following year and submit it to the prescribed authority and the ZP concerned within the prescribed time. Likewise, the GP shall have to prepare a report and submit the same to the PS concerned within the prescribed time.

Institutionalised public participation: the Gram Sabha and the Gram Sansad

Every GP constituency must have a *Gram Sansad* that will meet twice a year. It is to be comprised of all the voters in the concerned constituency. The GP has to give wide publicity regarding the date, time, agenda and venue of the *Sansad* meeting at least seven days in advance by notifying in the GP Notice Board and by beat of drums etc. The *Pradhan* or the *Upapradhan* generally presides over the meetings. The WBP (Amendment) Act,1997 stipulates that every member elected from the constituency shall attend each meeting of the *Gram Sansad*. After the completion of the half-yearly meeting of the *Gram Sansads*, the GP has to hold an annual meeting of the *Gram Sabha* (consisting of persons registered in the electoral roll pertaining to the area of the Gram panchayat), ordinarily in December every year at a time and place notified in advance, giving wide publicity for this meeting and announcing the agenda beforehand. As we indicate above, the recent amendments to the Act further institutionalise participation via the creation of a Block *Sansad* and a Zilla *Sansad* and through introducing another institutional layer of planning, namely, the Village Development Council. The latter will include, among others, members from local NGOs and community based organisations, ostensibly for the purpose of establishing a bridge between elected representatives and civic bodies.

Development plans and PRIs : The District Planning Committee (DPC) and the District Council of Panchayats (DCP)

The DPC, indirectly elected, and having some nominated members (from municipalities and from amongst MPS and MLAs, and from scholars and activists), is the apex planning body at the district level. The DPC plays the vital role of coordinating all developmental plans in the district as a whole. Under the West Bengal District Planning Committee Act, 1994, DPCs have been set up in all the districts (except Darjeeling which has its own planning structure under the Hill Council Act of 1988). The WB Panchayat (Amendment) Act 1994 inserted a new Section 214A, providing for the setting up of a body (something like a Public Accounts Committee) at the district level called the DCP. The DCP examines the accounts of the Panchayats within the district.

Reservation and rotation of seats in PRIs

The West Bengal Panchayat (Amendment) Act, 1992 makes it mandatory to provide for reservation of seats at each level of the panchayat for some population groups, namely, Scheduled Castes, Scheduled Tribes, Scheduled Caste women, Scheduled Tribe women, women in non-SC/ST categories, in proportion to their share in the population. The delimitation of constituencies, reservation of seats and the rotation of chairpersons of GPs, PSs and ZPs are effected on the basis of a Roster for reservation, as per the WB Panchayat (Election) Rules, 1974. However, there are some practical problems and anomalies encountered in the process of ascertaining the reserved categories, as has been pointed out on several occasions in the floor of the State Legislative Assembly.

Panchayat finances and the State Finance Commission

Panchayat finances include grants by the state or Central government (in case of the GP, also from the ZP or PS), loans granted by the state or Central Government and receipts on account of taxes (for example, the GP has been granted power to levy taxes on lands and buildings within its jurisdictions), fees, rates and tolls levied by it and receipts from other sources (including voluntary contributions and donations).

The State Finance Commission (SFC) will have to decide on the assignment of taxes, duties, fees and levies of panchayats. It has to determine which of the state-level taxes have to be shared between the state and the panchayats. It has also to decide about the grants-in-aid policy toward PRIs. There is a clause that enjoins the SFC to decide measures necessary to augment panchayat resources. For example, the SFC may recommend that the collection of entertainment tax will be vested with the state but its proceeds are to be distributed among local bodies. Similarly, the motor vehicle tax and the stamp duty - both state-level taxes – may be shared by local bodies in some proportion.

It is often claimed that a large percentage of the state plan outlay is channelled through PRIs. This is both a tall claim and a misnomer, observes one respected commentator on the subject. Because of many Central and state-sponsored schemes, a huge proportion of the plan outlay is spent on districts, but that does not necessarily mean that PRIs are at the helm of decision-making. Often, parastatal organisations and user groups (for example watershed committees) have more funds than PRIs.

In West Bengal the first State Finance Commission submitted its recommendations in 1996. It introduced the concept of entitlement. That is to say, in lieu of sharing individual taxes, 16 percent of net proceeds of all taxes in a year should be released to local bodies as untied fund. The SFC also emphasised the need for raising taxes, levies etc. by PRIs themselves and for generating voluntary contribution for development activities. In the recent years the state government has released Rs.100 crore to PRIs as untied fund, which has generated a fair degree of enthusiasm at the grassroots level, as Bandyopadhyay (2002) suggests in a workshop held in the recent past. In 2002, the second SFC endorsed the basic fund allocation structure proposed by the first SFC. It further recommended that a minimum of Rs.700 crore should be provided in the budget for devolution as untied entitlement. The respective shares of the GPs, PSs and ZPs in total allocation (as per its recommendations) should be in the ratio of 60, 20 and 20 percent. All these recommendations have to be viewed in the context of the huge revenue deficit of the state government and it remains to be seen to what extent it would implement these recommendations.

IV. Postscript : Some Pointers Towards Future Research

Finally, we hark back to our central concern for resourcing local public institutions for redistributive purposes. Put another way, we propose to explore the presumed relationship between fiscal autonomy and fiscal responsibility of LBs and their performance measured in terms of redistributive outcomes. The issue of fiscal autonomy and responsibility can be further disaggregated into four related but distinct parts :

(a) resource flow from the Centre via the centrally sponsored schemes and from the state government and through inter-tier devolution of funds; often resources are not devolved properly from district to lower levels or when devolved, funds are often tied. In other words, funds lose their untied character once they flow below the district;

(b) resource mobilisation - revenue autonomy, the local resource base etc. become relevant concerns here; also the issue of local capital accumulation and the flight of footloose capital from rural to urban and semi-urban areas for more profitable investment becomes germane to our research agenda;

although the 'local' is not necessarily connected with the 'global' in a direct and straightforward way, under the influence of new global forces, localities witness some visible changes. In West Bengal a major shift is under way from the regime of land reforms to one of land markets and contract farming. All this will have a direct bearing on resource mobilisation under PRI auspices; one may, however, ask what incentives the GP will have to use its power of revenue raising when transfer from above is assured. But given the huge burden of debt on both the Central and state governments, it is doubtful how long the fund flow will last. According to one estimate, the debt burden of the Central government is in the order of Rs. 8000 trillion. Of the total state-level debt burden, West Bengal's share is high – almost double the average burden. The per capita share of the debt burden in many other states is about Rs. 4000 whereas in West Bengal the corresponding figure is roughly about Rs. 9000;

(c) resource use – autonomy in spending decisions is the key question here. Are PRIs simply implementation agencies for development projects conceived at higher levels and therefore remain straight-jacketed within the confines of 'tied' grants or do the actual processes of budgetary allocations leave some room for flexibility such that in some situations enterprising PR representatives or local bureaucrats (e.g. BDOs) are able to get 'committed' funds released for other uses, driven by locally set priorities? The LBs are often devoid of autonomy in determining their spending priorities. The grants are generally tied (i.e., scheme-specific) and hence curb expenditure autonomy of PRIs (Jha, 2002). That is to say, the capacity of PRIs is limited in this context, as they are primarily implementer of government programmes and their role is largely in identifying beneficiaries for poverty alleviation programmes. But interestingly in using schematic funds there is some leeway in somehow getting tied grants untied.[31] Therefore, some room exists for using schematic budget in an innovative way. It is the careful analysis of such divergent budgetary practices, over and above the study of routine allocation of funds, which will hopefully illuminate our understanding of inter-state and even inter-tier variations in fiscal performance.

Another important element is to contrast citizens' resource mobilisation for local development projects – both formal and informal. Interviews with several experts and commentators indicate that while local resource mobilisation still remains a weak area, there exists a lot of scope for revenue generation on a voluntary basis. One influential minister notes in a recently held interview (conducted on November 13, 2002) that voluntary contributions may yield considerable amount, although this area remains relatively understudied. Also there exist wide variations across local bodies in this respect, accounting for corresponding differences in per capita revenue across panchayats (M. Shanthi, 2002).[32] D. Bandyopadhyay, in a workshop held in the recent past, gives an example of such innovative practices of revenue raising in one panchayat in West Bengal. Levying taxes on *paan* will be considered as agricultural income tax and therefore prohibited. So the panchayat president raises resources through donation of Rs.10 per head from those who grow *paan*. Social forestry proceeds may constitute another promising source of revenue. But one interviewee argues that too much emphasis on local resource mobilisation or generation of resources from social forestry etc. may lead to excessive of felling of trees and cause environmental damages.[33]

The question of resource use prompts us to raise three additional queries: (i) use for effective and equitable management of local public services (e.g., schools, health centres, drinking water facilities and so on); (ii) use for productivist purposes and strategies (as mentioned above, contract farming, agro-business etc are the emerging priorities in rural West Bengal) and their alleged benefits; and (iii) resource misuse and corruption. The fact of the widespread corruption and embezzlement of public resources associated with various local development programmes is well-known; such 'development rackets' are sometimes known to involve the local traders/contractors, the *sarpanch*, the BDO or the junior engineer, and the local landlord or upper-caste leader. Does decentralised spending start off a cycle of 'competitive corruption' or does it lead to redistributive gains?

(d) fiscal responsibility – alongside the issue of expenditure autonomy there remains the attendant question of expenditure transparency and accountability. Do local people have the right to information on past accounts and future spending priorities? Simply put, are the expenditure decisions transparent? Are the local authorities accountable to the people? Is there a scope for social audit of performance in addition to traditional audits? These issues will prompt us to focus on the mandatory village constituency meetings (i.e., *gram sansad* meetings) in the panchayat system of West Bengal. Gram sansad meetings are deliberative public meetings where the elected members of the GP and all the voters of a constituency meet (i) to review past and proposed programmes, (ii) to monitor the performance of elected representatives regarding the implementation of public projects and (iii) to inspect accounts of expenditure and budgets (Ghatak and Ghatak, 2002). Some recent studies indicate that until now such meetings are not well-attended; only about 20 percent of the voters routinely meet and adjourn. Some also note that 'green room' decisions in separate party meetings are held prior to *sansad* meetings, partly explaining people's lack of interest in such deliberations. Some of these worries may be somewhat premature, as one would expect a process of 'learning by doing' to take place after a reasonable time lag. All these will make the analysis of gram sansad meetings an integral component of our future research.

It is useful to bring out one related point here. In the mainstream literature on decentralisation, the alleged benefits of local level decision-making are to flow from its presumed information advantage, among others. But the standard focus is on the bottom-up generation of information to provide planners with more accurate details of local costs, needs and preferences. In the context of fiscal discipline and accountability however (and more generally in the case of the Right to Information movement), the emphasis is on demanding access to expenditure records, subjecting these to collective verification (i.e., social audit) and thus demanding accountability from local authorities.[34] The State-citizen channel may get clogged, even when the former is tax-financed and in a non-corporate economy through the 'contract Raj'. Thus, the thesis of State responsiveness is expected to work when people have 'unclassified' information which they can collectively scrutinise (the military budget, for example, is largely immune from public scrutiny) and then politically mobilise their concerns such that the State is compelled to respond.

Using the political and legislative narrative of the panchayats in West Bengal as a useful benchmark, we hope to take up these above-mentioned issues for further probing.

References

Bandyopadhyay, D., "Panchayats and Democracy: Elites versus Dalits", *Man and Development*, December. 1999.

________________, "Land Reforms and Agriculture : The West Bengal Experience", *Economic and Political Weekly*, Vol. 38, No. 9, 2003a, pp. 879-884.

________________, "Caucus and Masses : West Bengal Panchayats", *Economic and Political Weekly*, Vol. 38, no. 46, 2003b, pp. 4825-4826.

Bandyopadhyay, D, Saila K Ghosh and Budhhadeb Ghosh, "Dependency versus Autonomy: Identity Crisis of Indian Panchayats", *Economic and Political Weekly*, Vol. 38, no. 38, 2003,pp. 3984-3991.

Bardhan, P., "The Nature of Institutional Impediments to Economic Development", in Satu Kahkonen and Mancur Olson (eds.), *A New Institutional Approach to Economic Development*, Vistaar Publications, New Delhi, 2001, pp. 245-267.

Bhattacharya, Dwaipayan, "Politics of Middleness : The Changing Character of the Communist Party of India (Marxist) in Rural West Bengal (1977-90)", in Ben Rogaly, Barbara Harris-White and Sugata Bose (ed.), *Sonar Bangla? Agricultural Growth and Agrarian Change in West Bengal and Bangladesh*, New Delhi, Sage Publications, 1999, pp. 279-300.

Brautigam, Deborah, "Building Leviathan : Revenue, State Capacity and Governance", *The New Politics of Taxation and Accountability, IDS Bulletin*, Vol.33, no. 3, 2002.

Chatterjee, Arnab, "Old Wine : New Bottles : Panchayat Planning in West Beṅgal", *Economic and Political Weekly*, Vol. 38, no. 39, 2003.

Crook, Richard, C. and Alan Sturla Sverisson, "Decentralisation and Poverty Alleviation in Developing Countries : A Comparative Analysis or, is West Bengal Unique?", IDS Working Paper, No. 30, 2002.

Dreze, Jean and Amartya Sen, *India : Development and Participation*, New Delhi, Oxford University Press, 2002.

Frankel, Francine R., "Contextual Democracy : Intersections of Society, Culture and Politics in India", in Francine R. Frankel, Zoya Hassan, Rajeev Bhargava and Banveer Arora (eds.), *Transforming India : Social and Political Dynamics of Democracy*, Delhi, Oxford University Press, 2000.

Gazdar, Haris and Sunil Sengupta, "Agricultural Growth and Recent Trends in Well-being in West Bengal", in Ben Rogally, Barbara Harriss-White and Sugata Bose (eds.), *Sonar Bangla?* .

Ghatak, Maitreesh, and Maitreya Ghatak, "Recent Reforms in the Panchayat System in West Bengal : Toward Greater Participatory Governance?", *Economic and Political Weekly*, Vol. 37, no.1, 2002, pp.45-58.

Harriss, John, "Comparing Political Regimes Across Indian States", *Economic and Political Weekly*, Vol. 34, no. 48, 1999, pp.3367-3377.

Heller, Patrick, "Degrees of Democracy : Some Comparative Lessons from India", *World Politics*, Vol. 52, 2002.

Jenkins, Rob and Ann Marie Goetz, "Accounts and Accountability : Theoretical Implications of the Right to Information Movement in India", *Third World Quarterly*, Vol. 20, No.3, 1999.

Jha, Shikha, "Strengthening Local Governments : Rural Fiscal Decentralization in India", *Economic and Political Weekly*, Vol. 37, no. 26, 2002, pp. 2611-2623.

Joshi, Anuradha, "Progressive Bureaucracy : An Oxymoron? The Case of Joint Forest Management in India", mimeo, Department of Urban Studies and Planning, Cambridge, MIT, MA., 1999.

Kaviraj, Sudipto, "Dilemmas of Democratic Development in India", in Adrian Leftwich (ed.), *Democracy and Development*, Cambridge, Polity, 1996.

Kohli, Atul, *State and Poverty in India, Politics of Reform*, Cambridge, Cambridge University Press, Mass, 1987.

Kumar, G., "Constitutionalising Panchayats : The Response of State Legislatures", CSH Occasional Paper, no. 4, 2002.

Majumdar, Manabi, "Contours of Decentralisation", *The Hindu*, 27 December, 2000.

Mallick, Ross, *Development Policy of a Communist Government, West Bengal since 1977*, Cambridge University Press, 1993.

Moore, Mick and Lise Rakner, "Introduction : The New Politics of Taxation and Accountability in Developing Countries", *The New Politics of Taxation and Accountability, IDS Bulletin*, Vol. 33., no. 3, 2002.

Mukarji, Nirmal and D. Bandyopadhyay, *New Horizons for West Bengal Panchayats,* 1993.

Przeworski, Adam, Michael E. Alvarez, Jose Antonio Cheibub and Fernando Limongi, *Democracy and Development: Political Institutions and Well-being in the World, 1950-1990*, Cambridge, Cambridge University Press, 2000.

Sengupta, Sunil and Haris Gazdar, "Agrarian Poltics and Rural Development in West Bengal", in Jean Dreze and Amartya Sen (eds.), *Indian Development: Selected Regional Perspectives*, Delhi, Oxford University Press, 1996.

Seshiah, Shaila, "Contexts and Processes of Decentralisation in India", Development Research Centre for the Future State, *IDS*, Background Paper, 2003.

Varshney, Ashutosh, "Is India Becoming More Democratic?", *The Journal of Asian Studies*, Vol. 59, no.1 2000.

Webster, Neil, "Panchayati Raj in West Bengal : Popular Participation for the People or the Party?", in Kuldeep Mathur (ed.), *Development Policy and Administration*, New Delhi, Sage Publications,1996

Weiler, Hans N., "Control versus Legitimation : The Politics of Ambivalence", in Jane Hannaway and Martin Carnoy (eds.), *Decentralization and School Improvement : Can We Fulfil the Promise?*, San Francisco, Jossey-Bass Publishers, 1993.

West Bengal Legislative Assembly proceedings, relevant volumes.

West Bengal, Government of West Bengal, Law Department, The West Bengal Panchayat, Act 1973.

West Bengal, Government of West Bengal, Law Department, The West Bengal Panchayat (Second Amendment) Act, 1997.

West Bengal, Government of West Bengal, Law Department, The West Bengal Panchayat (Amendment) Act, 2003.

Notes

1. Stripped to its essence, the thesis propounds that the source of state revenue (e.g., tax, aid, loan etc.) determines biases – elitist or pro-poor – in public policies. There are several ways of raising revenue including aids and loans from international agencies which remain outside the purview of the present discussion, as also their effects on policy outcomes. Our focus in subsequent research is going to be on the tax-state and its tax-paying citizens. Put another way, the broad theme within which we situate our present analysis relates to the connection between fiscal process and political process, pursued not at the national but at the sub-national level. For an original and incisive analysis of the politics of taxation and the political mobilisation of taxpayer concerns in developing countries, see Brautigam (2002), and Moore and Rakner (2002).
2. As part of the larger project, two companion papers study Karnataka and Tamil Nadu respectively.
3. Apart from the possibility of 'elite capture' of public institutions, the costs of political action, time and resource constraints may also make participation by the poor difficult (Seshiah, 2003). Thus, citizen participation does not just happen even when the political space does emerge for it to do so. Developing effective citizenship and building democratic organisation take time and effort. Clearly, there is an element of 'learning by doing' here (Dreze and Sen, 2003). So any feasible plan of local governance must design its institutions such that they can be run efficiently by people like us who spend a great deal of time thinking about themselves and not about the promotion of local democracy (Majumdar, 2000).
4. The underlying motivation of this collaborative work is to develop state-specific political and legislative narratives of panchayat reforms in the three selected states, with the purpose of discerning

the political and social forces that have triggered the most recent spate of decentralisation reforms.

5. We are grateful to Dwaipayan Bhattacharya for his incisive comments on this.

6. See, for example, illuminating discussions in Dreze and Sen (2003), Frankel (2000), Harriss (1999), Heller (2002), Kohli (1987), and Varshney (2000) among others.

7. The impact of the Fifth Pay Commission recommendations on state finances and its implications for fiscal devolution are indeed far-reaching , as a participant insightfully observed in a meeting on fiscal devolution at MIDS, on April 16, 2002.

8. As a respected senior bureaucrat noted in course of an interview held in Bangalore, when decentralisation measures were under way in the state of Karnataka, Ministers for Agriculture, Horticulture, and Animal Husbandry all thought that their importance would be lost as some portion of their power would go to PRIs. (May 16, 2002). There indeed exists a possibility of competition and confrontation between the political leadership at different levels of government. In one reading, there is a systematic subversion of the Panchayats by the MPs and MLAs who feel threatened by the emerging grass-roots leadership. For example, the allotment of the Local Area Development Fund of MPs and MLAs – the 'pork-barrel' funds that keep on increasing - is a way, some feel, of perpetuating a system of Panchayat subservience (Bandyopadhyay, Ghosh and Ghosh, 2003).

9. As the organisational structure of the state panchayat stands now, the *Gram* panchayat or the village council constitutes the lowest level of electoral unit in the system covering 10-12 villages and is led by an elected *Pradhan*,. The Panchayat *Samiti* exists at the block level extending across 115 villages and is headed by an elected *Sabhapati*. The *Zilla Parishad*– a district-level unit – is at the apex of the PR system and is headed by an elected *Sabhadhipati* (Ghatak and Ghatak, 2002).

10. These were conceived as mere extension agencies of the existing development administration, for enhancing the efficacy of the latter (Bandyopadhyay, 1999).

11. One of our interviewees (interview held on 16 May, 2002) speculated in a similar vein that Rajiv Gandhi wanted to create a

channel between the common man and elected representatives which remained clogged at that point and hence felt motivated to re-establish that link through panchayats. (Interview on May 16, 2002).

12. This interview was conducted on 16 May in Bangalore, 2002.
13. This is based on an interview held on 11 November, 2002.
14. In general, the reason for the 'second generation' panchayat reforms in different parts of the country during this time is attributed to attempts by non-Congress forces to establish a political support base at the local level (Mathew, 1994).
15. The discussion in the rest of the paragraph is based on conversations with D. Bandyopadhyay and other participants in a meeting at the Centre for Studies in Social Sciences, Calcutta, on 11 November, 2002.
16. A respected commentator on agrarian reforms in West Bengal, however, remarked at the April 2003 workshop that it was rather the metropolitan reformers who lacked interest in land. This echoes the argument that the reformist external power might play a decisive role in challenging the traditional, parochial local power base. In his study of the politics of land reforms in West Bengal, Kohli (1987), however, claims that the main opposition to agrarian reform came from the lower level administration, especially from the frontline workers who were linked with landed interests in villages. The reason why land reforms have been successful in West Bengal, he further argues, is because the political party largely bypassed and neutralised the bureaucracy in their implementation (as discussed in Joshi, 1999).
17. This remark is based upon conversations with a senior politician and scholar in an interview on 11 November, 2002.
18. The discussion in the remainder of the paragraph draws on Webster (1996).
19. This comment was made by a leading economist in an interview in Kolkata held on November 12, 2002.
20. These observations are based on insightful comments of two senior administrators-cum-scholars during interviews held in Bangalore on May 16 and 17, 2002.
21. In this context, it is interesting to refer to Kumar (2002, p.6) who alludes to a similar constellation of personalities that partly

influenced the success of the 73rd Amendment Bill, when it was sent to a Joint Parliamentary Committee (JPC) for examination, "The JPC was headed by Nathuram Mirdha, a former Chief Minister of Rajasthan. Among its members were Mani Shankar Aiyar, Deve Gowda, P.M. Sayeed, Sudhir Roy *et al.* It may also be mentioned that Rajasthan was the first state in the country where the three-tier PRI system was inaugurated by the first Prime Minister on October 2, 1959. Aiyar, a Congress member, had worked closely with Rajiv Gandhi to prepare the 64th Amendment. Deve Gowda was from the Karnataka branch of the Janata party, which earned kudos for resurrecting panchayats in the state in the latter half of the 1980s. Generally speaking, the Committee was broad-based with members well exposed to the concepts as well as praxis of panchayati raj in the country."

22. In a recent interview, one senior politician in West Bengal talks about the need to guard against 'cronyism– a danger that the party bosses may easily slide into. Similarly, a seminar participant observed that PRIs are functioning as the 'elected sterile bureaucracy', whereas local party committees are calling the shots.
23. A similar point was made by an interviewee on November 11, 2002 in the city of Kolkata.
24. It is generally observed that if the state government accords sufficient importance to PRIs, bureaucrats accept them.
25. He makes this remark in an interview with us on November 9, 2002 in Kolkata.
26. The following discussion on Assembly debates pertaining to the conformity legislation draws largely on Kumar (2002).
27. At the April, 2003 Workshop at MIDS, a senior bureaucrat, with close knowledge of state-level happenstances during the passage of conformity legislations, recounted his conversation with the honourable minister on this issue. He also confirmed that originally the Left Front Government did not support the 1992 Amendment Act; it was of the view that decentralisation initiatives need to emanate from 'political will' and not the 'Constitutional Bill'. Several adjustments were made at the Central Secretariat at that time, he claimed, to incorporate the demands of the LFG. Still there was substantial delay on the part of the West Bengal government before

it finally enacted the conformity legislation. The honourable minister allegedly remarked that the Government wanted to have the panchayat election first (it was held in May 1993) and then have the amendment, as the latter would require, as per the newly introduced reservation rules, fielding of a large number of woman and SC/ST candidates, capable and competent to successfully contest in elections. The participant further wondered why the Left Coalition seemed to be not quite ready to field suitable candidates from the traditionally deprived backgrounds even after such a long and uninterrupted spell of power.

28. This interview was conducted on November 12, 2002 in Kolkata.
29. This is based on an interview held in Kolkata on 13 November, 2002.
30. Observation along this line was made by D. Bandyopadhyay in a workshop on Fiscal Devolution organised at MIDS on April 16, 2002.
31. M. Shanthi made this point with supportive evidence in a workshop on fiscal devolution.
32. This interview was conducted in Kolkata on November 14, 2002.
33. On an illuminating analysis of the difference between the Right to Information movement and the conventional view of community participation and generation of information from grass roots, See Jenkins and Goetz (1999).

7

Democratic Governance: Reforming the Accountability Domain

I. Ramabrahmam

S. Sudhakar Babu

Introduction

In the changing economic scenario marked by privatisation and the advent of market economy, public finance plays a significant role in the development process, especially in the arena of social infrastructure, to ensure minimum needs to the deprived[1]. Governance reforms too have to be seen in the context of the growing need for better management of public finances. The World Bank defined good governance as the one that epitomises open and enlightened policy-making, a bureaucracy imbued with a professional ether acting in furtherance of the public good, the rule of law, transparent processes, and a strong civil society participating in public affairs. Poor governance (on the other hand) is characterised by arbitrary policy-making, unaccountable bureaucracies, unenforced or unjust legal systems, the abuse of executive power, a civil society unengaged in public life, and widespread corruption[2].

Mohit Bhattacharya[3] stated in an interesting article entitled "Nexus between accountability and good governance: conceptual with two connotations: answerability and enforcement" that instead of keeping accountability as a managerial concept it should be viewed as a concept for strengthening democracy by empowering people. V.S. Prasad[4] in his article entitled "Governance for Development : Key concerns" stated that public administration should not be viewed as a stand-alone activity as it becomes imperative on the part of government to perform a multi-dimensional role in the present changing reformed-based scenario. In the chapter titled "Effective Governance : the New Public Management Perspective", Uma Madury[5] maintains that the new public management thinking has a key role to play with the supportive strategy formulated for the development in the context the reforms initiated to hone greater significance of effective governance.

Asian Development Bank (ADB) clarifies the concept of governance by identifying accountability as one of the elements for the efficiency. It reads that accountability means establishing criteria to measure the performance of public officials as well as oversight mechanisms to ensure that the standards are met :

1. Economic accountability – relates to the effectiveness of policy formulation and efficiency in resource use.
2. Financial accountability – covers accounting systems for expenditure central and internal and external audits.
3. Participation - covers the involvement of citizens and civil society in the development process.
4. Predictability - refers to the existence of laws, regulations and policies to regulate the society and their fair and consistent application.

Kuldeep Mathur[6] in his article entitled "Good Governance and Pursuit of Transparency in Administration: The Indian Efforts" highlights that the scope of governance is vast, as it is yet to materialise the goods of efficiency, effectiveness and accountability. He further states that the goals of governance will have to be extended beyond efficiency, effectiveness, economy and accountability which would further lead to the inclusion of responsiveness, empowerment and participation.

For the successful combating of corruption and to democratise the effective participation of civil society it was adopted in Sarajevo[7] in February 2000, the Stability Pact Anti-Corruption Initiative(SPAI) as a regional process through which governments of the region, local and international civil society organisations, bilateral and agencies, and international organisations combine their efforts to curb the corruption.

The comprehensive approach addresses five main areas:

1. Adoption and implementation of international legal instruments containing anti-corruption related provisions;
2. Promotion of good governance;
3. Strengthening the rule of law;
4. Promotion of transparency and integrity in business operations, and
5. Development of an active civil society.

It sought for the governmental transparency and co-operative partnerships between governments and civil society. An active civil society helps make government accountable for its decisions and actions. To have transparency in the aspect of finance the Republic of Montenegro[8] has distributed the public funds to NGOs to improve the capacity and maturity of civil society to work as anti-corruption initiatives to have better governance.

The above studies on governance reforms state explicitly that governance is an exercise of authority through formal and informal traditions and institutions for common good. Governance encompasses the processes of selecting, monitoring and replacing the methods of functioning. Governance reforms also touch upon the process of evolving suitable capacity-building packages for formulation of sound public policies. Some of these include voice and accountability through civil society, ensuring political stability, effectiveness in governance, focusing on quality policy-making, public service delivery, quality regulations, controlling of corruption and effective management of finances. In other words, governance reforms aim at knowledge building, effective leadership and work towards collective action. The accountability dimension in these reforms calls for critical focus as the objective is to ensure effective management of public finance. The normative model of good governance includes developing result-orientation, flexibility and open approach to alternatives, *performance audit* and creating a competitive environment. The broad policy model in most developing countries is that priority sectors like social sector should receive attention in resource allocation. The latter part is how the resources allocated are actually managed to achieve the desired outcomes.

Management of limited finances, therefore, assumes critical importance. In India, the Union and state legislatures vote the budgeted amounts to respective departments needed for the identified programmes. While this itself is a huge exercise, what happens subsequently appears to be of little interest to the academia, except the auditing under broad rubric referred to as financial administration. Scant attention is given to the details, such as, the outcomes of such allocations in qualitative terms, though there is a change in the structure of budget. Performance-based auditing, utilisation of funds for the purpose for which the legislative arms accord approval are of course reported. Since audit by constitutional authority such as the Comptroller and Auditor General (CAG) itself is post-facto, analysis is often restricted to the observable norms and violations, wherever occurred. The discussion in this paper centres around the provisions viz., Articles 148, 149, 150, 151 of the Indian Constitution, which concern the procedures involved in placing the reports of CAG on the table of parliament/respective state legislatures The processes include preparation of civil audit reports, transactional audit appraisals, performance appraisals etc[9]. These reports are referred to the Public Accounts Committee (PAC) to ensure the accountability of executive to the legislature.

Initiation of Governance Reforms

It will be interesting to observe as to how a state government perceives the *accountability* domain called auditing and how these reports are increasingly perceived as those which have to be received, analysed and replied. It deserves attention as the processes of audit appear to be regarded as 'unavoidable formality' despite introduction of governance reforms. Good governance, as articulated in several documents published by state governments (see White Paper on Governance and Public Management Strategy, Government of Andhra Pradesh, www.aponline.gov.in) demands that the administration is responsive, transparent, accountable besides being projected of late as simple and moral (acronym is 'SMART'). This article attempts to examine whether the stated new principles of governance are translated into action. Further, the scope of this paper is limited to the state of Andhra Pradesh (AP) as the state is showcased as one of the four states which initiated major governance reforms. The other states which generally get included in this credo are Karnataka, Madhya Pradesh and Delhi (National Capital Region). The period of study is restricted to four years, i.e., from 1999 to 2003 as during this period the Government of India as well as some states attempted major changes in the administrative structures and functions and initiated interventions through training programmes in financial administration.

According to Article 148 of Constitution of India, the CAG of India controls the entire financial system of the country. Late Dr. B.R. Ambedkar once observed that CAG shall be the most important officer under the Constitution. He/she is the guardian of public purse. It is CAG's responsibility to see that not a paisa is spent out of Consolidated Fund of India or of a state government without authority of appropriate legislature. The main function of the CAG is to audit and report on all expenditure from the Consolidated Fund of India and of each state and each Union Territory; audit and report on all expenditure from the contingency funds and Public Accounts of Union and states; to audit the receipts and expenditure of Union and each state and satisfy himself that the rules and procedures in that behalf are designed to secure an effective check on assessment, collection and proper allocation of revenue; to audit and report on all trading, manufacturing, profit and loss accounts kept by the Departments of Union and state governments[10].

The functions are a clear indication of the independence the CAG commands for regulating finances of Union and state governments. However, it must be stated that the CAG in India is limiting its role to the role of an Auditor than of Comptroller, unlike the case with the CAG in UK. The CAG in UK controls the receipts and issue of public money. This power of control over issue of public money by CAG in UK effectively prevents withdrawal of money for unauthorised purposes and also checks excess withdrawal of grants to those approved by Parliament. It appears that the British arrangement protects the public money much more effectively. In contrast, in India the CAG's role is limited to auditing. In UK the system of control over public issue continues[11].

CAG: Consensus on the Role

The functions of CAG are also a subject of controversy because it is widely perceived as a stumbling block to development administration. It is stated that when the Statute confers powers on an authority to sanction expenditure, the audit which questions the propriety is not in consonance with responsibilities of administration. Noted theorist in Public Administration, Paul Appleby, saw a link between economy and efficiency. He stated it in so many words: "Auditors do not know and cannot be expected to know very much about good administration. Auditing is a necessary but highly *pedestrian* function with a narrow perspective and very limited usefulness"[12].

However, there is a broad consensus on the role of Audit by the Union and state administration. Further, there is no controversy over the core activity of CAG, which is to examine how far the tax payers money is utilised and whether money mobilised through taxes is judiciously spent or not. The organisation of work is done through various Accountant Generals attached to each state/Union Government.The finance accounts as well as the appropriation accounts are scrutinised besides maintaining the Provident Fund account. The methodology is test-checking of the items of expenditure. There is no major deviation in this methodology since independence despite initiation of governance reforms.

The Structure of Audit Reports

Reports of the CAG for a year are prepared and presented to the Governor of a state under Article 151 of the Constitution.

The authors have selected reports of the CAG on financial management of AP for a macro-view of the processes involved in this accountability system. This period may be regarded as crucial to the students of Public Administration as many reforms were attempted in the domain of financial administration too. The reports cover test auditing on financial transactions on matters arising from examination of finance and accounts, and appropriation of accounts of the state government for an year (ending on March 31 of each year). The period of study is restricted to 1999-2003 for the reasons already stated. The reports selected covered implementation of policies and programmes in social sector besides PWD, Irrigation Department, audit of stores and stock, audit of autonomous bodies and departmentally run commercial undertakings. Further, they contained observations arising out of audit of statutory corporations, boards and government companies and also revenue receipts.

Table 1
Audit Reports of Andhra Pradesh: An Overview of Structure and Contents of the Reports

Year	*No. of Audit Paragraphs*	*No. of pages of Reports*	*Performance Review*	*Subjects/Departments Covered*
1999-2000	43	257	5	Education, Health & Family Welfare
2000-2001	44	255	6	CMEY, Medical, Health & Family Welfare
2001-2002	35	216	4	Agriculture, Cooperation, IT, Education & Technical Education
2002-2003	36	210	4	Health, AIDS, Home, Agriculture, Cooperatives, Irrigation, Environment

(Source: *Reports of Comptroller and Auditor General of India; Government of India* for the years 2000, 2001, 2002 and 2003: for more information http://cagindia.org/states/andhrapradesh/2003)

The following table gives an overview of the Audit Reports presented in case of AP for the year 1999 to 2003. It is not out of place to mention that major governance reforms are initiated in the state and intensive efforts are made to implement them since 1999.

New Methodologies for Measuring Impact of Public Expenditure

The mandate of the CAG is to give a feedback on governance deficit in social sector, that is, health, education and so forth. An assessment of performance of the government in this sector is necessary to understand how the taxpayers' money is utilised for their benefit especially in the context of reforms initiated for effective governance. Further, this exercise is expected to ensure enhanced accountability and result-oriented performance. UC Agarwal, former Secretary to Government of India and Editor of *Indian Journal of Public Administration*, in an interesting article, entitled "Governance for Development: Constitutional Goals and Directives" mentioned that 'the primary aim of any good state ... is to promote the general well-being of the people through provision of proper health care, educational facilities, access to basic needs'[13] Quoting the Directive Principles the author observes that 'the principles of governance are meant to promote social harmony among all citizens by reducing inequalities and providing equal opportunities'. This goal can be visualised only by stepping up investment in social sector. A greater thrust to this sector ensures education and health for all (a larger canvas of social sector includes Family Welfare, Water Supply and Sanitation)[14]. Let us look at the allocations for the crucial sector in order to get an overview. It must be remembered that the promised 6% GDP for education remained a mirage. Perhaps the low allocation to education explains the poor ranking of India in Human Development Index (HDI) in the *Human Development Reports*, computed by UNDP.

The objective of all development is human development, encompassing the quality of life, the level of well-being and access to basic social services. It is further pointed out that a renewed thrust to social sector ensures overall development. It needs to be stated in this context that the *Human Development Reports* of the United Nations Development Programme (UNDP) continue to

Table 2

Social Sector Expenditure by Union & State Governments

Sl. No.	*Sector*	*1995-96 (as % GDP)*	*2003*
1.	Education	2.7	3.1
2.	Health		

Sl. No.	*Sector*	*As % of total Expenditure*	
1.	Education	11.3	2.2
2.	Health	4.3	4.6

Source: U.C. Agarwal, *Governance for Development*, IJPA, Vol. L No.1, 2004 p.17.

raise alarm over the poor status of HDI of India. It is common knowledge that the quality of life is closely linked to one's educational and health status. While the macro-level concerns on the status of India vis-à-vis other countries in literacy etc. are documented and reported through the UNDP's Human Development Index, several state governments within the country are lagging behind in the social policy matrix. For example, the performance of AP in social sector is a matter of deep concern as the state is occupying a lowly twenty eighth position in literacy and other indicators like health, life expectancy, infant mortality etc. While higher allocations are demanded for better results in social sector what needs to be studied is whether sound financial management ensures checking the wastage of public funds. Efficient management of allocated funds can be assessed through the reports of the CAG, besides independent research studies.

The Reports of the CAG on Andhra Pradesh

The CAG report for the year 2002-2003, relating to AP's general financial status, does not miss the social scientists' prying eyes. It was pointed out that the financial management of the state calls for a critical look by policymakers. It showed increasing liabilities and decreasing development expenditure. This means that there is little money left for the social sector. The borrowings of the government doubled from Rs.28,297 crores in 1998 to Rs. 54,831 crores in 2003. The actual availability of funds was sharply reduced as those borrowings were used for revenue deficits, loan repayments and interest payment. Less than 5 per cent of the borrowed money (as reported by the CAG) is available for development. It was stated in the report that non-development expenditure increased 8 per cent while development expenditure declined by 3 per cent. While liabilities grew by 16 per cent, assets grew only by 12 per cent widening the gap between assets and liabilities.[15]

Downsizing as a Governance Reform

Noting that government did not fill up the vacant posts since almost a decade, the CAG recorded that this governance initiative had a negative impact on the administrative system in almost all departments including Health, Education. The report in the process documented how the inadequate number of staff affected the goal-attainment. Let us refer to some of the critical sectors. Commenting on the low investment in core sectors like agriculture the latest report noted that plan outlay for this sector has been coming down and now stood at 3 per cent. This has resulted in huge shortfalls in physical performance with net sown area decreasing by over 13 lakh hectares between 1998-1999 and 2002-2003. Perhaps the current crisis in agriculture could be traced to low public investment, which was already raised in the CAG report. Observers might argue that had the CAG report been taken seriously there would have been a stepping up of public investment in agriculture, rescuing the farmers, to some extent, from the situation which compels them to commit suicide. Needless to mention, the failure of the monsoon has adversely affected the farm sector. But nonetheless, if one takes a look at the CAG report, one would not miss the point that there was, in fact, a decline in area under canal irrigation. An amount of Rs.8,692 crores is reported to have been blocked in 23 incomplete irrigation projects.[16]

Unresponsiveness of Bureaucracy to CAG, Reports

The CAG report also noted the unresponsiveness of the state administration to the repeated reminders regarding misallocation and misuse of funds on twenty four specific objectives brought to the notice of the state legislature.[17] This may be quite common to all the layers of government but it will be seen in a different light in the case of state governments which have initiated governance reforms as one of the aims for sound management of finances. However, the comments/observations made by Comptroller and Auditor General on the lapses committed by the government seem to have been taken seriously by the present government. But it remains to be seen whether necessary steps will be initiated to take corrective measures.

Social Sector: Key to Development

It must again be noted that the social agenda for good governance covers measures for controlling population growth, rural and urban poverty, illiteracy, ill-health, uneven development, empowerment of women and weaker sections, minorities and general concern about human development — all of which can be lumped under the social sector. The champions of human development argue that formal sanctions do not matter. It is the end result that matters. The position of AP in this case too continues to be a cause for alarm. Let us look at AP's expenditure on social sector vis-à-vis other states in South India and also at national level. The *National Human Development Report* (2002) provides Human Development Index at the state levels. It shows that AP's place was lower than all India in the past two decades. While its rank was 8 in 1981 and 9 in 1991, it declined to 11th place according to the media reports. Tamil Nadu, and even *BIMARU* states including Madhya Pradesh and Rajasthan improved their relative position. (See for details Mahendradev & Sridevi : Social Sector Expenditures in A.P., Centre for Economic and Social Studies, Hyderabad, 2004, pp. 4-7).

From the preceding table one can infer that AP spends much lower compared to other southern states. Expenditure on education and health as percentage of GSDP is low. However, AP spends more on rural development. It should also be stated at this juncture that the social sector is not receiving priority in terms of allocations. Even the allocations are not spent to the extent the legislatures approved. There are cases of misappropriation in the social welfare

Table – 3
Per Capita Real Expenditure on Social Sector in South

Social Sector in Southern States as % of GSDP							
	1980-81	*1985-86*	*1990-91*	*1995-96*	*1999-00*	*2000-01*	*2001-02 (RE)*
Education, Sports, Art and Culture							
Andhra Pradesh	117	179	207	200	305	317	329
Karnataka	126	185	242	289	400	425	399
Kerala	230	308	371	394	573	532	524
Tamil Nadu	136	214	314	312	494	456	453
Medical, Public Health &Family Welfare							
Andhra Pradesh	62	63	67	70	107	113	115
Karnataka	52	72	75	87	129	122	136
Kerala	87	92	103	113	155	139	134
Tamil Nadu	62	104	95	100	135	123	126
Water Supply and Sanitation							
Andhra Pradesh	0	27	21	29	37	35	48
Karnataka	0	28	18	37	71	49	46

(Contd.)

(Contd. Table-3)

Social Sector in Southern States as % of GSDP							
	1980-81	*1985-86*	*1990-91*	*1995-96*	*1999-00*	*2000-01*	*2001-02 (RE)*
Kerala	0	17	31	28	40	33	29
Tamil Nadu	0	0	36	37	35	70	68
Other Services							
Andhra Pradesh	84	128	144	248	245	240	249
Karnataka	62	120	133	150	176	187	198
Kerala	81	179	107	109	164	153	159
Tamil Nadu	55	144	173	188	221	223	235
Total Social Services							
Andhra Pradesh	263	396	440	547	693	705	740
Karnataka	240	405	469	563	777	783	779
Kerala	399	596	612	643	932	856	846
Tamil Nadu	253	463	617	637	886	871	882
Rural Development							
Andhra Pradesh	0	79	97	67	98	111	131

(Contd.)

(Contd. Table-3)

Social Sector in Southern States as % of GSDP							
	1980-81	*1985-86*	*1990-91*	*1995-96*	*1999-00*	*2000-01*	*2001-02 (RE)*
Karnataka	0	69	76	56	59	56	51
Kerala	0	58	59	53	189	162	125
Tamil Nadu	0	63	79	46	62	88	52
Total Social Sector							
Andhra Pradesh	263	475	537	614	791	816	871
Karnataka	240	474	545	619	836	839	831
Kerala	399	654	671	696	1121	1019	972
Tamil Nadu	253	526	696	682	949	959	935

Details as quoted in Sridevi N, *AP Finances: An Overview*, *Veekshanam*, December 1-31, 2003, p. 8-10. Also see Mahendra Dev & Sridevi, *Social Sector Expenditures in Andhra Pradesh*, Paper presented at the Annual Conference of AP Economic Association, Chittoor, 2003.

segment to the extent of Rs. 2,438 crores[18]. In their anxiety to spend money on populist schemes perhaps the governments across the country frequently violate norms of expenditure and sometimes incur excess expenditure. It may be pointed out here that despite tall claims about governance reforms in the financial sector, the state government is yet to regularise excess amount of expenditure to the extent of Rs. 2001.80 crores for the years from 1990-1991 to 1998-1999[19]. However, as per Article 205 of Constitution, it is mandatory for the state governments to get the legislatures' approval. This may be the same case with other states as well but cannons of sound financial management demand that there is broad compliance with existing legal framework.

The next table presents an overview of the major observations made by the CAG regarding incomplete irrigation projects, what policy scientists describe as *sunk costs*. The investment made has no economic return. This points to the low impact of reforms in financial management.

Further, dreaded diseases like AIDS are spreading for want of proper monitoring, according to the CAG report. Pointing out to the lack of direction to the National AIDS Control mechanism it was stated that since the state was unable to utilise the funds in time and completely, the implementation process was affected. The report documented that while 485 were affected with AIDS in 1999, the number increases to 1,478 in 2003 and till the year 2002 as many as 297 people died of AIDS. This is a serious point to the efforts made by the state governments. The performance of the state governments in areas like transport, registration, commercial taxes, and autonomous bodies companies was also pointed out by the CAG in its report.[20]

The performance of AP in education and health sectors is particularly causing concern. While schools continue to request for teaching and learning material, money received from the Central Government remained unutilised owing to the failure of the agencies to formulate guidelines. Experts say that the acquisition of the material would have prevented drop-outs as innovative materials evolved would have sustained the enthusiasm of the children.[21] It was pointed out in an earlier report that programmes

Table 4
Overview of other Important Audit Observations

	1999-2000*	(Rupees in Crores)
1. Incomplete Irrigation Projects(since 1971). Amount spent: Rs. 4,482.33 cores.	10 13	1999-2000: Rs. 4,482.33 2001-2002: Rs. 8,104.15 2002-2003: Rs. 8,692.42
2. Excess Provision for regularisation by the State Legislative Assembly 1999-2000	(i) Excess amount of Rs. 2,001.80 crores for the year 1990-1991 to 1998-99 was yet to be regularised.	
2000-2001	Rs. 1,562 crores to be regularized through expenditure sanction for 1997-98 to 1999-2000	
2001-2002	Rs. 1,976.35 crores to be regularised through expenditure sanction for 1997-1998 to 2000-2001	
2002-2003	Rs. 2,404.04 crores to be regularised through expenditure sanction for 1997-1998 to 2001-2002	

on primary education are not efficiently managed by the Government of AP[22], up to 67 per cent of plan funds were not spent. Budget estimates and allocations were finalised by the Finance Department without consulting the Education Department. It was clearly pointed out that nearly 40 per cent of children in the relevant age group were never enrolled. The drop-out rate was very high among SC/STs. Funds meant for disabled were never released. Intake of children in urban areas is less than 50 per cent and independent surveys show negative growth in enrolment, non-appointment of female teachers in 35 per cent of schools and ineffective training. It was also reported that there was a shortage of 8,000 teachers upsetting the teacher-student ratio. There was no drinking water facility in 56 per cent of schools test-checked. 69 per cent of funds provided by the Central Government, on the recommendations of the Tenth Finance Commission, was not spent. It was clearly stated that management of human resources was highly deficient in the department[23]. Programmes for strengthening social capital were also neglected. In another report it was stated that central assistance received by the state in 1999 for disbursement as a one time functional grant to water users' associations was not disbursed.[24] Schemes meant for empowerment of youth under CMEY (Chief Minister's Empowerment of Youth) too suffered from bureaucratic apathy. The report also noted that the budget estimates and provisions of funds were made without assessing the requirements. Large sums remained unspent. While the state government's ways and means position was critical money for the CMEY was lying unutilised in savings bank and fixed deposit accounts[25] while in some instances there were cases of misappropriation. Performance parameters were not evolved to measure the impact of these important and innovative programmes. It is ironical that the agency, which is expected to closely monitor the programme does not have list of beneficiary groups.

Thus, in a number of areas there is need for comprehensive plan to strengthen mechanisms for effective management of finances of the state. The management of finances assumes critical importance in the context of the need for observing propriety and economy. The post-globalisation scenario is presenting a challenging situation: introduction of governance reforms in various sectors, on the one hand, and planning state intervention in priority sectors, on the other hand, appeals for more transparent modules for the accountability domain. While introduction of governance reforms called for organisation or capacity-building programmes, these are done mostly in a routine way. Employees at various levels seem to be attending to these programmes as a ritual. One should take up a project on the long-term impact of the training programmes. A cursory look at the annual audit reports submitted to the state legislature highlights the need for a more professional approach in responding to the remarks they contain. Principles of New Public Management also demand that governments need to run on three principles: economy, efficiency and effectiveness. The CAG reports broadly promote these three goals. Insofar as priorities are concerned, the state agencies may have to go for a comprehensive *plan of action* for achieving the goal of universalisation of elementary education involving state agencies, civil society groups and business groups too. Optimisation of resources can be expected if all the partners work for a 'convergence model' for better performance in the social sector. The promised 6 per cent of GDP to education as promised in CMP (Common Minimum Programme) can be effectively put to use if only the present management practices for utilisation of finances undergo change.

Meanwhile, the students of governance have to note the interesting developments which are going to influence the accountability domain of Indian administration. One relates to the reform of administration of Government of India's expenditure with the focus on efficient utilisation of financial outlays to enhance intended outcomes. The Finance Minister of the Union Government presented to Parliament the Outcome Budget 2005-06, outcomes being identified and targets set by the Ministries and Departments. This exercise is limited for the present programmes like Sarva Siksha Abhiyan, National Rural Employment Guarantee Programme, Mid-day Meal, Integrated Child Development, National Highways and selected components of *Bharat Nirman*.

This initiative introduces a new dimension to accountability. It is indeed a governance reform as the Programme Outcome and Response Monitoring Division (PORM), a new unit created in the Planning Commission, serves a useful function of keeping an eye on the targets and the processes of implementation. It must also be added here that outlays do not necessarily get translated into outcomes. The new unit, the Planning Commission's Programme Outcome and Response Monitoring Division can ensure delivery of outcomes which help in evolving cost effective measures to fill implementation deficits. This is especially so in the social sector. It also helps the CAG to investigate what causes the gap between expectations and outcomes and helps in developing a strategic administrative action plan. This facilitates long term institutional and capacity-building measures for putting in place a corrective mechanism. The civil society too can take note of the deficit in the process of implementation and can put pressure on the system for better outcomes.

The initiative must be seen again in the context of India's place in the HDI. As per the HDI of the year 2005, out of 177 countries, India is occupying 127th place (Human Development Report, 2005, UNDP). This only shows the need for overhauling our implementation strategies and taking stronger measures for better performance in this vital sector. The second major development that calls for mention here is a move by the Central Government to bring in a bill to dispense with the role of CAG of India in auditing the accounts of the public sector undertakings (PSUs) in India and Government of India companies. A Committee has been constituted recently to draft a bill to do away with the role of the CAG in about 1200 Government companies and PSUs, based on the recommendations of the J.J. Irani Committee. Similar attempts were made earlier in the years 1997, 2001 and 2003 to introduce such a measure. However, the respective Parliamentary Standing Committees stonewalled the measure aimed at entrusting the CAG's functions to the Chartered Accountants. The Parliamentary observers were of the opinion that the Irani Committee recommendations are very hasty, as a level-playing field to PSUs can be accorded only by removing the supplementary audit. Further, it was pointed out by the observers that the Chartered Accountants do not go into all aspects and certainly cannot discharge social responsibilities or watchdog functions of statutory CAG.

The aforementioned points indicate the changes that are likely to come into the domain of accountability. In an interesting work entitled *Controlling Government's Spending*, Premchand[26] observes that audit reports are frequently delayed and most of them concentrate on financial and regulatory audit. This, he adds, does not include policy aspects and it mostly depends for its success on the legislative support. It may be interesting here to observe that the performing aspects of programmes and projects, and their linkages of financial resources are not specified. For instance, except the media, the people have very little information for assessing the efficiency or outcomes of a project. In one of the media reports[27] it was pointed out that the Rs. 650 crore educational intervention, channeled through the District Primary

Education Project for stepping up universalisation of elementary education, has not succeeded to the extent the policymakers visualised. It was pointed out that more than 60 per cent cannot even write, read or attempt numeracy. The report shows that the District Primary Education Programme (DPEP) in Bihar, West Bengal and Rajasthan is faring better, compared to AP. As the student progresses from class to class, the percentage of those who are not proficient in all the three Rs. i.e., reading, writing and numeracy, is increasing. This vindicates reports submitted by the CAG on the DPEP.

Conclusion

The major challenge of the democratic governance is to continue with the reforms, improve the growth, financial health of the systems, to enable competition and acceleration of economic growth while ensuring the accountability. With the idea that accountability has a central point for the effective governance, it emerges as response to many factors - global concerns about the crisis of governance in many sectors. Challenges to democratic governance and accountability amount to the recognition of its potentials in the process of globalisation and sustainable development. Effective responses to those challenges can be the basis for new models of governance and problem-resolving desperately required in the rapidly changing scenario of the world.

Notes and References

1. Since April 1974 the Government of India introduced a revised accounting structure to ensure better financial control and accountability. A five-tier classification was adopted, i.e., sectoral; major head; minor head; sub-head; and detailed head of accounts. Sectoral classification has grouped the functions of government under General Services, social & community services and economic services. For details see Sarada A, Public Finance in India, New Delhi, Kanishka, 2004, pp. 144-145.
2. Pradeep Sahi and Uma Medury (eds.), *Governance for Development: Issues and Strategies*, , New Delhi, Prentice-Hall of India Private Limited, 2003, p. ii.

3. Mohit Bhattacharya, "Nexus between accountability and good governance: conceptual with two connotations: answerability and enforcement", in *Governance for Development*, pp. 32-33.
4. V.S. Prasad ,*Governance for Development : Key Concerns,* pp. 12-14.
5. Uma Medury, "Effective Governance: the New Public Management Perspective" in *Governance for Development*, 2003, pp. 21-23.
6. Kuldeep Mathur, "Good Governance and Pursuit of transparency in Administration: The Indian Efforts", in *Governance for Development*, pp. 47-49.
7. See 'Foreword' of *Anti-Corruption Measures In South Eastern Europe Civil Society's Involvement*, Organization for Economic Co-operation and Development (OECD), 2003.
8. *The Enabling environment for Civil Society's participation in fight against corruption in South Eastern Europe*, Organization for Economic Co-operation and Development (OECD), 2003, p. 10.
9. Hoshiar Singh and Pradeep Sachdeva, *Administrative Theory*, Allahabad, Kitab Mahal, 1999, p. 309.
10. Durga Das Basu, *Constitution of India: An Introduction*, New Delhi, Wadhwa & Co., July 1993, pp. 195-198.
11. Ibid., p. 198.
12. Vide Re-examination of India's Administrative System, with special reference to administration of government's Industrial and Commercial Enterprises, Government of India,1956, pp. 12-13, 27-29.
13. UC Agarwal "Governance for Development", *Indian Journal of Public Administration*, Golden Jubilee Special Number on Governance, January-March 2004, Vol. L. No. 1, p. 28.
14. Ibid., p. 28.
15. Government of Andhra Pradesh, *Report of the Comptroller & Auditor General of India (Civil)*, 2003, pp 2-23. Out of the developmental expenditure of Rs.18,504 crores, during the reporting year 2002-2003, social services accounted for 51 per cent, expenditure on General Education, Health, Medical and Family Welfare, Water Supply and Sanitation constituted 72 per cent to the expenditure on social sector. Despite lions share to this sector, the end result appears to be discouraging. Also see, *The Hindu* (Hyderabad), July 29, 2004.

16. Ibid., p. 15.
17. Ibid., p.131.
18. See Mahendra Dev and Sridevi, *Social Sector Expenditures in Andhra Pradesh*, Paper presented at the Annual Conference of AP Economic Association, Chittoor, 2003.
19. Ibid.
20. Government of Andhra Pradesh, *Report of the Comptroller and Auditor General of India (Civil)*, 2003, Ibid., p. 131.
21. *Report of the Comptroller and Auditor General of India*, 2003, pp. xxi-xxii.
22. See *Report of CAG*, 2002, p. xviii.
23. See *Report of CAG*, 2002, p. 54.
24. See *Report of CAG*, 2001, p. 99.
25. See *Report of CAG*, 2001, p. 2.
26. Premchand A., *Controlling Government's Expenditure: The Ethos, Ethics and Economics of Expenditure Management*, New Delhi, Oxford Publishing House, 2005, p. 217.
27. See *Eenadu Daily* (Hyderabad), July 31, 2004

8

Righting Governance or Governing Rights? Tripura (2000)

Samir Kumar Das

The classical liberal theory views rights necessarily in opposition to the state and its governance. Thus, rights are considered as inalienable and the state is always looked upon as a potential encroacher on individual rights. The state in other words, is always held in suspicion. Proponents of the theory were therefore keen on delimiting the authority of the state and providing the individual citizens with certain 'basic' rights in case, the state encroaches on their inalienable rights. The 'basic' rights are means of securing the rights that the individual citizens view as the conditions of survival and efflorescence of their personalities. 'Right to rebellion' is one such right that invests the individual citizen with the right to defy a state – of course under certain conditions - that takes away or threatens to take away her inalienable rights. Rights in liberal political parlance are seen as conditions that need to be wrested away from the state through constant movements and struggles. Social contract may institute the political body called the state, but is no permanent guarantee against the violation and transgression of rights by the state. It is interesting to note that rights, according to the liberal political theory, are located outside the framework of state and its governance. The state is called upon to respect them as much as the people are expected to assert them by way of constantly redefining and widening their horizon and thereby almost proportionally restricting and delimiting the scope of the state and its governance. Consequently, no effort is made to take rights into the framework of governance, for the individual's entitlement to rights does not depend on what the state should do – its governance – but rather on what it should not.

Present-day advocacies for governance particularly of 'good governance' turn the classical liberal problematic literally by its head by way of subordinating and surrendering as it were the discourse of rights to the imperative of governance and not vice versa. Governance, according to these advocacies, is the condition of individual and in some cases, group rights and denial of rights is attributed to failures in governance. While governance, as we know, has become multi-centred in the age of globalization with the state and its *government* being one - and not necessarily the most important - of the many centres and agencies, the recent accent on rights forms an inseparable part of the discourse of governance. Rights are thus sought to be taken into the heart of the framework of governance and the assumption is that rights cannot be enjoyed without governance being substantially improved and bettered. Governance, in other words, is sought to be *righted* in all these pleas and advocacies. Rights are what the tools and instruments of governance provide to us; they come as 'services' rendered by the agencies of governance. Consequently, the citizen is seen as the 'user and consumer' of these services.[1] Governance therefore deprives the rights of their most valued property – the agency and subjectivity of citizens. The introductory part of this paper proposes to probe into these pleas and advocacies being made for righting governance.

Perhaps, UNDP's *Human Development Report* of 1999 was the first of its kind to have made a comprehensive advocacy for 'putting human concerns and human rights at the centre of international policy and action.' It urged upon the states and all relevant multilateral agencies for being guided by what it calls, 'a new global ethic' of values enshrined in the UN Charter and the Universal Declaration of Human Rights. It felt 'the need for translating them into the principles and practices of global governance'.[2] Here, rights as we have said do not denote the outside of governance. On the contrary, they are supposed to provide the criteria (among others, of course) on the basis of which the 'goodness' of 'good governance' can be judged, measured, evaluated and accordingly acted upon - whether by offering aid or censoring the states. The UNDP formulations on defining rights as criteria of governance have been inspired by the writings of such human development economists as Amartya Sen, Mahbub Ul Haq and Partha Dasgupta etc. who sought to re-conceptualise rights on the basis of what is now being fashionably called, the human rights index (HRI). HRI has been variously defined as political freedom index (PFI) by Mahbub Ul Haq[3] and citizenship index (CI) by Partha Dasgupta.[4] In the same year *Human development in South Asia* published from Mahbub Ul Haq Human Development Centre, for example, lays down: "For good civic governance to flourish, a solid framework of human rights must be established."[5] Governance, according to this framework, is a function of constantly refining and improving upon its tools and instruments designed to the objective of 'realizing rights'. The Centre calls for improving and bettering governance primarily through more efficient law enforcement and adjudication and most importantly, civil society vigilantism. *The UNDP Report* of 2000 makes it clearer:

> *Human development ... brings dynamic, long-term perspective to the fulfillment of rights. It directs attention to the socio-economic context in which rights can be realized – or threatened. The concepts and tools of human development provide a systematic assessment of economic and institutional constructs to the realization of rights – as well as of the resources and policies available to overcome them.*[6]

We argue that these attempts at righting governance – current and fashionable as they may be since the end of the last decade - are also means of *governing*[7] rights in at least two mutually overlapping ways: First, the governance-oriented theory of rights refuses to take note of the fact that the emergence of rights-perspective necessarily triggers off certain social transformations that unless taken care of, are bound to implicitly push a significant number of people outside the realm of governance. It assumes often misleadingly, that all societies are necessarily rights-based societies. Rights-consciousness, as we argue, threatens to tear a hitherto existent placid and face-to-face society of neighbours apart. The tools and instruments of governance force the society to remain divided into two unbridgeable quantities and throw a vast multitude of people from out of its ambit. Governance at the same time serves as the principle of exclusion.

Second, the perspective on rights does not per se offer any means of reconciling the contending and at times, rivaling rights claims in the society – particularly those of the natives and the immigrants in a state like Tripura. While it disrupts and breaches a hitherto existent society of neighbours, the perspective does not have the capacity for holding the society together. On the other hand, a society of neighbours can no longer serve as the basis of making and most importantly, reconciling our contending rights claims. Human development perspective of course speaks of the necessity of creating and resuscitating civil societies as instruments of governance supplementing and more often than not taking upon itself the functions of the government by the state. Thus, the report on *Human Development in South Asia 1999: The Crisis of Governance*, prepared by the Mahbub Ul Haq Human Development Centre,. argues:

As demonstrated in the 1997 and 1998 Reports on Human Development in South Asia, self-organization within civil society, including private sector, helps fill the void left by the limited role South Asian governments (with the notable exception of Sri Lanka) have played in providing social services to the poor and investing in their nation's abundant human capital.[8]

It essentially views civil society as a single, monolithic and albeit unproblematic unit that also serves as an efficient vehicle of development. Civil society seldom exists in such an unproblematic manner in any society including the societies mentioned above. The actually existing civil societies are much messier than what human development protagonists would have us believe. The civil society that the above reports and probably many more following them promise to build and rejuvenate is simply oblivious to the imperative necessity of reconciling the contending and often rivaling rights claims. The agenda of civil society building (CSB) is therefore seriously flawed in the discourse of governance.

Insofar as the act of governance throws a vast multitude of people from out of its ambit, the latter, one must remember, do not necessarily constitute what Partha Chatterjee would have called, the 'political society'. For, they are too insignificant to force the civil society and the actors and stakeholders of governance to enter into some form of strategic alliance and compromise with them. Civil and political societies although take on two distinct courses are, as he argues, locked up in an intricate web of compromises and alliances between them having implications for both of them. Political society is an object not of law but of what he calls, 'paralegal arrangements'.[9] But, the society of neighbours that is thrown into disarray by the governance-induced rights-consciousness is forever lost in oblivion and the tools and instruments of governance are simply incapable of making them find a place in its ambit. They suffer a double jeopardy: they lose the world of their own – that of the society of neighbours with the advent of rights consciousness and at the same time are denied entry into the world composed of the rights-bearing agents of governance – the civil society in Chatterjee's sense.

A Society of Neighbours

Rights are claimed when they are or face the threat of being violated. What we get without making any claim to it, is better called, opportunities or privileges rather than rights. The claimants of rights are therefore in a necessarily oppositional relationship with those from whom they claim their rights. One has to be a stranger in order to be able to voice and articulate one's rights claims. A neighbour is always bound by the protocols of decency and neighbourliness that, as we will see, also restrain her from making the claim for fear of alienating others or what Tocqueville describes as 'his indiscretion':

> *The stranger often learns truths in the home of his host that the latter would perhaps conceal from a friend; with a stranger one is relieved of obligatory silence; one does not fear his indiscretion because he is passing through.*[10]

A society of strangers as the site where rights claims are articulated and negotiated by the contending parties threatens to breach and disrupt our everyday neighbourly relations. While the truth of violations is always difficult to be established, making the rights claims in the first place has not been an easy proposition in modern history. This paper makes a plea for reconstructing civil society and develops its argument on the assumption that civil society makes the voicing of rights claims possible. A civil society that makes rights claims possible, is not a society of neighbours but one of what Tocqueville would have called, 'strangers'. A society of neighbours, as Tocqueville warns us, is not the same as a civil society.

The argument that we seek to drive home in this paper is simple: much of our present-day enthusiasm with governance and civil society fails to see the limits it *inherently* imposes on prevailing modes of representation by some groups of people in it and thereby in the sphere of institutional politics. It draws our attention to the existence of some alternative spaces that apparently lie outside the scope of conventionally understood civil society. For want of a better term, we describe it as a society of neighbourliness. For it is a space where the people lead their everyday lives by almost constantly rearticulating and renegotiating the otherwise given communal solidarities and most importantly, make their everyday living possible. I will argue that it is a space, which involves a good deal of crossing of the given ethnic and communal lines and with it a considerable blurring of their differences. The re-articulation of course assumes different forms in different parts of India and there is enough scope for further research on a comparative basis. But whatever be its particular form, it never transcends itself into a civil society understood in the classical liberal sense of the term. We need however to note that these solidarities look immensely fragile and are seen often to cave in, in the face of severe ethnic and communal conflicts. If anything seems to characterize the ethnic conflicts in today's India, it is certainly the suddenness and unexpected nature of their occurrence. In almost every case, the ethnic and communal riots take us by surprise, as if we are not prepared for them. They spring a surprise precisely because the communities conflicting between them always perceive themselves as 'good neighbours' to each other till the moment conflict breaks out between them. Any commonplace narrative of conflict prefers to source it to an outsider - a third party. Makiko Kimura's study on the riots of Nellie in February 1983 follows the same commonplace narrative.[11] While the Tiwas (Lalungs) whom she interviewed, were by their admission, in good terms with the Bengali Muslims living in the same locality and attribute the riots to the incitement of the All-Assam Students' Union (AASU) leaders who had come from outside and instigated them, the outsiders refused to accept the responsibility of the killing on such a wanton scale. The genealogy of conflict in other words is thus located outside the conflicting parties. The paper merely underscores the importance of turning our attention to this evidently fragile neighbourly space and of course its limited efficacy for being a guarantee of rights.

A society of neighbours is not the place where people can communicate amongst themselves in the language of rights. A closed society of neighbours hardly confers recognition on the rights claims of the strangers. A society of strangers, according to Bryant, is what makes the circulation of rights claims possible within a society. When everyone is regarded as a potentially rights-bearing entity, no one is supposed to be discriminated against on the ground of being a stranger to others. Being neighbourly to each other cannot be the ground for claiming rights. As he argues:

Within defined boundaries, it treats strangers with different interests and sensibilities as all the same, as citizens with the rights that all citizens possess, as persons worthy of our consideration because they are human beings, or whatever.[12]

Besides, neighbourliness in political theory has been defined in contradistinction with civility. While neighbourliness is governed by the principle of equality where differences between individuals are seldom taken into account, civility, according to Hannah Arendt, is the realm where individuals and groups clamour for recognition of their individual identities.[13] Neighbourliness therefore is a private virtue; civility is not. Neighbourliness first of all requires the submergence of individuality. Neighbourly activities are always informed by the identity of perspectives. The persons who are neighbours to each other are not supposed to disagree or differ on their perspectives. Secondly, while neighbourliness is governed by the imperative of living like neighbours that at the same time makes 'living' possible, civility is governed by certain impersonal rules on the basis of which individual excellence is recognized and rewarded. Although this makes living possible, it also prevents us from claiming those rights that pose a threat to our neighbourly coexistence. Neighbourliness draws us closer together; our rights awareness keeps us separate and separable entities. The rules of civility also benefit the 'strangers and anonymous others who live in a community or pass through, or others in far-away places'.[14] The rules exist independently of those who are supposed to be bound by it. Neighbourliness, one must note, also allows a certain bending (and not necessarily breaking) of these rules if that helps in ensuring the coexistence of neighbours. There are no given rules in the case of neighbours. The given-ness of rules cannot be the reason for the breach of neighbourly trust and relations. Rules too are improvised in keeping with the requirements of neighbours and neighbourly coexistence. It is over and above a commitment to the imperative of living like neighbours and in certain contexts, living together and responding to what the imperative demands from us. Thus to cite a recent example, in Belgachhia (a neighbourhood in north Kolkata, West Bengal, India) back in 2003, the organisers of a local Puja committee (namely, Olaichanditala Sarbojanin Durgotsab Committee) reportedly ran short of funds almost to the point of cancelling the annual Durga Puja (a Hindu religious festival) in the locality. When the Muslim neighbours came to the rescue and saw to it that it was celebrated with the same fanfare and gaiety, did they come forward because Islam had said so? Islam as a religion is opposed to idolatry and the counterexamples of Muslims refusing to bail out the Hindus in similar distress or vice versa are by no means rare. The rules of Islam were not considered as relevant at least momentarily in the interest of good neighbourliness. Yet the Muslims came forward with a wonderful neighbourly gesture. They had thought it imperative to respond to it and steer their Hindu neighbours from out of an unprecedented financial hardship.

We define neighbourliness as a commitment in which we as moral beings are bound together by the overarching imperative of living and coexisting with others irrespective of their caste, creed, religion, ethnicity or place of birth. It is this imperative that is powerful enough to create new religions and break the older ones. It is interesting to see how the imperative shapes our concerns for others in the light of the burgeoning researches particularly in West Bengal on the periodic marketplaces (*haat*)[15], colonies and settlements established in the wake of Partition by the refugees (1947)[16] and the celebratory congregations, religious festivals and assemblies (*melas* and *parbans*)[17]. First of all, it frees us of the obligation of being overtly rational. It is a space where we do not mind losing out in terms of our rational and utilitarian calculations. Thus, the local marketplace is not only a place for buying and selling of goods and services and thereby maximizing our mutually contradictory interests; it is also the site of local culture, cult and entertainment that binds us together notwithstanding our contradictory interests as buyers and sellers.

Secondly, it is a space where one's being a Hindu or a Muslim is simply irrelevant to one's membership to it. It does not mean that one has to cease to be a Hindu or a Muslim for that matter, to be a member of this space. It only means that this does not necessarily become either a constraint or a privilege for those who happen to be its members.

Thirdly, it is a space that facilitates communication. It does not guarantee rights in the sense in which we have used the term. It is on the contrary, a space where *freedoms* rather than rights are protected, safeguarded and secured. It is by way of enjoying these freedoms that we can live as neighbours. The freedoms are the enabling conditions of coexistence, not the reasons per se justifying and supporting our rights claims. Liberal theory – whether classical or its newer variety, fails to recognize that there could be many societies where freedoms as minimal conditions of living and coexistence are sufficient: their value is not determined by the contribution they make towards the articulation and voicing of rights claims. These are not after all rights-based societies. The problem is that liberal theory in its penchant for reason rules out the presence of such societies, which are governed by the minimal rules of freedom. The anthropology of liberal theory is therefore partial at its best and jaundiced at its worst. Freedoms in such societies are valuable per se; they are not supposed to be a means to any further end of claiming rights. For Habermas on the other hand, living and coexistence in the society per se does not hold out any pleasure for us unless it promises the fulfillment of reason and accomplishment of our rights claims. For him, living per se does not offer any pleasure and excitement unless backed by reasons. Habermas's is more a theory of reason than a theory of neighbours living together and enjoying the charm and pleasure of togetherness. He too - like his Enlightenment predecessors - was interested in founding a society on the basis of reason and the language of rights. Enjoyment of rights presupposes the existence of a 'culture of rights' that binds the society together and prevents it from falling apart.[18]

We may end up this brief outline by way of deriving at least three major implications of the concept of neighbourliness mentioned here: One, it should not be confused with what Habermas described as, 'plebian public sphere'.[19] Although substantially restricted to the underclass, our concept of neighbourliness shows a remarkable dissimilarity to his idea that even the 'plebian public sphere' remains wedded to 'bourgeois intentions'. The bourgeois pursuit of rights for example, is ruled out in this space. It is a society that is minimal in the sense that it is not organized on the basis of any maximalist project of reason. Two, it is true that neighbourliness cuts across the ethnic lines. But, it cannot be called, rational in the sense of completely cutting across the ethnic and community lines and basing itself on universal reason. In this connection, we have to distinguish the communal from what we choose to call, the communitarian. Briefly stated, while the communal pits us against each other along the already enumerated ethnic and communal lines, the communitarian is what defines a larger cultural ethos - its perceived universe - and inspires people to relate to and be at peace with each other. More than a bounded solidarity, communitarian ties prepare us for coexistence and a much larger, relatively open and unbounded solidarity that cuts across given ethnic and communal lines. Thus, when the 'beggars' (the homeless) on the Calcutta streets open common kitchen run on whatever they collect from begging and dine together irrespective of their caste and communal ties, they bring as it were a new community into existence.[20] In many ways, however the nature of solidarity resembles that of narrowly defined communities in India. But, these are essentially neighbourly solidarities that are situated between the narrow ethnic solidarities on one hand and the broad civic solidarities on the other. Three, it is a space that is extremely fragile in the sense that it looks disappointingly incapable of withstanding the challenges coming from the communal. The frequent occurrence of communal riots exposes the fragility of the neighbourly space and takes everyone involved in them by surprise. Makiko Kimura's study on Nellie riots, Assam (1983) demonstrates how both the aggressors and the victims – more than the outsiders - were surprised for their involvement in them.

I will now take the following case, which is by no means unique to the history of contemporary India, as our point of entry into the space of neighbourliness mentioned above. It aptly sums up how the existing neighbourly ties between the Bengali Muslims and the Jamatias in Tripura could not withstand the conflicts that finally set them apart.

Tripura Women's Commission[21] initiated a suo moto investigation on the basis of a report of gang rape of some young Bengali-speaking Muslim women in a remote village called, Raiyabari, of the district of South Tripura. *Syandan* — a local daily carried out the report as a news item on 11 January 2000 and the investigation team that was set up for the purpose left for the village on 22 January 2000. It was reported that a group of armed militants belonging to the National Liberation Front of Tripura (NLFT) had allegedly committed atrocities on the women including several minor girls. Interestingly not a single complaint was lodged either by the victims or any of the villagers even after nearly all of them (123 families in all) had left Raiyabari and decided to settle in Udaipur – the nearest town. Raiyabari - as a member of the investigating team wrote in the fragmentary notes of her personal diary, became 'deserted, empty and solitary'.[22] While militant raids in the village for extortion were not infrequent, atrocities on the women reported in the local press mentioned above were certainly the first of its kind. Two of the National Liberation Front of Tripura (NLFT) militants named by the rape victims to the investigating team were Halflong Jamatia and Chhalgazi Jamatia – both of whom were pretty well known to the victims and their families as good neighbours. According to Zahera – a rape victim herself, both of them used to come to their house and take food like the sweet pancakes etc. (*pitha-titha*). Even at the peak of fierce interethnic tensions, the local Jamatias (the tribals) have by their own admission offered them food and shelter whenever their lives were at risk. The above case is neither new nor unique in the otherwise long history of interethnic conflicts in contemporary India. Indeed as I will argue, it aptly sums up the complexities involved in the relation of rights to governance and vice and versa by way of bringing almost all the relevant discourses into play.

Neighbours Fall Apart

At one level, the case cited above throws light on the ambivalence between the central NLFT leadership and the Jamatias of Raiyabari neighbourhood that the former looks upon as the potential base for its cadreship and support. It took quite a long time for the Bengali-speaking Muslims of Raiyabari to take the painful decision of actually leaving their village and finally migrating to Udaipur. The initial extortion raids by the tribal militants that finally culminated in the unprecedented incident of gang rape were powered by the imaginary of ethnic homeland and coupled with it, the imperative necessity of cleansing the village that supposedly falls under its proposed area, of 'the Muslims' who as the Roy Commission set up by the State Government for conducting a judicial inquiry as per the recommendations of the Women's Commission, paraphrases, 'drove out their forefathers by way of paying nominal prices'.

It took equally long for the Jamatias of the neighbourhood to actually carry out the raids and finally the atrocity of gang rape. While much has been said about the rights of rape victims, nothing whatsoever has been mentioned about the powerful imaginary of ethnic homeland that circulates around the thesis of 'colonization by the Bengalis' and serves as the fountainhead of collective rights. The fear of being outnumbered and thereby losing their language and culture dates back to the merger of the princely state into the Indian Union. The Tribal Convention organized in February 1980 at Toidu, Tripura resolved to drive out the 'foreigners' (defined as those who have migrated to Tripura after the day of her merger in 1949) from Tripura. The riots of 1980 including the one in Mandai closely followed the Convention. In the pamphlet entitled 'Tripuray ganahatyar janya Mandai ki ekmatra sakshi?' (Is Mandai the only witness to the genocide in Tripura?), Harinath Debbarma – a tribal leader himself, accused the State administration and the security forces for having perpetrated atrocities in the tribal areas.[23] The same foreigners' issue figured centrally in the speech that Bijoy Hrangkhawl - an ex-insurgent himself, had delivered at a meeting of the Indigenous Group of Populations in Geneva in 2002. This happens to be the running theme of tribal politics whether of its insurgent or of its parliamentary variety.

In Tripura long back in 1876-77, the indigenous people formed more than two-third of the total population of 91,759. More than hundred years later in 1991, they constituted less than one third of the state's population of 2,757,205. Immigration from outside the tiny princely state was encouraged by the Maharaja and his nobility when they used to depute the Bengalis mostly as priests and in different advisory capacities. Two legislative edicts were passed by the palace in 1917 and 1925 making way to the massive acquisition of land for tea cultivation. This actually opened the floodgates of immigration mostly from the plains. Moreover, Bengali being the language of administration, the immigration of land-hungry peasants from East Bengal continued unabated. Besides the peasants, artisans also joined the golden trek driven out from native land by recurrent famines, usury and landlords' oppression. By 1930, as the number of immigrants had risen alarmingly and the indigenous people were facing the threat of being pushed away from their traditionally held land, the Maharaja declared the famous policy of tribal land reservation by the government decrees of 1931 and 1943 for the Tripuris, Jamatias,

Reangs, Noatias and the Halams. Massive internal displacement took place in the first half of the 1940s when the Reangs – the largest indigenous community in Tripura – revolted against the Maharaja and the movement was brutally suppressed. Reangs in large number left Amarpur and Udaipur in South Tripura and emigrated in thousands towards the north and also towards the Chittagong Hill Tracts and the Lushai Hills. Thus, Udaipur's Reang population remained stagnant between 1931 (i.e. 2151) and 1961 (i.e. 2374) while in the same thirty years the Reang population in Dharmanagar rose from 735 to 18,834. With the great partition, began the fresh waves of migration in the state, and finally in the eighties, Buddhist Chakma refugees entered in sizeable numbers from the Chittagong Hill Tracts in the wake of the conflict there and army operation against the rebellion. The Tripura Upajati Juba Samity (TUJS) formed in 1967 led in 1978 to the first ever militant movement against the immigrants organized by the Tripura National Volunteers (TNV), which soon started attacking settlers and symbols of government authority, including at times security forces. Land question became crucial, and with *jhum* (swidden or slash-and-burn) cultivation being systematically disturbed and finally destroyed, clashes began to erupt. The percentage increase in Tripura's population (77.19) during 1981-1991 has been the highest, trailed by the other two border states of Assam (53.26) and Meghalaya (75.43) in the region. Each district during this decade registered a rate of increase that is higher than the national average.

The Mandai riots of June 1980 were the first of their kind in which the Bengali settlers were targeted in a large and massive genocide. It also caused enormous displacement. The Dinesh Singh Committee estimated that nearly 3,72,000 persons had been affected by the riots of whom about 1,50,000 people belonged to indigenous communities. Nearly 2,00,000 people had to be sheltered in camps. The number of total relief camps was 141; nearly 35,000 houses were gutted; and the estimated loss of property stood at a staggering Rs. 21 crores (1 crore = 100,000,00). About 13,000 persons lost their lives.[24] Again in 1989 and 1990, an estimated 2614 families were displaced from severely affected areas such as Khowai, Sadar and Bishalgarh subdivisions due to interethnic clashes. By 2000, the civil-political-military movement of the indigenous people against the settlers had acquired a certain stridency so much so that a ragtag combination of political forces with the name of Indigenous People's Front of Tripura won the elections of the Tripura Tribal Autonomous District Council. The decade of 1980s was marked by violence, large-scale settler-native conflicts, army operations, rape of women by the security forces and militants, kidnapping and increasing ethnic polarisation. And in 2000 and 2001, as many as 692 civilians were killed over and above 47 security personnel and 84 militants who also had lost their lives. The TUJS demanded from the Government of India more powers to the Autonomous District Council, barbed wire fencing of the entire length of the 856 km long boundary with Bangladesh, 'pushback' of immigrants who had arrived after 1971 (a remarkable climb down from its earlier demand of making 1949 as the cutoff year), and the introduction of the inner-line permit system to the Tribal Council area. In December 1999, the NLFT leaders launched a programme of 'ethnic cleansing' in the Autonomous District Council areas of Tripura following their decision in a secretly held conclave in Chittagong Hill Tracts of Bangladesh. The events of Raiyabari were one in the series of many that took place as fallouts of this secret programme.

If the indigenous people of Tripura feel alarmed at the almost incessant immigration of the Bengalis predominantly from across the international borders, this has also lent to the politics of settlers a certain stridency and organisation. In desperation, a section of immigrant Bengalis set up an outfit of "Bengali Extremists" in order "to retaliate the killings and acts of depredations". Amra Bangali (literally, 'We, the Bengalis') – the militant orgnisation claiming to represent the ethnic Bengalis pointed to the 'historically, Bengali-dominated' character of Tripura since the days of the Maharaja. The entire Tripura formed part of the map of 'Bangalisthan' (the land of the Bengalis) alongside Bangladesh, West Bengal, parts of Assam, Bihar and Orissa. Land has been made an issue in the settlers' politics. It was also pointed out by Amra Bangali that if Tripura Tribal Autonomous Council is formed, its jurisdiction would spread over two-third of Tripura's land mass and the Bengalis would be deprived of their right to land and representation.[25] The 'long term political impact' of 'competitive violence' is 'yet unknown'.[26]

The imaginary of ethnic homeland produces not only riots but also rights. Riots, as I argue, are centred on the contentious rights claims. 'Colonialism - whether by the Bengalis or by the Hindi-speaking settlers or by New Delhi' or any of their combination is perhaps the most important running theme of insurgent discourses in contemporary India. The case gives us some idea of how the insurgent discourse of rights slowly though not irreversibly, grips the imagination of the local tribals – the Jamatias of the neighbourhood. Our tools and procedures of governance do not seem to have any clue for taking them into account and examining how they stand in a perpetually uneasy relation to other and no less significant discourses of victimhood.

It is important to see how good neighbourliness that existed between the Jamatias and the Bengali-speaking Muslims of Raiyabari suddenly gave way to production of two mutually divergent rights discourses and violence between them. Although the split appears to be externally engineered by the NLFT leadership and in many other cases by Amra Bangali, an ultra-chauvinist organization claiming to represent the ethnic Bengalis, it seems to be aided and abetted by a number of local factors. It happens to be the commonest narrative on any ethnic riot in India. However, two points are of particular significance in this context: One, sheer good neighbourliness was not enough to withstand the pressure of ethnic schism that was apparently developing everywhere outside, except Raiyabari. Good neighbourliness after all is not predicated on the language of rights. There are times when good neighbourliness is earned at the expense of one's rights. Most of the Bengali-speaking Muslims of Assam returned Assamese as their mother tongue till the 1991 census fearing that anything to the contrary might enrage the Varna-Hindu Assamese community. Secondly, ethnic schism in the Northeast is the nursery where consciousness about collective rights takes its roots. Indeed, we may argue that this consciousness can come about only by way of fracturing the good neighbourliness.

The Naga case may be cited as one in contrast. Their respect for the Indian state's right to represent the Indian nation not only speaks of their obeisance to the principle of equality but their earnestness in seeing the Indian nation and the communities the Nagas represent as 'good neighbours' and 'great friends'. The present cease-fire and peace talks according to Kaka D. Iralu have given the 'golden opportunity' of 'restoring peaceful coexistence' with India to the Nagas.[27] Their insistence on such values as friendship, neighbourliness and camaraderie seems to be issued from the overarching principle of equality that informs most of the insurgent discourses of Northeastern India.[28]

The conventional understanding of democratic governance hardly tells us anything about how such mutually exclusive collective rights claims are to be negotiated and settled without taking resort to violence. It is no use addressing the problem of ethnic violence if democratic governance does not address the question of rights. Civil society that is sought to be 'built' (CSB) is hardly sensitive to this problem. While civil society institutions emerging from within the confines of their respective ethnic communities can hardly be expected to address the question of incompatibility between diverse rights discourses (they in many cases are part of the problem), such statutory bodies as the ones mentioned above are more concerned with what Bhabha calls, 'cases' rather than 'causes'[29] and refuse to recognize that the cases of violation are only symptomatic of this deep yet negotiable, incompatibility.

Trust and the Politics of Truth

At another level, the case points to the difficulties the victims or the villagers face in taking up the matter with the relevant political and administrative authorities or in filing their complaints with the local police station and in seeking remedies. While not a single complaint was lodged 'officially', the police according to the report of the Roy Commission, of course received 'complaints orally'. This leads to a divergence between the official and the oral and in the hierarchy between them the official is invariably privileged over the oral. As the Roy Commission finds out: "Since no such information regarding rape on them was given in writing, police might not have been in a position to take any action." It also points out that in the absence of any official complaint the police cannot be blamed for its inaction. There is reason to believe that governance helps in reproducing the hierarchy by way of pushing orality further into the margins and excising it as it were, from its ambit. Notwithstanding the intervention by the Women's Commission, the charges against the accused could not be sustained in the Roy Commission, though of course Halflong Jamatia – one of the accused was subsequently killed in an encounter with the police. As the personal diary referred to above, observes:

I trusted their words. The chairperson of the State Women's Commission trusted them. The State Women's Commission too trusted them. But no one else trusted them. Neither the Government, nor the single-member judicial inquiry commission.

Ironically, truth process seldom coincides with justice process and she as a member-secretary of Tripura Women's Commission can do very little in this respect. This probably is the tragedy that every human rights institution or individual on earth is faced with, including the proverbial Truth and Reconciliation Commission of South Africa. This is symbolic of the deeper problem of converting victims' personal narratives into proofs and evidences of human rights violations. Human rights, as Rorty reminds us, are less about evidences and more about 'the long, sad and sentimental stories' being narrated to us by them. These are less about proofs and more about 'empathy'.[30]

Governance and the Fear Game

At yet another level, governance has to do with the question of enabling the victims and the villagers to lodge their complaints, seek appropriate legal remedies and thereby get entitled to the services that such service-providers as the state are supposed to offer and deliver. The enjoyment of one's rights is contingent on the services delivered by the government agencies. That is why the ratio between a police station and the number of people living within its jurisdiction becomes important. What is it that kept the victims and the villagers from officially registering their complaints while contacting them orally? It is certainly not a question of distance that has to be covered in order to lodge a formal complaint. After all, they contacted the police orally. It is not because rape victims are liable to suffer from the social stigma they do, like in other parts of India. The 'Muslim society' according to the personal diary cited above did not 'desert' them. When a whole community is shamed, it becomes nobody's shame within the community. The Nagas of the present state of Nagaland were 'waiting' for their ethnic cousins displaced in Manipur in June 2001 to come and take shelter there.[31] A report prepared by the Naga People's Movement for Human Rights (NPMHR) observes: "So far the contribution (for providing relief and rehabilitation to the displaced Nagas, SKD) has been internally generated from the Naga communities in and around the affected areas."[32] The shame of losing their homes without putting up the semblance of a battle after all did not haunt them. Shame shared in common by one and all in fact gives the community an occasion to rivet its bonds of unity. It is not because rape for them does not acquire the same humiliation and opprobrium as it is in most of the societies. According to Women's Commission, Zahera Bibi 'did not tell anybody about the incident (let alone officially registering any complaint, SKD) fearing further torture on her in-laws who stayed in Raiyabari still then'. Of course the police reportedly did nothing to allay fears from their minds and the Killa police station was inadequately equipped to do that. As the Roy Commission maintains: '... the strength of the police forces being inadequate, the police kept mum in spite of receiving oral complaints'. As a result, the Commission also found that the police did not pay heed to the complaints 'very seriously'. Zaheras everywhere are the victims of a perpetual asymmetry of fear that weighs against them. They always face the problem of establishing violations into legally entertainable 'truths'. Fear and torture have always served as the time-honoured technologies of extracting the official truth of order and tranquility.

But how do they overcome fear? It is interesting to see how the very act of overcoming fear implies certain bypassing of the established tools and instruments of democratic governance. In this game of fear being met by counter-fear, Zaheras are bound to lose. In the ratio between the number of people and the number of police stations, fear is only seen as a service to be rendered in order to counter fear perpetrated by the militant cadres and seeing it as a 'service' does not in any way reduce its fearfulness. Their experience of being perpetually caught in the asymmetry of fear leads them to lose faith in the fear game and introduce and be part of a new game and a game, which situates itself outside the ambit of democratic governance. The rules of the game are also remarkably different. This is how Meenakshi Sen Bandyopadhyay describes Soma – another rape victim, in her personal diary:

Good to see that she is no longer the yesterday's rape victim - ailing, fearful and puzzled – a straight young woman appears before us. She earns by serving as a domestic help. She is shining with the light of self-confidence.

Now I do not have anything to write in my notebook. They do not know of the provisions for rehabilitating the rape victims prescribed by the Supreme Court; they do not know that even the very ruthless fact of their being raped is doubted. They did not wait for any government aid. Although Muslims by religion, their families did not desert them – stigmatize or humiliate them. They wanted to live and also stood up. My eyes were constantly looking for her - she has grown taller as if her head has risen towards the sky.

They have come back to life all on their own – did not care for any assistance whether governmental or non-governmental. They have proven that life is ever unstoppable, eternally flowing.

They are yet to find a place in the world of democratic governance. They have not waited for it either. It is now for the proponents and practitioners of democratic governance to come to terms with these new realities and subjecting it to the principles of rights audit.

Notes and References

[All translations from non-English sources are mine, SKD]

1. Niraja Gopal Jayal's presentation to the seminar on 'Images of India in the 21st century' organised by the Department of Political Science, University of Calcutta, on 8 October 2004.

2. UNDP, *Human Development Report 1999*, London, Oxford University Press, 1999.
3. Mahbub Ul Haq, *Reflections on Human Development,* New Delhi, OUP, 1995.
4. Partha Dasgupta, *An Inquiry into Well-being and Destitution,* Oxford, Clarendon Press, 1995.
5 Mahbub Ul Haq Human Development Centre, *Human Development in South Asia 1999*, Oxford, Oxford University Press, 1999, p. 131.
6. UNDP, *Human Development Report 2000*, London, Oxford University Press, 2000, p. 2.
7. I use the term in the same sense in which Foucault has used the term 'governmentality'.
8 Mahbub Ul Haq Human Development Centre, op. cit., p.128.
9. Partha Chatterjee, *The Politics of the Governed: Reflections on Popular Politics in the Most of the World*, New Delhi, Permanent Black, 2004.
10. Alexis De Tocqueville, *Democracy in America,* London, University of Chicago Press, 2000, p.14.
11. Makiko Kimura's address on 'Nellie riots' to the Centre for Studies in Social Sciences, Kolkata on November 24, 2004.
12. Christopher G. A. Bryant, 'Civic nation, civil society and civil religion' in John A. Hall, *Civil Society: Theory, History, Comparison,* Cambridge, Polity, 1995, p.147
13. Hannah Arendt, *The Human Condition*, Chicago, University of Chicago Press, 1958, p.41.
14. Ian Shapiro & Casiano Hacker-Cordon (eds.), *Democracy's Value*, Cambridge, Cambridge University Press, 1999, p. 146.
15. The collection entitled *Banglar Haat* (haats of Bengal) although not a very well researched volume provides an example. See, Pranab Sarkar (ed.), *Lok*, 'Banglar haat' (in Bengali) [*Haats* of Bengal], Book fair Number, 2002.
16. See, Pradip Kumar Bose (ed.), *Refugees in West Bengal: Institutional Practices and Contested Identities*, Kolkata, Calcutta Research Group, 2000.
17. See, Sudhir Chakrabarty, *Paschimbanger Mela O Mahotsab* (in Bengali), [The folk congregations and festivals of West Bengal], Kolkata, Pustak Bipani, 1996.

18. A fairly recent argument along this line has been made in the context of India by Rajeev Bhargava in 'The Right to Culture' in *Social Scientist*, 18 (10), October, 1990.
19. Thomas McCarthy, 'Introduction' to Jurgen Habermas, *The Structural Transformation of the Public Sphere: An Inquiry into Category of Bourgeois Society*, trans. by Thomas Burger with the assistance of Frederick Lawrence, London, Polity, 1989, p. XVIII.
20. I have borrowed from the survey conducted by Debamoy Ganguly submitted as part of the M.A. dissertation (entitled 'Street Dwellers of Kolkata: A Survey') to the Department of Political Science, University of Calcutta in 2003 on the street-dwellers of Kolkata.
22. The reports of all commissions referred to in this paper are yet unpublished and have been read from the original.
23. I am grateful to Meenakshi Sen Bandyopadhyay, then the member secretary of Tripura Women's Commission, for giving me access to her personal diaries.
24. The pamphlet does not contain any of the publication data.
25. All figures are taken from Government of Tripura, *Relief and Rehabilitation of People Affected by 1980 Disturbances*, Agartala, Government of Tripura, 1982.
25. Jiban Chakrabarty, *Tripura: Tiris Theke Asi* (in Bengali), [Tripura: from the Thirties to the Eighties], Agartala, Barnamala Prakashani, 1983.
26. Shibapada De, *Illegal migrations in the Northeast: a Study of Migrants from Bangladesh*, Kolkata, Maulana Abul Kalam Azad Institute of Asian Studies, p.132.
27. Kaka D. Iralu, *Nagaland and India: The Blood and Tears*, publication data not available, 2000, p.16.
28. Many Naga civil society leaders whom I had the opportunity of interviewing pointed out that 'the Nagas want to live like good neighbours to India'.
29. Homi Bhabha, 'Cultural choices and the revision of freedom' in Austin Sarat & Thomas R. Kearns (eds.), *Human Rights: Concepts, Contexts, Contingencies*, The Amherst Series in Law, Jurisprudence, and Social Thought, Ann Arbor, The University of Michigan Press, 2002, p. 45
30. Richard Rorty, *Truth and Progress: Philosophical Chapters,* Vol. 3. Cambridge, Cambridge University Press, 1998, pp. 167-85.

31. My interview with Achan Mungleng from Imphal in December 2004.
32. Naga People's Movement for Human Rights, 'Summary report on the conditions of the internally displaced persons (IDPs) from the Imphal valley to the Naga hills areas of Manipur – its repercussion on (sic) Indo-Naga ceasefire', 2001, mimeo.

PART - III

Landmark Act: Right to Information

MINISTRY OF LAW AND JUSTICE

(Legislative Department)

New Delhi, the 21st *June,* 2005/*Jyaistha* 31, 1927 (*Saka*)

The following Act of Parliament received the assent of the President on the 15th June, 2005, and is hereby published for general information:—

THE RIGHT TO INFORMAT!ON ACT, 2005

No. 22 of 2005

[15*th June*, 2005.]

An Act to provide for setting out the practical regime of right to information for citizens to secure access to information under the control of public authorities, in order to promote transparency and accountability in the working of every public authority, the constitution of a Central Information Commission and State Information Commissions and for matters connected therewith or incidental thereto.

WHEREAS the Constitution of India has established democratic Republic; AND WHEREAS democracy requires an informed citizenry and transparency of information which are vital to its functioning and also to contain corruption and to hold Governments and their instrumentalities accountable to the governed;

AND WHEREAS revelation of information in actual practice is likely to conflict with other public interests including efficient operations of the Governments, optimum use of limited fiscal resources and the preservation of confidentiality of sensitive information;

2 THE GAZETTER OF INDIA EXTRAORDINARY [PART II—
AND WHEREAS it is necessary to harmonise these conflicting interests while preserving the paramountcy of the democratic ideal; NOW, THEREFORE, it is expedient to provide for furnishing certain information to citizens who desire to have it. BE it enacted by Parliament in the Fifty-sixth Year of the Republic of India as follows:—

CHAPTER I
Preliminary

Short title, extent and commencement

1.(*1*) This Act may be called the Right to Information Act, 2005.

(*2*) It extends to the whole of India except the State of Jammu and Kashmir.

(*3*) The provisions of sub-section (*1*) of section 4, sub-sections (*1*) and (*2*) of section 5, sections 12, 13, 15,16, 24, 27 and 28 shall come into force at once, and the remaining provisions of this Act shall come into force on the one hundred and twentieth day of its enactment.

Definitions.

2. In this Act, unless the context otherwise requires,—

(*a*) "appropriate Government" means in relation to a public authority which is established, constituted, owned, controlled or substantially financed by funds provided directly or indirectly—

(i) by the Central Government or the Union territory administration, the Central Government;

(ii) by the State Government, the State Government;

(*b*) "Central Information Commission" means the Central Information Commission constituted under sub-section (*1*) of section 12;

(*c*) "Central Public Information Officer" means the Central Public Information Officer designated under sub-section (*1*) and includes a Central Assistant Public Information Officer designated as such under sub-section (*2*) of section 5;

(*d*) "Chief Information Commissioner" and "Information Commissioner" mean the Chief Information Commissioner and Information Commissioner appointed under sub-section (*3*) of section 12;

(*e*) "competent authority" means—

(i) the Speaker in the case of the House of the People or the Legislative Assembly of a State or a Union territory having such Assembly and the Chairman in the case of the Council of States or Legislative Council of a State;

(ii) the Chief Justice of India in the case of the Supreme Court;

(iii) the Chief Justice of the High Court in the case of a High Court;

(iv) the President or the Governor, as the case may be, in the case of other authorities established or constituted by or under the Constitution;

(v) the administrator appointed under article 239 of the Constitution;

(*f*) "information" means any material in any form, including records, documents, memos, e-mails, opinions, advices, press releases, circulars, orders, logbooks, contracts, reports, papers, samples, models, data material held in any electronic form SEC.1 THE GAZETTE OF INDIA EXTRAORDINARY 3 and information relating to any private body which can be accessed by a public authority under any other law for the time being in force;

(*g*) "prescribed" means prescribed by rules made under this Act by the appropriate Government or the competent authority, as the case may be;

(*h*) "public authority" means any authority or body or institution of self- government established or constituted—

(a) by or under the Constitution;

(b) by any other law made by Parliament;

(c) by any other law made by State Legislature;

(d) by notification issued or order made by the appropriate Government, and includes any—

(i) body owned, controlled or substantially financed;

(ii) non-Government organisation substantially financed, directly or indirectly by funds provided by the appropriate Government;

(*i*) "record" includes—

(a) any document, manuscript and file;

(b) any microfilm, microfiche and facsimile copy of a document;

(c) any reproduction of image or images embodied in such microfilm (whether enlarged or not); and
(d) any other material produced by a computer or any other device;
(*j*) "right to information" means the right to information accessible under this Act which is held by or under the control of any public authority and includes the right to—
(i) inspection of work, documents, records;
(ii) taking notes, extracts or certified copies of documents or records;
(iii) taking certified samples of material;
(iv) obtaining information in the form of diskettes, floppies, tapes, video cassettes or in any other electronic mode or through printouts where such information is stored in a computer or in any other device;
(*k*) "State Information Commission" means the State Information Commission constituted under sub-section (*1*) of section 15;
(*l*) "State Chief Information Commissioner" and "State Information Commissioner" mean the State Chief Information Commissioner and the State Information
Commissioner appointed under sub-section (*3*) of section 15;
(*m*) "State Public Information Officer" means the State Public Information Officer designated under sub-section (*1*) and includes a State Assistant Public Information Officer designated as such under sub-section (*2*) of section 5;
(*n*) "third party" means a person other than the citizen making a request for information and includes a public authority.

4 THE GAZETTER OF INDIA EXTRAORDINARY [PART II—

CHAPTER II

Right to information and obligations of public authorities

3. Subject to the provisions of this Act, all citizens shall have the right to information. Right to information

4. (*1*) Every public authority shall—
a) maintain all its records duly catalogued and indexed in a manner and the form which facilitates the right to information under this Act and ensure that all records that are appropriate to be computerised are, within a reasonable time and subject to availability of resources, computerised and connected through a

network all over the country on different systems so that access to such records is facilitated;

b) publish within one hundred and twenty days from the enactment of this Act,—

(i) the particulars of its organisation, functions and duties;

(ii) the powers and duties of its officers and employees;

(iii) the procedure followed in the decision making process, including channels of supervision and accountability;

(iv) the norms set by it for the discharge of its functions;

(v) the rules, regulations, instructions, manuals and records, held by it or under its control or used by its employees for discharging its functions;

(vi) a statement of the categories of documents that are held by it or under its control;

(vii) the particulars of any arrangement that exists for consultation with, or representation by, the members of the public in relation to the formulation of its policy or implementation thereof;

(viii) a statement of the boards, councils, committees and other bodies consisting of two or more persons constituted as its part or for the purpose of its advice, and as to whether meetings of those boards, councils, committees and other bodies are open to the public, or the minutes of such meetings are accessible for public;

(ix) a directory of its officers and employees;

(x) the monthly remuneration received by each of its officers and employees, including the system of compensation as provided in its regulations;

(xi) the budget allocated to each of its agency, indicating the particulars of all plans, proposed expenditures and reports on disbursements made;

(xii) the manner of execution of subsidy programmes, including the amounts allocated and the details of beneficiaries of such programmes;

(xiii) particulars of recipients of concessions, permits or authorisations granted by it;

(xiv) details in respect of the information, available to or held by it, reduced in an electronic form;

(xv) the particulars of facilities available to citizens for obtaining information, including the working hours of a library or reading room, if maintained for public use;

(xvi) the names, designations and other particulars of the Public Information Officers;

(xvii) such other information as may be prescribed; and thereafter update these publications every year;

c) publish all relevant facts while formulating important policies or announcing the decisions which affect public;

d) provide reasons for its administrative or quasi-judicial

SEC.1 THE GAZETTE OF INDIA EXTRAORDINARY 5

decisions to affected persons.

(*2*) It shall be a constant endeavour of every public authority to take steps in accordance with the requirements of clause (*b*) of sub-section (*1*) to provide as much information *suo motu* to the public at regular intervals through various means of communications, including internet, so that the public have minimum resort to the use of this Act to obtain information.

(*3*) For the purposes of sub-section (*1*), every information shall be disseminated widely and in such form and manner which is easily accessible to the public.

(*4*) All materials shall be disseminated taking into consideration the cost effectiveness, local language and the most effective method of communication in that local area and the information should be easily accessible, to the extent possible in electronic format with the Central Public Information Officer or State Public Information Officer, as the case may be, available free or at such cost of the medium or the print cost price as may be prescribed.

Explanation.—For the purposes of sub-sections (*3*) and (*4*), "disseminated" means making known or communicated the information to the public through notice boards, newspapers, public announcements, media broadcasts, the internet or any other means, including inspection of offices of any public authority.

5. (*1*) Every public authority shall, within one hundred days of the enactment of this Act, designate as many officers as the Central Public Information Officers or State Public Information Officers, as the case may be, in all administrative units or offices under it as may be necessary to provide information to persons requesting for the information under this Act.

(*2*) Without prejudice to the provisions of sub-section (*1*), every public authority shall designate an officer, within one hundred days of the enactment of this Act, at each sub-divisional level or other sub-district level as a Central Assistant Public Information Officer or a State Assistant Public Information Officer, as the case may be, to receive the applications for information or appeals under this Act for forwarding the same forthwith to the Central Public Information Officer or the State Public Information Officer or senior officer specified under sub-section (*1*) of section 19 or the Central Information Commission or the State Information Commission, as the case may be:

Provided that where an application for information or appeal is given to a Central Assistant Public Information Officer or a State Assistant Public Information Officer, as the case may be, a period of five days shall be added in computing the period for response specified under sub-section (*1*) of section 7.

(*3*) Every Central Public Information Officer or State Public Information Officer, as the case may be, shall deal with requests from persons seeking information and render reasonable assistance to the persons seeking such information.

(*4*) The Central Public Information Officer or State Public Information Officer, as the case may be, may seek the assistance of any other officer as he or she considers it necessary for the proper discharge of his or her duties.

(*5*) Any officer, whose assistance has been sought under sub-section (*4*), shall render all assistance to the Central Public Information Officer or State Public Information Officer, as the case may be, seeking his or her assistance and for the purposes of any contravention of the provisions of this Act, such other officer shall be treated as a Central Public Information Officer or State Public Information Officer, as the case may be.

Designation of Public Information Officers.

THE GAZETTER OF INDIA EXTRAORDINARY [PART II—

6. (*1*) A person, who desires to obtain any information under this Act, shall make a request in writing or through electronic means in English or Hindi or in the official language of the area in which the application is being made, accompanying such fee as may be prescribed, to—

(a) the Central Public Information Officer or State Public Information Officer, as the case may be, of the concerned public authority;

(b) the Central Assistant Public Information Officer or State Assistant Public Information Officer, as the case may be, specifying the particulars of the information sought by him or her:

Provided that where such request cannot be made in writing, the Central Public Information Officer or State Public Information Officer, as the case may be, shall render all reasonable assistance to the person making the request orally to reduce the same in writing.

(*2*) An applicant making request for information shall not be required to give any reason for requesting the information or any other personal details except those that may be necessary for contacting him.

(*3*) Where an application is made to a public authority requesting for an information,—

(i) which is held by another public authority; or

(ii) the subject matter of which is more closely connected with the functions of another public authority, the public authority, to which such application is made, shall transfer the application or such part of it as may be appropriate to that other public authority and inform the applicant immediately about such transfer:

Provided that the transfer of an application pursuant to this sub-section shall be made as soon as practicable but in no case later than five days from the date of receipt of the application.

Request for obtaining information.

Disposal of request.

7. (*1*) Subject to the proviso to sub-section (*2*) of section 5 or the proviso to subsection (*3*) of section 6, the Central Public Information Officer or State Public Information Officer, as the case may be, on receipt of a request undersection 6 shall, as expeditiously as possible, and in any case within thirty days of the receipt of the request, either provide the information on payment of such fee as may be prescribed or reject the request for any of the reasons specified in sections 8 and 9:

Provided that where the information sought for concerns the life or liberty of a person, the same shall be provided within forty-eight hours of the receipt of the request.

(*2*) If the Central Public Information Officer or State Public Information Officer, as the case may be, fails to give decision on the request for information within the period specified under sub-section (*1*), the Central Public Information Officer or State Public Information Officer, as the case may be, shall be deemed to have refused the request.

(*3*) Where a decision is taken to provide the information on payment of any further fee representing the cost of providing the information, the Central Public Information Officer or State Public Information Officer, as the case may be, shall send an intimation to the person making the request, giving—

(a) the details of further fees representing the cost of providing the information as determined by him, together with the calculations made SEC.1 THE GAZETTE OF INDIA EXTRAORDINARY 7 to arrive at the amount in accordance with fee prescribed under subsection (*1*), requesting him to deposit that fees, and the period intervening between the despatch of the said intimation and payment of fees shall be excluded for the purpose of calculating the period of thirty days referred to in that sub-section;

(b) information concerning his or her right with respect to review the decision as to the amount of fees charged or the form of access provided, including the particulars of the appellate authority, time limit, process and any other forms.

(*4*) Where access to the record or a part thereof is required to be provided under this Act and the person to whom access is to be provided is sensorily disabled, the Central Public Information Officer or State Public Information Officer, as the case may be, shall provide assistance to enable access to the information, including providing such assistance as may be appropriate for the inspection.

(*5*) Where access to information is to be provided in the printed or in any electronic format, the applicant shall, subject to the provisions of sub-section (*6*), pay such fee as may be prescribed: Provided that the fee prescribed under sub-section (*1*) of section 6 and sub-sections (*1*) and (*5*) of section 7 shall be reasonable and no such fee shall be charged from the persons who are of below poverty line as may be determined by the appropriate Government.

(*6*) Notwithstanding anything contained in sub-section (*5*), the person making request for the information shall be provided the information free of charge where a public authority fails to comply with the time limits specified in sub-section (*1*).

(*7*) Before taking any decision under sub-section (*1*), the Central Public Information Officer or State Public Information Officer, as the case may be, shall take into consideration the representation made by a third party under section 11.

(*8*) Where a request has been rejected under sub-section (*1*), the Central Public Information Officer or State Public Information Officer, as the case may be, shall communicate to the person making the request,—

(*i*) the reasons for such rejection;

(*ii*) the period within which an appeal against such rejection may be preferred; and

(*iii*) the particulars of the appellate authority.

(*9*) An information shall ordinarily be provided in the form in which it is sought unless it would disproportionately divert the resources of the public authority or would be detrimental to the safety or preservation of the record in question.

8. (*1*) Notwithstanding anything contained in this Act, there shall be no obligation to give any citizen,—

(*a*) information, disclosure of which would prejudicially affect the sovereignty and integrity of India, the security, strategic, scientific or economic interests of the State, relation with foreign State or lead to incitement of an offence;

(*b*) information which has been expressly forbidden to be published by any court of law or tribunal or the disclosure of which may constitute contempt of court;

Exemption from disclosure of information.

8 THE GAZETTER OF INDIA EXTRAORDINARY [PART II—

(*c*) information, the disclosure of which would cause a breach of privilege of Parliament or the State Legislature;

(*d*) information including commercial confidence, trade secrets or intellectual property, the disclosure of which would harm the competitive position of a third party, unless the competent authority is satisfied that larger public interest warrants the disclosure of such information;

(*e*) information available to a person in his fiduciary relationship, unless the competent authority is satisfied that the larger public interest warrants the disclosure of such information;

(*f*) information received in confidence from foreign Government;

(*g*) information, the disclosure of which would endanger the life or physical safety of any person or identify the source of information or assistance given in confidence for law enforcement or security purposes;

(*h*) information which would impede the process of investigation or apprehension or prosecution of offenders;

(*i*) cabinet papers including records of deliberations of the Council of Ministers, Secretaries and other officers:

Provided that the decisions of Council of Ministers, the reasons thereof, and the material on the basis of which the decisions were taken shall be made public after the decision has been taken, and the matter is complete, or over:

Provided further that those matters which come under the exemptions specified in this section shall not be disclosed;

(*j*) information which relates to personal information the disclosure of which has no relationship to any public activity or interest, or which would cause unwarranted invasion of the privacy of the individual unless the Central Public Information Officer or the State Public Information Officer or the appellate authority, as the case may be, is satisfied that the larger public interest justifies the disclosure of such information:

Provided that the information which cannot be denied to the Parliament or a State Legislature shall not be denied to any person.

19 of 1923. (2) Notwithstanding anything in the Official Secrets Act, 1923 nor any of the exemptions permissible in accordance with sub-section (*1*), a public authority may allow access to information, if public interest in disclosure outweighs the harm to the protected interests.

(*3*) Subject to the provisions of clauses (*a*), (*c*) and (*i*) of sub-section (*1*), any information relating to any occurrence, event or matter which has taken place, occurred or happened twenty years before the date on which any request is made under secton 6 shall be provided to any person making a request under that section:

Provided that where any question arises as to the date from which the said period of twenty years has to be computed, the decision of the Central Government shall be final, subject to the usual appeals provided for in this Act. SEC.1 THE GAZETTE OF INDIA EXTRAORDINARY 9

Grounds for rejection to access in certain cases.

9. Without prejudice to the provisions of section 8, a Central Public Information Officer or a State Public Information Officer, as the case may be, may reject a request for information where such a request for providing access would involve an infringement of copyright subsisting in a person other than the State.

Severability

10. (*1*) Where a request for access to information is rejected on the ground that it is in relation to information which is exempt from disclosure, then, notwithstanding anything contained in this Act, access may be provided to that part of the record which does not contain any information which is exempt from disclosure under this Act and which can reasonably be severed from any part that contains exempt information.

(*2*) Where access is granted to a part of the record under sub-section (*1*), the Central Public Information Officer or State Public Information Officer, as the case may be, shall give a notice to the applicant, informing—

(a) that only part of the record requested, after severance of the record containing information which is exempt from disclosure, is being provided;

(b) the reasons for the decision, including any findings on any material question of fact, referring to the material on which those findings were based;

(c) the name and designation of the person giving the decision;

(d) the details of the fees calculated by him or her and the amount of fee which the applicant is required to deposit; and

(e) his or her rights with respect to review of the decision regarding non-disclosure of part of the information, the amount of fee charged or the form of access provided, including the particulars of the senior officer specified under sub-section (*1*) of section 19 or the Central Information Commission or the State Information

Commission, as the case may be, time limit, process and any other form of access.

Third party information.

11. (*1*) Where a Central Public Information Officer or a State Public Information Officer, as the case may be, intends to disclose any information or record, or part thereof on a request made under this Act, which relates to or has been supplied by a third party and has been treated as confidential by that third party, the Central Public Information Officer or State Public Information Officer, as the case may be, shall, within five days from the receipt of the request, give a written notice to such third party of the request and of the fact that the Central Public Information Officer or State Public Information Officer, as the case may be, intends to disclose the information or record, or part thereof, and invite the third party to make a submission in writing or orally, regarding whether the information should be disclosed, and such submission of the third party shall be kept in view while taking a decision about disclosure of information:

Provided that except in the case of trade or commercial secrets protected by law, disclosure may be allowed if the public interest in disclosure outweighs in importance any possible harm or injury to the interests of such third party.

(*2*) Where a notice is served by the Central Public Information Officer or State Public Information Officer, as the case may be, under sub-section (*1*) to a third party in respect of any information or record or part thereof, the third party shall, within ten days from the date of receipt of such notice, be given the opportunity to make representation against the proposed disclosure.

(*3*) Notwithstanding anything contained in section 7, the Central Public Information Officer or State Public Information Officer, as the case may be, shall, within forty days after receipt of the request under section 6, if the third party has been given an opportunity to make representation under sub-section (*2*), make a decision as to whether or not to disclose the information or record or part thereof and give in 10 THE GAZETTER OF INDIA EXTRAORDINARY [PART II—

writing the notice of his decision to the third party.

(*4*) A notice given under sub-section (*3*) shall include a statement that the third party to whom the notice is given is entitled to prefer an appeal under section 19 against the decision.

CHAPTER III

The Central Information Commission

12. (*1*) The Central Government shall, by notification in the Official Gazette, constitute a body to be known as the Central Information Commission to exercise the powers conferred on, and to perform the functions assigned to, it under this Act.

(*2*) The Central Information Commission shall consist of—

(a) the Chief Information Commissioner; and

(b) such number of Central Information Commissioners, not exceeding ten, as may be deemed necessary.

(*3*) The Chief Information Commissioner and Information Commissioners shall be appointed by the President on the recommendation of a committee consisting of—

(i) the Prime Minister, who shall be the Chairperson of the committee;

(ii) the Leader of Opposition in the Lok Sabha; and

(iii) a Union Cabinet Minister to be nominated by the Prime Minister.

Explanation.—For the purposes of removal of doubts, it is hereby declared that where the Leader of Opposition in the House of the People has not been recognised as such, the Leader of the single largest group in opposition of the Government in the House of the People shall be deemed to be the Leader of Opposition.

(*4*) The general superintendence, direction and management of the affairs of the Central Information Commission shall vest in the Chief Information Commissioner who shall be assisted by the Information Commissioners and may exercise all such powers and do all such acts and things which may be exercised or done by the Central Information Commission autonomously without being subjected to directions by any other authority under this Act.

(*5*) The Chief Information Commissioner and Information Commissioners shall be persons of eminence in public life with wide knowledge and experience in law, science and technology, social service, management, journalism, mass media or administration and governance.

(*6*) The Chief Information Commissioner or an Information Commissioner shall not be a Member of Parliament or Member of the Legislature of any State or Union territory, as the case may be, or hold any other office of profit or connected with any political party or carrying on any business or pursuing any profession.
(*7*) The headquarters of the Central Information Commission shall be at Delhi and the Central Information Commission may, with the previous approval of the Central Government, establish offices at other places in India.
Constitution of Central Information Commission.

SEC.1 THE GAZETTE OF INDIA EXTRAORDINARY 11
13. (*1*) The Chief Information Commissioner shall hold office for a term of five years from the date on which he enters upon his office and shall not be eligible for reappointment:
Provided that no Chief Information Commissioner shall hold office as such after he has attained the age of sixty-five years.
(*2*) Every Information Commissioner shall hold office for a term of five years from the date on which he enters upon his office or till he attains the age of sixty-five years, whichever is earlier, and shall not be eligible for reappointment as such Information Commissioner:
Provided that every Information Commissioner shall, on vacating his office under this sub-section be eligible for appointment as the Chief Information Commissioner in the manner specified in sub-section (*3*) of section 12:
Provided further that where the Information Commissioner is appointed as the Chief Information Commissioner, his term of office shall not be more than five years in aggregate as the Information Commissioner and the Chief Information Commissioner.
(*3*) The Chief Information Commissioner or an Information Commissioner shall before he enters upon his office make and subscribe before the President or some other person appointed by him in that behalf, an oath or affirmation according to the form set out for the purpose in the First Schedule.
(*4*) The Chief Information Commissioner or an Information Commissioner may, at any time, by writing under his hand addressed to the President, resign from his office:

Provided that the Chief Information Commissioner or an Information Commissioner may be removed in the manner specified under section 14.

(*5*) The salaries and allowances payable to and other terms and conditions of service of—

(a) the Chief Information Commissioner shall be the same as that of the Chief Election Commissioner;

(b) an Information Commissioner shall be the same as that of an Election Commissioner:

Provided that if the Chief Information Commissioner or an Information Commissioner, at the time of his appointment is, in receipt of a pension, other than a disability or wound pension, in respect of any previous service under the Government of India or under the Government of a State, his salary in respect of the service as the Chief Information Commissioner or an Information Commissioner shall be reduced by the amount of that pension including any portion of pension which was commuted and pension equivalent of other forms of retirement benefits excluding pension equivalent of retirement gratuity:

Provided further that if the Chief Information Commissioner or an Information Commissioner if, at the time of his appointment is, in receipt of retirement benefits in respect of any previous service rendered in a Corporation established by or under any Central Act or State Act or a Government company owned or controlled by the Central Government or the State Government, his salary in respect of the service as the Chief Information Commissioner or an Information Commissioner shall be reduced by the amount of pension equivalent to the retirement benefits:

Provided also that the salaries, allowances and other conditions of service of the Chief Information Commissioner and the Information Commissioners shall not be varied to their term of office and conditions of service.

12 THE GAZETTER OF INDIA EXTRAORDINARY [PART II—

disadvantage after their appointment.

(*6*) The Central Government shall provide the Chief Information Commissioner and the Information Commissioners with such officers and employees as may be necessary for the efficient performance of their functions under this Act, and the salaries and allowances payable to and the terms and conditions of service of the officers and other employees appointed for the purpose of this Act shall be such as may be prescribed.

14. (*1*) Subject to the provisions of sub-section (*3*), the Chief Information Commissioner or any Information Commissioner shall be removed from his office only by order of the President on the ground of proved misbehaviour or incapacity after the Supreme Court, on a reference made to it by the President, has, on inquiry, reported that the Chief Information Commissioner or any Information Commissioner, as the case may be, ought on such ground be removed.

(*2*) The President may suspend from office, and if deem necessary prohibit also from attending the office during inquiry, the Chief Information Commissioner or Information Commissioner in respect of whom a reference has been made to the Supreme Court under sub-section (*1*) until the President has passed orders on receipt of the report of the Supreme Court on such reference.

(*3*) Notwithstanding anything contained in sub-section (*1*), the President may by order remove from office the Chief Information Commissioner or any Information Commissioner if the Chief Information Commissioner or a Information Commissioner, as the case may be,—

(a) is adjudged an insolvent; or

(b) has been convicted of an offence which, in the opinion of the President, involves moral turpitude; or

(c) engages during his term of office in any paid employment outside the duties of his office; or

(d) is, in the opinion of the President, unfit to continue in office by reason of infirmity of mind or body; or

(e) has acquired such financial or other interest as is likely to affect prejudicially his functions as the Chief Information Commissioner or a Information Commissioner.

(*4*) If the Chief Information Commissioner or a Information Commissioner in any way, concerned or interested in any contract or agreement made by or on behalf of the Government of India or participates in any way in the profit thereof or in any benefit or emolument arising therefrom otherwise than as a member and in

common with the other members of an incorporated company, he shall, for the purposes of sub-section
(*1*), be deemed to be guilty of misbehaviour.
Removalof Chief Information Commissioner or Information Commissioner.

CHAPTER IV

The State Information Commission

15. (*1*) Every State Government shall, by notification in the Official Gazette, constitute a body to be known as the .... (name of the State) Information Commission to exercise the powers conferred on, and to perform the functions assigned to, it under this Act.
(*2*) The State Information Commission shall consist of—
(a) the State Chief Information Commissioner, and
(b) such number of State Information Commissioners, not exceeding ten, as may be deemed necessary. Constitution of State Information Commission.

SEC.1 THE GAZETTE OF INDIA EXTRAORDINARY 13
(*3*) The State Chief Information Commissioner and the State Information
Commissioners shall be appointed by the Governor on the recommendation of a committee consisting of—
(i) the Chief Minister, who shall be the Chairperson of the committee;
(ii) the Leader of Opposition in the Legislative Assembly; and
(iii) a Cabinet Minister to be nominated by the Chief Minister
Explanation.—For the purposes of removal of doubts, it is hereby declared that where the Leader of Opposition in the Legislative Assembly has not been recognised as such, the Leader of the single largest group in opposition of the Government in the Legislative Assembly shall be deemed to be the Leader of Opposition.
(*4*) The general superintendence, direction and management of the affairs of the State Information Commission shall vest in the State Chief Information Commissioner who shall be assisted by the State Information Commissioners and may exercise all such powers and do all such acts and things which may be exercised or

done by the State Information Commission autonomously without being subjected to directions by any other authority under this Act.

(*5*) The State Chief Information Commissioner and the State Information Commissioners shall be persons of eminence in public life with wide knowledge and experience in law, science and technology, social service, management, journalism, mass media or administration and governance.

(*6*) The State Chief Information Commissioner or a State Information Commissioner shall not be a Member of Parliament or Member of the Legislature of any State or Union territory, as the case may be, or hold any other office of profit or connected with any political party or carrying on any business or pursuing any profession.

(*7*) The headquarters of the State Information Commission shall be at such place in the State as the State Government may, by notification in the Official Gazette, specify and the State Information Commission may, with the previous approval of the State Government, establish offices at other places in the State. Term of office and conditions of service.

16. (*1*) The State Chief Information Commissioner shall hold office for a term of five years from the date on which he enters upon his office and shall not be eligible for reappointment: Provided that no State Chief Information Commissioner shall hold office as such after he has attained the age of sixty-five years.

(*2*) Every State Information Commissioner shall hold office for a term of five years from the date on which he enters upon his office or till he attains the age of sixty-five years, whichever is earlier, and shall not be eligible for reappointment as such State Information Commissioner: Provided that every State Information Commissioner shall, on vacating his office under this sub-section, be eligible for appointment as the State Chief Information Commissioner in the manner specified in sub-section (*3*) of section 15: Provided further that where the State Information Commissioner is appointed as the State Chief Information Commissioner, his term of office shall not be more than five years in aggregate as the State Information Commissioner and the State Chief Information Commissioner.

(*3*) The State Chief Information Commissioner or a State Information Commissioner,

14 THE GAZETTER OF INDIA EXTRAORDINARY [PART II—
shall before he enters upon his office make and subscribe before the Governor or some other person appointed by him in that behalf, an oath or affirmation according to the form set out for the purpose in the First Schedule.

(*4*) The State Chief Information Commissioner or a State Information Commissioner may, at any time, by writing under his hand addressed to the Governor, resign from his office: Provided that the State Chief Information Commissioner or a State Information Commissioner may be removed in the manner specified under section 17.

(*5*) The salaries and allowances payable to and other terms and conditions of service of—

(a) the State Chief Information Commissioner shall be the same as that of an Election Commissioner;

(b) the State Information Commissioner shall be the same as that of the Chief Secretary to the State Government: Provided that if the State Chief Information Commissioner or a State Information Commissioner, at the time of his appointment is, in receipt of a pension, other than a disability or wound pension, in respect of any previous service under the Government of India or under the Government of a State, his salary in respect of the service as the State Chief Information Commissioner or a State Information Commissioner shall be reduced by the amount of that pension including any portion of pension which was commuted and pension equivalent of other forms of retirement benefits excluding pension equivalent of retirement gratuity:

Provided further that where the State Chief Information Commissioner or a State Information Commissioner if, at the time of his appointment is, in receipt of retirement benefits in respect of any previous service rendered in a Corporation established by or under any Central Act or State Act or a Government company owned or controlled by the Central Government or the State Government, his salary in respect of the service as the State Chief Information Commissioner or the State Information Commissioner shall be reduced by the amount of pension equivalent to the retirement benefits: Provided also that the salaries, allowances and other conditions of service of the State Chief Information

Commissioner and the State Information Commissioners shall not be varied to their disadvantage after their appointment.

(*6*) The State Government shall provide the State Chief Information Commissioner and the State Information Commissioners with such officers and employees as may be necessary for the efficient performance of their functions under this Act, and the salaries and allowances payable to and the terms and conditions of service of the officers and other employees appointed for the purpose of this Act shall be such as may be prescribed.

17. (*1*) Subject to the provisions of sub-section (*3*), the State Chief Information Commissioner or a State Information Commissioner shall be removed from his office only by order of the Governor on the ground of proved misbehaviour or incapacity after the Supreme Court, on a reference made to it by the Governor, has on inquiry, reported that the State Chief Information Commissioner or a State Information Commissioner, as the case may be, ought on such ground be removed.

(*2*) The Governor may suspend from office, and if deem necessary prohibit also from attending the office during inquiry, the State Chief Information Commissioner or a State Information Commissioner in respect of whom a reference has been made to the Supreme Court under sub-section (*1*) until the Governor has passed orders on receipt of the report of Removal of State Chief Information Commissioner or State Information Commissioner

SEC.1 THE GAZETTE OF INDIA EXTRAORDINARY 15

the Supreme Court on such reference.

(*3*) Notwithstanding anything contained in sub-section (*1*), the Governor may by order remove from office the State Chief Information Commissioner or a State Information Commissioner if a State Chief Information Commissioner or a State Information Commissioner, as the case may be,—

(a) is adjudged an insolvent; or

(b) has been convicted of an offence which, in the opinion of the Governor, involves moral turpitude; or

(c) engages during his term of office in any paid employment outside the duties of his office; or

(d) is, in the opinion of the Governor, unfit to continue in office by reason of infirmity of mind or body; or

(e) has acquired such financial or other interest as is likely to affect prejudicially his functions as the State Chief Information Commissioner or a State Information Commissioner.

(*4*) If the State Chief Information Commissioner or a State Information Commissioner in any way, concerned or interested in any contract or agreement made by or on behalf of the Government of the State or participates in any way in the profit thereof or in any benefit or emoluments arising therefrom otherwise than as a member and in common with the other members of an incorporated company, he shall, for the purposes of sub-section

(*1*), be deemed to be guilty of misbehaviour.

Powers and functions of Information Commissions.

CHAPTER V

Powers and functions of the Information Commissions, appeal and penalties

18. (*1*) Subject to the provisions of this Act, it shall be the duty of the Central Information Commission or State Information Commission, as the case may be, to receive and inquire into a complaint from any person,—

(a) who has been unable to submit a request to a Central Public Information Officer or State Public Information Officer, as the case may be, either by reason that no such officer has been appointed under this Act, or because the Central Assistant Public Information Officer or State Assistant Public Information Officer, as the case may be, has refused to accept his or her application for information orappeal under this Act for forwarding the same to the Central Public Information Officer or State Public Information Officer or senior officer specified in subsection

(*1*) of section 19 or the Central Information Commission or the State

Information Commission, as the case may be;

(b) who has been refused access to any information requested under this Act;

(c) who has not been given a response to a request for information or access to information within the time limit specified under this Act;

(d) who has been required to pay an amount of fee which he or she considers unreasonable;

(e) who believes that he or she has been given incomplete, misleading or false information under this Act; and

(f) in respect of any other matter relating to requesting or obtaining access to records under this Act.

(*2*) Where the Central Information Commission or State Information Commission, as the case may be, is satisfied that there are reasonable grounds to inquire into the matter, it may initiate an inquiry in respect thereof.

16 THE GAZETTER OF INDIA EXTRAORDINARY [PART II—

(*3*) The Central Information Commission or State Information Commission, as the case may be, shall, while inquiring into any matter under this section, have the same powers as are vested in a civil court while trying a suit under the Code of Civil Procedure, 1908, in respect of the following matters, namely:—

5 of 1908

(a) summoning and enforcing the attendance of persons and compel them to give oral or written evidence on oath and to produce the documents or things;

(b) requiring the discovery and inspection of documents;

(c) receiving evidence on affidavit;

(d) requisitioning any public record or copies thereof from any court or office;

(e) issuing summons for examination of witnesses or documents; and

(f) any other matter which may be prescribed.

(*4*) Notwithstanding anything inconsistent contained in any other Act of Parliament or State Legislature, as the case may be, the Central Information Commission or the State Information Commission, as the case may be, may, during the inquiry of any complaint under this Act, examine any record to which this Act applies which is under the control of the public authority, and no such record may be withheld from it on any grounds.

Appeal **19**. (*1*) Any person who, does not receive a decision within the time specified in subsection (*1*) or clause (*a*) of sub-section (*3*) of section 7, or is aggrieved by a decision of the Central Public Information Officer or State Public Information Officer, as the case may be, may within thirty days from the expiry of such period or from the receipt of such a decision prefer an appeal to such officer who is senior in rank to the Central Public Information Officer or State Public Information Officer as the case may be, in each public authority:

Provided that such officer may admit the appeal after the expiry of the period of thirty days if he or she is satisfied that the appellant was prevented by sufficient cause from filing the appeal in time.

(*2*) Where an appeal is preferred against an order made by a Central Public Information Officer or a State Public Information Officer, as the case may be, under section 11 to disclose third party information, the appeal by the concerned third party shall be made within thirty days from the date of the order.

(*3*) A second appeal against the decision under sub-section (*1*) shall lie within ninety days from the date on which the decision should have been made or was actually received, with the Central Information Commission or the State Information Commission:

Provided that the Central Information Commission or the State Information Commission, as the case may be, may admit the appeal after the expiry of the period of ninety days if it is satisfied that the appellant was prevented by sufficient cause from filing the appeal in time.

(*4*) If the decision of the Central Public Information Officer or State Public Information Officer, as the case may be, against which an appeal is preferred relates to information of a third party, the Central Information Commission or State Information Commission, as the case may be, shall give a reasonable opportunity of being heard to that third party.

(*5*) In any appeal proceedings, the onus to prove that a denial of a request was justified shall be on the Central Public Information Officer or State Public Information Officer, as the case may be, who denied the request.

(*6*) An appeal under sub-section (*1*) or sub-section (*2*) shall be disposed of within thirty days of the receipt of the appeal or within such extended period not exceeding a total of forty-five days from the date of filing thereof, as the case may be, for reasons to be SEC.1 THE GAZETTE OF INDIA EXTRAORDINARY 17 recorded in writing.

(*7*) The decision of the Central Information Commission or State Information Commission, as the case may be, shall be binding.

(*8*) In its decision, the Central Information Commission or State Information Commission, as the case may be, has the power to—

(*a*) require the public authority to take any such steps as may be necessary to secure compliance with the provisions of this Act, including—

(i) by providing access to information, if so requested, in a particular form;

(ii) by appointing a Central Public Information Officer or State Public Information Officer, as the case may be;

(iii) by publishing certain information or categories of information;

(iv) by making necessary changes to its practices in relation to the maintenance, management and destruction of records;

(v) by enhancing the provision of training on the right to information for its officials;

(vi) by providing it with an annual report in compliance with clause (*b*) of subsection (*1*) of section 4;

(*b*) require the public authority to compensate the complainant for any loss or other detriment suffered;

(c) impose any of the penalties provided under this Act;

(d) reject the application.

(*9*) The Central Information Commission or State Information Commission, as the case may be, shall give notice of its decision, including any right of appeal, to the complainant and the public authority.

(*10*) The Central Information Commission or State Information Commission, as the case may be, shall decide the appeal in accordance with such procedure as may be prescribed.

Penalties **20**. (*1*) Where the Central Information Commission or the State Information Commission, as the case may be, at the time of deciding any complaint or appeal is of the opinion that the Central Public Information Officer or the State Public Information Officer, as the case may be, has, without any reasonable cause, refused to receive an application for information or has not furnished information within the time specified under sub-section (*1*) of section 7 or malafidely denied the request for information or knowingly given incorrect, incomplete or misleading information or destroyed information which was the subject of the request or obstructed in any manner in furnishing the information, it shall impose a penalty of two hundred and fifty rupees each day till application is received orinformation is furnished, so however, the total amount of such penalty shall not exceed twenty-five thousand rupees:

Provided that the Central Public Information Officer or the State Public Information Officer, as the case may be, shall be given a reasonable opportunity of being heard before any penalty is imposed on him:

Provided further that the burden of proving that he acted reasonably and diligently shall be on the Central Public Information Officer or the State Public Information Officer,

as the case may be.

(2) Where the Central Information Commission or the State Information Commission, as the case may be, at the time of deciding any complaint or appeal is of the opinion that the Central Public Information Officer or the State Public Information Officer, as the case

18 THE GAZETTER OF INDIA EXTRAORDINARY [PART II—

may be, has, without any reasonable cause and persistently, failed to receive an applicationm for information or has not furnished information within the time specified under subsection (*1*) of section 7 or malafidely denied the request for information or knowingly given incorrect, incomplete or misleading information or destroyed information which was the subject of the request or obstructed in any manner in furnishing the information, it shall recommend for disciplinary action against the Central Public Information Officer or the State Public Information Officer, as the case may be, under the service rules applicable to him.

CHAPTER VI
Miscellaneous

Protection of action taken in good faith.

21. No suit, prosecution or other legal proceeding shall lie against any person for anything which is in good faith done or intended to be done under this Act or any rule made thereunder.

Act to have overriding effect

22. The provisions of this Act shall have effect notwithstanding anything inconsistent therewith contained in the Official Secrets

Act, 1923, and any other law for the time being in force or in any instrument having effect by virtue of any law other than this Act.

Bar of jurisdiction of courts

23. No court shall entertain any suit, application or other proceeding in respect of any order made under this Act and no such order shall be called in question otherwise than by way of an appeal under this Act. Act not to apply to certain organisations

24. (*1*) Nothing contained in this Act shall apply to the intelligence and security organisations specified in the Second Schedule, being organisations established by the Central Government or any information furnished by such organisations to that Government: Provided that the information pertaining to the allegations of corruption and human rights violations shall not be excluded under this sub-section: Provided further that in the case of information sought for is in respect of allegations of violation of human rights, the information shall only be provided after the approval of the Central Information Commission, and notwithstanding anything contained in section 7, such information shall be provided within forty-five days from the date of the receipt of request.

(*2*) The Central Government may, by notification in the Official Gazette, amend the Schedule by including therein any other intelligence or security organisation established by that Government or omitting therefrom any organisation already specified therein and on the publication of such notification, such organisation shall be deemed to be included in or, as the case may be, omitted from the Schedule.

(*3*) Every notification issued under sub-section (*2*) shall be laid before each House of Parliament.

(*4*) Nothing contained in this Act shall apply to such intelligence and security organisation being organisations established by the State Government, as that Government may, from time to time, by notification in the Official Gazette, specify:

Provided that the information pertaining to the allegations of corruption and human rights violations shall not be excluded under this sub-section: SEC.1 THE GAZETTE OF INDIA EXTRAORDINARY 19 Provided further that in the case of information sought for is in respect of allegations of violation of human rights, the information shall only be provided after the approval of the State Information Commission and, notwithstanding anything contained in section 7, such information shall be provided within forty-five days from the date of the receipt of request.

(*5*) Every notification issued under sub-section (*4*) shall be laid before the State Legislature.

25. (*1*) The Central Information Commission or State Information Commission, as the case may be, shall, as soon as practicable after the end of each year, prepare a report on the implementation of the provisions of this Act during that year and forward a copy thereof to the appropriate Government.

(*2*) Each Ministry or Department shall, in relation to the public authorities within their jurisdiction, collect and provide such information to the Central Information Commission or State Information Commission, as the case may be, as is required to prepare the report under this section and comply with the requirements concerning the furnishing of that information and keeping of records for the purposes of this section.

(*3*) Each report shall state in respect of the year to which the report relates,—

(a) the number of requests made to each public authority;

(b) the number of decisions where applicants were not entitled to access to the documents pursuant to the requests, the provisions of this Act under which these decisions were made and the number of times such provisions were invoked;

(c) the number of appeals referred to the Central Information Commission or State Information Commission, as the case may be, for review, the nature of the appeals and the outcome of the appeals;

(d) particulars of any disciplinary action taken against any officer in respect of the administration of this Act;

(e) the amount of charges collected by each public authority under this Act;

(f) any facts which indicate an effort by the public authorities to administer and implement the spirit and intention of this Act;

(g) recommendations for reform, including recommendations in respect of the particular public authorities, for the development, improvement, modernisation, reform or amendment to this Act or other legislation or common law or any other matter relevant for operationalising the right to access information.

(*4*) The Central Government or the State Government, as the case may be, may, as soon as practicable after the end of each year, cause a copy of the report of the Central Information Commission or the State Information Commission, as the case may be, referred to in sub-section (*1*) to be laid before each House of Parliament or, as the case may be, before each House of the State Legislature, where there are two Houses, and where there is one House of the State Legislature before that House.

(*5*) If it appears to the Central Information Commission or State Information Commission, as the case may be, that the practice of a public authority in relation to the exercise of its functions under this Act does not conform with the provisions or spirit of this Act, it may give to the authority a recommendation specifying the steps which ought in its opinion to be taken for promoting such conformity.

Monitoring and Reporting Appropriate Government to prepare programmes

26. (*1*) The appropriate Government may, to the extent of availability of financial and other resources,—

(*a*) develop and organise educational programmes to advance the understanding of the public, in particular of disadvantaged communities as to how to exercise the rights contemplated under this Act;

20 THE GAZETTER OF INDIA EXTRAORDINARY [PART II—

(*b*) encourage public authorities to participate in the development and organisation of programmes referred to in clause (*a*) and to undertake such programmes themselves;

(*c*) promote timely and effective dissemination of accurate information by public authorities about their activities; and

(*d*) train Central Public Information Officers or State Public Information Officers, as the case may be, of public authorities and produce relevant training materials for use by the public authorities themselves.

(*2*) The appropriate Government shall, within eighteen months from the commencement of this Act, compile in its official language a guide containing such information, in an easily comprehensible form and manner, as may reasonably be required by a person who wishes to exercise any right specified in this Act.

(*3*) The appropriate Government shall, if necessary, update and publish the guidelines referred to in sub-section (2) at regular intervals which shall, in particular and without prejudice to the generality of sub-section (*2*), include—

(a) the objects of this Act;

(b) the postal and street address, the phone and fax number and, if available, electronic mail address of the Central Public Information Officer or State Public Information Officer, as the case may be, of every public authority appointed under sub-section (*1*) of section 5;

(c) the manner and the form in which request for access to an information shall be made to a Central Public Information Officer or State Public Information Officer, as the case may be;

(d) the assistance available from and the duties of the Central Public Information Officer or State Public Information Officer, as the case may be, of a public authority under this Act;

(e) the assistance available from the Central Information Commission or State Information Commission, as the case may be;

(f) all remedies in law available regarding an act or failure to act in respect of a right or duty conferred or imposed by this Act including the manner of filing an appeal to the Commission;

(g) the provisions providing for the voluntary disclosure of categories of records in accordance with section 4;

(h) the notices regarding fees to be paid in relation to requests for access to an information; and

(i) any additional regulations or circulars made or issued in relation to obtaining access to an information in accordance with this Act.

(*4*) The appropriate Government must, if necessary, update and publish the guidelines at regular intervals.

27. (*1*) The appropriate Government may, by notification in the Official Gazette, make rules to carry out the provisions of this Act.

(*2*) In particular, and without prejudice to the generality of the foregoing power, such rules may provide for all or any of the following matters, namely:—

(a) the cost of the medium or print cost price of the materials to be disseminated under sub-section (*4*) of section 4;

(b) the fee payable under sub-section (*1*) of section 6;

(c) the fee payable under sub-sections (*1*) and (*5*) of section 7;

(d) the salaries and allowances payable to and the terms and conditions of serviceof the officers and other employees under

sub-section (*6*) of section 13 and Power to make rules by appropriate Government

SEC.1 THE GAZETTE OF INDIA EXTRAORDINARY 21
sub-section (*6*) of section 16;

(e) the procedure to be adopted by the Central Information Commission or State Information Commission, as the case may be, in deciding the appeals under sub-section (*10*) of section 19; and

(f) any other matter which is required to be, or may be, prescribed.

28. (*1*) The competent authority may, by notification in the Official Gazette, make
rules to carry out the provisions of this Act.

(*2*) In particular, and without prejudice to the generality of the foregoing power, such rules may provide for all or any of the following matters, namely:—

(i) the cost of the medium or print cost price of the materials to be disseminated under sub-section (*4*) of section 4;

(ii) the fee payable under sub-section (*1*) of section 6;

(iii) the fee payable under sub-section (*1*) of section 7; and

(iv) any other matter which is required to be, or may be, prescribed Power to make rules by competent authority.

29. (*1*) Every rule made by the Central Government under this Act shall be laid, as soon as may be after it is made, before each House of Parliament, while it is in session, for a total period of thirty days which may be comprised in one session or in two or more successive sessions, and if, before the expiry of the session immediately following the session or the successive sessions aforesaid, both Houses agree in making any modification in the rule or both Houses agree that the rule should not be made, the rule shall thereafter have effect only in such modified form or be of no effect, as the case may be; so, however, that any such modification or annulment shall be without prejudice to the validity of anything previously done under that rule.

(*2*) Every rule made under this Act by a State Government shall be laid, as soon as may be after it is notified, before the State Legislature. Laying of rules.

30. (*1*) If any difficulty arises in giving effect to the provisions of this Act, the Central Government may, by order published in the

Official Gazette, make such provisions not inconsistent with the provisions of this Act as appear to it to be necessary or expedient for removal of the difficulty:

Provided that no such order shall be made after the expiry of a period of two years from the date of the commencement of this Act.

(*2*) Every order made under this section shall, as soon as may be after it is made, be laid before each House of Parliament.

Power to remove difficulties.

Repeal **31**. The Freedom of Information Act, 2002 is hereby repealed. 5 of 2003 22 THE GAZETTER OF INDIA EXTRAORDINARY [PART II—

THE FIRST SCHEDULE

[*See* sections 13 (*3*) and 16(*3*)]

Form of oath or affirmation to be made by the Chief Information Commissioner/the Information Commissioner/the State Chief Information Commissioner/the State Information Commissioner

"I, ..., having been appointed Chief Information Commissioner /Information Commissioner / State Chief Information Commissioner / State Information Commissioner swear in the name of God solemnly affirm that I will bear true faith and allegiance to the Constitution of India as by law established, that I will uphold the sovereignty and integrity of India, that I will duly and faithfully and to the best of my ability, knowledge and judgment perform the duties of my office without fear or favour, affection or ill-will and that I will uphold the Constitution and the laws." SEC.1 THE GAZETTE OF INDIA EXTRAORDINARY 23

THE SECOND SCHEDULE (*See* section 24)

Intelligence and security organisation established by the Central Government

1. Intelligence Bureau.
2. Research and Analysis Wing of the Cabinet Secretariat.
3. Directorate of Revenue Intelligence.
4. Central Economic Intelligence Bureau.
5. Directorate of Enforcement.
6. Narcotics Control Bureau.
7. Aviation Research Centre.
8. Special Prontier Force.

9. Border Security Force.
10. Central Reserve Police Force.
11. Indo-Tibetan Border Police.
12. Central Industrial Security Force.
13. National Security Guards.
14. Assam Rifles.
15. Special Service Bureau
16. Special Branch (CID), Andaman and Nicobar.
17. The Crime Branch-C.I.D.-CB, Dadra and Nagar Haveli.
18. Special Branch, Lakshadweep Police.

Bibliography

[The bibliography is only meant to provide a brief idea of the current trends in the theoretical literature on democratic governance. Eds.]

The Burden of Democracy, by Pratap Bhanu Mehta, New Delhi, Penguin, 2003.

The volume has a dual focus—first, social hierarchy that has penetrated into the social relation resulting in persistence of social inequality; second, the functioning of the state and democracy in India. The author argues that the state has kept the nation together and provided a legal-political framework. But at the same time he asserts that the state is disproportionately captured by the dominant groups. His central point is that democracy has raised popular expectation but the developing state has failed to satisfy it.

Seeing the State: Governance and Governmentality in India, by Stuart Corbridge, Glyn Williams, Manoj Srivastava, René Véron, Cambridge,Cambridge University Press, 2005.

The volume considers in some detail what it means to talk of seeing the state, and how this lens might deepen the understanding of 'the politics of the governed'. Based on the review of some of the existing literature on the everyday state and society in India it also draws attention to the ways in which encounters with the state are produced by dispersed state agencies amid conditions of greater or lesser institutional scarcity. In the process it considers how recent debates in development studies have sought to attend to these conditions, and provide 'remedies' for state 'failure'.

Politics of the Governed, by Partha Chatterjee, New Delhi, Permanent Black, 2004.

Partha Chatterjee insists that poorer people in most of the world are very often compelled to meet the state as members of social groups 'that transgress the strict lines of legality in struggling to live and work'. Civility and pluralism not being the defining features of their lives they inhabit the rough and tumble worlds of political society, where governmental agencies are met by wit and by stealth, and not uncommonly by violence. The volume views Democratic Governance and its hype from a very different angle and posits the concept of 'political society' at a time when the concept of civil society dominates much of social science literature.

Success of India's Democracy, by Atul Kohli, Cambridge, Cambridge University Press, 2001.

As a sort of sequel to Kohli's earlier writings on Indian democracy and the problem of governability the volume tends to concentrate on exploring the ways in which power is distributed in India, and their implications on governance.

Public Institutions in India: Performance and Design, edited by Devesh Kapur and Pratap Bhanu Mehta, Delhi, Oxford University Press, 2005.

The volume assesses the parliament, presidency, institutions of internal accountability, the judiciary, police, and the civil service in addition to economic institutions such as the Reserve Bank of India, keeping in mind the variables like autonomy, accountability, and information-sharing. It also reveals how electoral uncertainty has resurrected the public institutions like the Election Commission and the Supreme Court. However, surprisingly, academic institutions like universities remain outside the purview of the volume. But it provides interesting insights to the games institutions play in a democratic polity.

Governance in India: Culture, Context and Comparative Theory, by Subrata.K.Mitra, London, Routledge, 2006. In view of India's challenging, if not faltering, steps as the world's largest democracy— with instances of communal riots, separatist insurgency and caste conflict and so forth— the volume examines how India has been able to sustain democratic governance while undergoing substantial social, economic and political changes. The medium identified in this context is the neo-institutional rational choice model of governance, bounded by local culture and context.

Governance in India, by Marina Pinto, New Delhi, Sage Publications, 2000.

The volume examines the administrative structure of the country's four metropolitan cities - Kolkata, Delhi, Chennai & Mumbai and it makes a critique of the structures of municipal governance for failure to deliver efficient and effective governance. The author argues that compared to the governance scenario in rural India, which has made some headway in democracy decentralisation through the Panchayati Raj, the urban governance scenario is disappointing.

Does Civil Society Matter?: Governance in Contemporary India, edited by Rajesh Tandon and Ranjita Mohanty, New Delhi, Sage, 2003.

The volume provides and basically underlines the parameters and challenges of governance in India with judicious emphasis on the conceptual and empirical dimensions. The themes in the volume include crisis of governance, corruption and the Right to Information, civil society and *Dalit* protest. The volume calls for broader conceptualisation of the term "governance" from its currently narrow confines.

Investigating Social Capital: Comparative Perspective on Civil Society, Participation and Governance, edited by Sanjeev Prakash, University of Bergen, 2004.

It contains critical analysis of social capital & helps to clarify the concept in terms of empirical studies of civil society, voluntary organisation & democratic institutions in the developed world.

Administrative Reforms, by Amita Singh, Sage Publications, New Delhi, 2003.

The volume analyses the impact of globalisation on governance, with specific focus on the public-sector reforms. The ten essays in this book dwell on urban governance, energy & environmental governance, and service delivery systems, which have been subject to intensive reforms in recent years.

Public Accountability and Transparency: The Imperative of Good Governance, by Madhav Godbole, New Delhi, Orient Longman, Hyderabad, 2003.

The book deals with two critical categories of good governance, covering a wide range of institutions, both governmental and non-governmental. The percept of public accountability and transparency are examined in wider context of parliamentary institutions and procedure with practices of electoral reforms. He also describes the present shortcomings and weaknesses along with the manner in which this can be remedied.

Towards Good Governance and Sustainable Development, by Prabhat Datta, Kolkata, Dasgupta and Company, 2003.

The book is a collection of twelve articles pertaining to the central theme of the volume. It has two sections- one dealing with India and the other dealing with West Bengal. All these articles examine the issues with reference to rural and urban areas of governance.

Democratic Governance in India: Challenges of Poverty, Development and Identity, edited by Niraja Gopal Jayal and Sudha Pai, New Delhi, Sage Publications, **/2001?**

The essays highlight a variety of social movements and new institutional experiments that are now seeking to wrest the states' responsibility of securing development and alleviating poverty.

Democratic Governance, by James March and John Olsen, Free Press Publications, 2001.

In the volume J. March and J. Olsen construct a foundation for both theoretical formulation and deliberation on the broad theoretical concerns of democratic governance.

Multiculturalism, Liberalism and Democracy, edited by Rajeev Bhargava, Amiya Kumar Bagchi and R. Sudershan, Delhi, Oxford University Press, 1999.

The assumption that guides the volume is that 'multiculturalism' as a concept or strategy should somehow help us address our collective goals better than mere 'liberalism' or 'democracy'.

Civil Society, Public Sphere and Citizenship, by Rajeev Bhargava and Helmut Reifeld, New Delhi, Sage Publication, 2005. The essays examine the relationship between the state and society in India, discuss ideas of citizenship and study the broad area known as public sphere.

Panchayati Raj: Women Changing Governance, by Devaki Jain, Priya, 1996.
Panchayati Raj in India offers an opportunity to women to change the face of political leadership, but it still has to ensure that these are spaces where women can go to negotiate for power. The volume focuses on this complex issue.

Tradition, Self-governing Institutions among the Hill Tribes of North-East India, edited by Atul Goswami, Manohar, 2002.

The volume contains papers on traditional self-governing institutions among the hill tribes of north-east India, which critically examine the relevance of these institutions in the tribal society in transition.

Decentralisation and Local Governance, by L.C. Jain, Manohar, 2005.

The volume examines decentralised governance primarily in the context of a dynamic and globalising world. The analysis is based on empirical studies and decentralisation paradigms and models of developed and developing countries with focus on India's Panchayati Raj Institutions.

Good Governance, Democratic Societies and Globalization, edited by Surendra Munshi and Biju Paul Abraham, New Delhi, Sage Publications, 2004.

The collection of essays, with interdisciplinary orientation, addresses economic, political and social issues of contemporary significance.

Governance: South Asian Perspective, edited by Hasrat Abdul Hye, Delhi, Manohar, 2002,
The anthology reflects important issues of governance from the South Asian perspectives based on the experiences of the past and the imperatives of the present.

Governance in India: A Theatre of the Absurd, by Amrit Lal, New Delhi, Shipra Publications, 2004.
This book represents a highly critical view of what goes on in the name of governance in India.

Debating Governance, edited by Paul Hirst, Oxford, Oxford University Press, 2000.
The collection of essays seeks to highlight the various complex linkages of governance with special emphasis on democracy.

Democratic Governance and International Law, by Gregory H. Fox, Cambridge, Cambridge University Press, 2000.
The volume explores the impact of the post-Cold War "democratic revolution" on the international law and poses the question whether a commitment to democracy is consistent with the structure and rules of the international legal system.

Democratic Governance and Social Inequality, edited by Joseph S. Tulchin and Amelia Brown, Lynne Rienner Publishers, 2002.

The volume lives up to its title in exploring and exposing the complex and still-to-be-solved relations between democratic governance and social inequality.

Understanding Governance: Policy Networks, Governance, Reflexivity and Accountability, by R. Rhodes, Buckingham, Open University Press, 1997.

For the World Bank perspective on governance:

Governance: The World Bank's Experience, World Bank, Washington D.C., 1994;

Governance Matters, World Bank Policy Research Working Paper 2196, by Daniel Kaufman, Aart Kray and Pablo Zoida-Lobaton, World Bank, Washington D.C., 1999.

Index

Q

R

U

V

W

Z